Understanding and Promoting Transformative Learning

Patricia Cranton

Understanding and Promoting Transformative Learning

A Guide for
Educators of Adults

JOSSEY-BASS
A Wiley Company
www.josseybass.com

Published by

JOSSEY-BASS
A Wiley Company
989 Market Street
San Francisco, CA 94103-1741

www.josseybass.com

Jossey-Bass books and products are available through most bookstores. To contact Jossey-Bass directly, call (888) 378-2537, fax to (800) 605-2665, or visit our website at www.josseybass.com.

Substantial discounts on bulk quantities of Jossey-Bass books are available to corporations, professional associations, and other organizations. For details and discount information, contact the special sales department at Jossey-Bass.

We at Jossey-Bass strive to use the most environmentally sensitive paper stocks available to us. Our publications are printed on acid-free recycled stock whenever possible, and our paper always meets or exceeds minimum GPO and EPA requirements.

Jossey-Bass also publishes its books in a variety of electronic formats. Some content that appears in print may not be available in electronic books.

Library of Congress Cataloging-in-Publication Data

Cranton, Patricia.
    Understanding and promoting transformative learning : a guide for educators of adults / Patricia Cranton — 1st ed.
        p.   cm. — (The Jossey-Bass higher and adult education series)
    Includes bibliographical references and index.
    ISBN 0-7879-0017-6
    1. Adult learning. 2. Transfer of training. 3. Adult education
I. Title. II. Series
LC5225.L42C72 1994
374—dc20   94-21300
                                                                                                          CIP

HB Printing   10 9 8 7 6 5 4 3   Code 9499

The Jossey-Bass
Higher and Adult Education Series

Consulting Editor
Adult and Continuing Education

Alan B. Knox
University of Wisconsin, Madison

Contents

ix

Preface

In recent years, exciting new theoretical developments have been introduced into the field of adult education, primarily through the writings of Jack Mezirow. With the exception of Mezirow and his associates' edited book (1990) and Brookfield's *The Skillful Teacher* (1990), little literature is available for the practitioner interested in the application of these developments. There is a need to bring new ideas to practicing adult educators and students of adult education in a way that does not diminish the complexity of the ideas but still provides practical suggestions that educators can consider and use.

Background

Historically, particularly in Britain and Europe, adult education has been seen as a political movement — a movement toward freedom and liberation that is both personal and social. For the past several decades, however, North American adult education has adopted the model of meeting the needs of learners. Malcolm Knowles's influential writings (1975, 1980) led practitioners to work from the assumptions that adults are self-directed and that they have immediate goals and problems to solve; in other words, that they know what they want to learn. Although

Knowles himself did not intend for his basic assumptions to be viewed in such a black-and-white manner (he speaks of *a potential for* and a *continuum of* self-directed learning), other authors and practitioners have translated his concepts into formulas for effectiveness. Over the years, dozens of practical guides for adult educators based on Knowles's work have been published. Practitioners routinely implement these suggestions and consider them to be *the* principles of adult education.

Transformative learning is defined as the development of revised assumptions, premises, ways of interpreting experience, or perspectives on the world by means of critical self-reflection. Mezirow began developing a theory of transformative learning in 1975, and his work became more widely known with the publication of *Fostering Critical Reflection in Adulthood* (1990). The book contains several practical strategies for encouraging transformative learning. Mezirow's *Transformative Dimensions of Adult Learning* (1991), which describes his theory in detail, is one of the most important recent contributions to the literature. He does not describe strategies for practitioners or learners, however; perhaps this partially explains why transformative learning theory has not been widely researched or discussed in the literature. Yet this theory could change the direction of adult education practice.

Need

If we agree with Mezirow that transformative learning is the goal of adult education, then the theory must be described so that it reaches practitioners. There is no need for another how-to book or another simplification of transformative learning like those that follow Knowles's model of adult learning. It is not my intention to provide such a synopsis here. There is a need, however, for a description of the transformative learning process as educators observe it, within familiar contexts — as well as guidelines and strategies for working toward transformative learning.

Purpose and Audience

My intent in this book is to do the following:

- To explain transformative learning theory by distinguishing it from and relating it to current adult education perspectives
- To describe how learners undergo transformative learning
- To examine individual differences in the way learners work toward transformative learning
- To present strategies and techniques for fostering and supporting transformative learning
- To discuss the role of the adult educator as transformative learner

The primary audience for the book is practicing adult educators and students of adult education. With the tremendous growth in the numbers of adults participating in retraining programs, academic upgrading, and career changes, many North American colleges, school systems, government agencies, and businesses now offer certificate programs, professional development courses, or workshop series for their educators and trainers. *Understanding and Promoting Transformative Learning* is ideal for that audience.

Another audience comprises university faculty members and graduate students in departments of adult education. The book could serve as a textbook or supplementary textbook for master's-level graduate courses.

Finally, instructional developers at institutions of higher education, staff developers with school boards, trainers involved in human resource development in business and industry, and professional developers in the health professions will find the book useful for their practice.

Overview of the Contents

The book is divided into two parts. Part One (Chapters One through Five) describes transformative learning theory and its context. Chapter One provides an overview of perspectives on adult learning and places transformative learning within that context. Chapter Two presents Mezirow's (1991) theory of transformative learning. In Chapter Three, I show that transformative learning theory exists within a broader context and discuss types of learning, types of reflection, critical responses to the theory, and the relationship between transformative learning and other current concepts in adult education. In Chapter Four, I present a taxonomy of transformative learning as a way of classifying the many facets of the phenomenon. This chapter also describes from the learner's perspective the process of working toward transformation. In Chapter Five, Jung's psychological type theory is used to explain how individuals engage in transformative learning in different ways.

In Part Two (Chapters Six through Ten), the focus shifts to the educator's role in promoting transformative learning. In Chapter Six, teaching roles are discussed in relation to the three perspectives on learning presented in Chapter One: subject-oriented, consumer-oriented, and reformist roles. Chapter Seven describes the process of fostering learner empowerment. I argue that learners must be empowered before they can engage in critical self-reflection and that critical self-reflection, in turn, increases empowerment. Chapter Eight describes some strategies already suggested in the literature and illustrates how they can be applied to stimulate transformative learning: questioning techniques, consciousness-raising exercises, and experiential activities. Chapter Nine describes strategies that the educator can use to provide support for the transformative learning process, as well as practical techniques for encouraging learners to support each other. Chapter Ten applies the process of transformative learning to the educators' role in an effort to foster critical self-reflection and possibly transformation among educators.

Acknowledgments

I would like to acknowledge each of the more than one hundred adult learners with whom I have worked over the years for helping me to shape and inform my theory of practice. Specifically, I want to thank the learners, friends, and colleagues who worked with me to understand and apply transformative learning theory: Janice Clark, Valerie Grabove, Ellen Herbeson, Carolin Kreber, and Susan Wilcox.

I want to thank Jack Mezirow for stimulating the transformation of my meaning perspective on being an adult educator. I benefited greatly from the feedback of the reviewers whom Jossey-Bass asked to assess the manuscript. I am also grateful for the assistance I received from Gale Erlandson, senior editor; Ann Richardson, editorial assistant; Susan Abel, senior production editor; and Alan Knox, consulting editor for the Jossey-Bass Higher and Adult Education Series.

Finally, I am deeply indebted to Robert Knoop for his insights, support, and challenges to my thinking.

St. Catharines, Ontario Patricia Cranton
July 1994

The Author

Patricia Cranton is professor of education and director of the Instructional Development Office at Brock University. She received her B.Ed. degree (1971) from the University of Calgary in English literature and mathematics, her M.Sc. degree (1973), also from the University of Calgary, in computer applications, and her Ph.D. degree from the University of Toronto in measurement, evaluation, and computer applications.

Cranton's main research interests have been the evaluation of teaching in higher education; instructional development; self-directed learning; and transformative learning theory. She was selected as a Distinguished Scholar at Brock University in 1991 in recognition of her research and writing; she received the Ontario Confederation of University Faculty Associations Teaching Award in 1993 for an outstanding contribution to university teaching. Cranton's books include *Planning Instruction for Adult Learners* (1989) and *Working with Adult Learners* (1992).

Cranton was at McGill University from 1976 to 1986 in the Centre for Teaching and Learning and the Department of Educational Psychology and Counselling.

Understanding and Promoting
Transformative Learning

Part 1

Adult Learning as a Process of Transformation

The purpose of Part One is to describe the process of transformative learning both from the theoretical perspective presented by Mezirow (1991) and, building on that, from the learner's perspective. I first set transformative learning into the broader context of other perspectives on adult learning. I then describe Mezirow's theory and integrate it with types of learning, types of reflection, and other current adult learning concepts. I next view the process from the learner's perspective and examine what it is like to engage in critical self-reflection and potentially in transformation. And finally, I discuss individual learner differences in the process by examining Jung's theory of psychological type.

ONE

The Many Dimensions
of Adult Learning

Perspectives on adult learning have changed dramatically over the decades. Adult learning has been viewed as a process of being freed from the oppression of being illiterate, a means of gaining knowledge and skills, a way to satisfy learner needs, and a process of critical self-reflection that can lead to transformation. The phenomenon of adult learning is complex and difficult to capture in any one definition. The emphasis on a particular perspective is simply a product of the social context of the time in which it dominated educational practice (Jarvis, 1992), and each is valid in that context. Adult learning could be viewed as political rebellion in a social system that depends on maintaining the power of an elite few by withholding information from the illiterate masses. Adult learning could be viewed as the acquisition of knowledge and skills in a society that espouses the value of equal access to information by all members of the society. Adult learning could be viewed as the fulfilling of expressed learner needs in a culture that emphasizes consumerism and the immediate gratification of needs. And finally, adult learning could be seen as a process of critical reflection during a time when individuals are questioning their political and economic systems.

Adult learning could be any or all of these processes, as well as others such as personal or professional development and

3

consciousness-raising. Whether or not the literature of the decade advocates a particular type of adult learning, individuals will continue to acquire specific sets of knowledge, engage in learning to solve immediate problems, and question their own and others' assumptions and values.

The purpose of this book is to examine the process of transformative learning and to propose ways in which the educator can challenge learners to engage in it. Transformative learning occurs when, through critical self-reflection, an individual revises old or develops new assumptions, beliefs, or ways of seeing the world. The interest here is in the process of critical self-reflection, the potential learning and development that can occur through this process, and the strategies by which an educator can stimulate and support transformative learning. Part One of this book describes transformative learning; Part Two examines the educator's role in promoting transformative learning. I will make the case that transformative learning is one of the critical goals of adult education.

Educators should not see transformative learning as the only goal of education, however; people learn in different but interwoven ways. To this end, three broad perspectives on adult learning will be proposed in this chapter: *subject-oriented learning, consumer-oriented learning,* and *emancipatory learning.* (In Chapter Six, the educator roles relevant to each type of learning will be discussed.) Before I introduce these perspectives, I will examine some of the extensive efforts, primarily in the 1980s, to delineate unique aspects of adults as learners. The goal in this chapter is to review the traditional literature and, in subsequent chapters, to show how transformative learning theory expands our understanding of adult learning.

Adult Learning as a Distinctive Process

Adult learners are any individuals who participate in any informal or formal learning activity. An adult learner might take classes to fulfill requirements in a Ph.D. program, participate in a training session her organization requires that she attend, learn how to ski, or join a self-help group in order to understand her reactions to the death of her spouse. Although the literature continues to describe adult learners as affluent, well-educated, white, and middle-class (Brookfield, 1986; Long, 1983; Merriam and Caffarella, 1991), by definition and in practice, learning in some form is an aspect of virtually every person's life.

Given the complexity of human differences, the diverse contexts within which people live and work, and the many types of adult learning, can any general characteristics of adult learning be identified? Educators and educational theorists have struggled to do so for decades. Much of their writing does not rest within a theoretical framework, articulate a philosophical perspective on types of knowledge, or consider social context. Nevertheless, this work does form a sizable portion of the adult education literature and cannot be neglected. Many practitioners will recognize at least some of the proposed distinctive characteristics of adult learning, although the universality of the characteristics may be debatable.

Adult learning is often seen to be *voluntary* (see Cross, 1992). Individuals choose to become involved in either informal or formal learning activities as a result of a desire to grow, change, or develop, or as a response to a professional or practical need. Some external stimulus, such as the loss of a job or a change in personal circumstances, may prompt the person to engage in learning. Since adult learning is considered to be voluntary, adult learners are assumed to be highly motivated and interested in content that is relevant to their immediate needs. In practice, of course, we all have met people who do not see the decision to attend a course or workshop as voluntary. Also, most of us have worked with voluntary learners who do not exhibit a keen interest or strong motivation.

Adult learning is usually described as *self-directed*. The concept of self-directed learning has permeated theory and practice to such an extent that it is almost equated with adult education. Unfortunately, the definitions of self-directed learning are varied and confused. Knowles's (1975, 1980) original conception was that of a process by which learners make each of the instructional design decisions (identifying needs, setting objectives, gathering materials, selecting methods, and evaluating progress) for their own learning. Knowles did not see all adults as being immediately capable of self-directed learning but rather as having a preference for it once they had the skills to engage in it. Practitioners tended to overlook this point and implemented self-directed learning programs in a variety of contexts and a variety of ways (see Piskurich, 1993). Knowles's work was criticized (see Brookfield, 1986); self-directed learning has been redefined, analyzed, and thoroughly discussed (see Brookfield, 1993; Candy, 1991). It remains a common descriptor, albeit with a variety of interpretations, of adult learning in general.

Many writers argue that adult learning is *practical* in nature, an idea that began with Dewey (1916) and has been perpetuated by various interpretations and misinterpretations of Dewey's work. Theorists have assumed that adults have immediate problems to solve (Knowles, 1980; Wlodkowski, 1990) and that they primarily want to apply their learning to their work or personal lives the next day. This assumption about adult learning is validated to some extent by the popularity of self-help books and the nature of most continuing education offerings. Recent theorists, such as Mezirow (1991), have continued to include *action* as a vital component of adult learning. It can also be argued, of course, especially in light of theorizing about individual psychological types (see Chapter Five) and learning styles, that not everyone prefers, or is even interested in, practical learning.

A strong humanist influence, for example, through Rogers (1969), on the adult education literature led to the notion that adult learning is *participatory* or collaborative in nature (see Meyers and Jones, 1993). Practitioners commonly employ group work and other interactive strategies; they describe themselves as facilitators of a process in which learners share experiences, resources, and expertise as equal members of a group. They consider a comfortable atmosphere (both physical and psychological) to be important in adult learning. However, learning through participation with others may not be preferred. Again, a person's psychological type is an important factor in that preference.

Educators often suggest that adult learning involves a

sharing of experiences and resources. This view assumes (see Knowles, 1984) that adults bring a rich and varied set of life experiences to the learning environment, and that they wish to share these resources with other learners and benefit from the experiences of other members of the group. Such a process makes the learning concrete and relevant rather than abstract or theoretical and thus unrelated to the learner's life (Kolb, 1984). This notion, too, has greatly influenced adult education practice. However, there is little evidence that all adults learn in this way, and Kolb describes this process as only one part of a learning cycle rather than as a universal learner characteristic. Also, Knox (1977) finds that adult learners tend to relate new tasks to previously learned tasks and that prior learning can either enhance or interfere with new learning.

Adult learning is often unrelated to individuals' *self-concept;* low self-concept is seen as inhibiting learning, and increased self-concept is described as a product of learning. In Knox's (1977) study of adult development, he concludes that adults tend to underestimate their abilities, overemphasize their past school experience, and therefore learn less than they are capable of learning. This idea that self-concept influences learning appears throughout the literature (Brundage and Mackeracher, 1980; Merriam and Caffarella, 1991; Wlodkowski, 1990).

Similarly, learning is described as being threatening or *anxiety-provoking* for adults. Smith (1982) observes that anxiety may be produced by attempts to become more autonomous, by personal or job-related stress, or by associations with childhood school experiences. Transformative learning has been seen as a painful process (Mezirow, 1991), and Brookfield (1990) proposes that resistance to learning can be a consequence of anxiety or fear of change.

The diversity of adults' *learning styles* is often included in discussions of the nature of adult learning (Kolb, 1984; Perry, 1988). Unfortunately, there is confusion about what constitutes a learning style, and the concept provides us with little more than a way to say that people learn differently. The practical literature usually advises educators to adopt a variety of teaching roles in order to meet the needs of learners with different styles: "The principle of diversity should be engraved on every teacher's heart" (Brookfield, 1990, p. 69).

Practical literature proliferated in the 1980s, providing educators with a variety of principles of adult education. Brundage and Mackeracher (1980), for example, developed a list of thirty-six such principles. Primarily, this literature stemmed from the North American consumer-oriented perspective; that is, it was an attempt to describe adult learning and determine the needs of adult learners so that educators could then provide for the consumer of education. In the late 1980s and early 1990s, this approach came into question (Brookfield, 1986, 1987, 1993; Mezirow, 1991; Mezirow and Associates, 1990). Brookfield (1986, p. 32) describes our search for generic characteristics of adult learning as "inextricably bound up with the quest for professional identity on the part of adult educators." He concludes that "such a revelation is unlikely to transpire for some considerable time, and it may be that the most empirically attestable claim that can be made on behalf of adult learning styles concerns their range and diversity" (p. 33). Educational writers have again begun to search for theoretically and philosophically based ways of understanding adult learning.

Perspectives on Adult Learning

Theories of learning abound, and they come into and go out of fashion in education and psychology. The behaviorists of the 1950s saw learning as a change in behavior that occurs as organisms respond to stimulation from the environment. The humanists of the 1960s viewed learning as personal development resulting from interaction with others or as nondirective facilitation of self-awareness. The cognitive psychologists of the 1970s described learning as changes in memory and as a product of individual information processing mechanisms. Learning has also been described as change in attitudes or skills; as individuation, that is, the development of the individual as distinct from the collective; as a developmental process of moving from a world of absolutes to a relativistic world, and as a process of construing meaning or interpreting reality.

Such a list of theories quickly becomes confusing and contradictory rather than helpful for someone trying to understand the meaning of adult learning. However, most such perspectives can be classified or clustered as components of larger systems.

The philosophical concepts of positivism and constructivism provide one means of grouping theories of learning. Positivism is most easily understood by thinking of scientific or instrumental knowledge, that is, knowledge of invariant laws and objective data derived empirically. Learning is a process of accumulating this information. Behavioristic and information processing theories of learning fall under the positivistic paradigm. On the other hand, in the constructivist perspective knowledge is constructed by the individual who perceives the world, and there is no objective reality. Learning is a process of construing meaning and transforming understanding. Humanistic and contextual theories of learning fit nicely into the constructivist paradigm. As I will discuss in Chapter Two, Mezirow's theory of transformative learning is based on constructivism.

Habermas (1971) proposes three domains of knowledge that provide another means of classifying theories of learning. *Technical knowledge* includes information about cause and effect relationships in the environment (the positivistic paradigm). Behavioristic learning theories are concerned with the acquisition of technical knowledge. *Practical knowledge* is concerned with understanding what others mean; this includes understanding social norms, values, and political concepts, as well as making ourselves understood (a component of the constructivist paradigm). Humanistic learning theories are concerned, in part, with Habermas's practical knowledge. *Emancipatory knowledge* is gained through critical self-reflection and can also be seen as a component of the constructivist paradigm. Mezirow's theory of transformative learning is primarily concerned with emancipatory knowledge.

Mezirow (1991) discusses three domains of learning that are based on Habermas's work: *instrumental* (gaining of technical knowledge), *communicative* (gaining of practical knowledge), and *emancipatory*. This way of understanding human interests, knowledge, and learning provides an invaluable framework for the educator, and I will discuss that in more detail in Chapter Three. However, it is also valuable to place adult learning in the context of adult education literature and practice; for this discussion, I will propose another typology.

The goals of adult education have changed over the decades. In addition, learning now takes place in such diverse settings as business and industry training sessions, university and college degree programs, labor education classes, community action groups, self-help groups, and literacy programs (Brookfield, 1986). Writers and theorists have responded to this diversity by devising classification systems. Fenstermacher and Soltis (1992), for example, develop a framework in which they describe the executive, therapeutic, and liberationist views of teaching. I will introduce the broader perspectives of subject-oriented, consumer-oriented, and emancipatory adult learning and integrate those perspectives with the positivist and constructivist paradigms, as well as the instrumental, communicative, and emancipatory domains of learning. My aim in doing this is to place transformative learning theory in the historical and social context of adult education practice.

Subject-Oriented Adult Learning

The goal of subject-oriented learning is the acquisition of content, whether that is facts, concepts, problem-solving strategies, or technical or practical skills. The educator speaks of covering the material, and the learners see themselves as gaining knowledge or skills. Subject-oriented learning has long been the focus of college and university education (see Banta and Associates, 1993; Wilcox, 1990). The goals of continuing professional education are seen to include the mastery of theoretical knowledge and the acquisition of problem-solving skills (Jarvis, 1983). An effective training program in business and industry often is described as one that helps trainees become "more productive employees, not one in which employees become critically reflective and develop insights concerning their own lives . . . " (Brookfield, 1986, p. 191).

Many examples of subject-oriented learning come easily

to mind. An apprentice mechanic, welder, electrician, or carpenter is engaged in learning the skills of the trade. The student of nursing, physiotherapy, dentistry, or medicine is focused on the subject of the profession. The management trainee is most likely acquiring knowledge about the organization and the skills specific to a managerial position in that organization. The undergraduate student of history, sociology, or even philosophy often is occupied in accumulating knowledge about that discipline — its history, its theorists, and its concepts. The college instructor enrolled in a course on curriculum development expects to learn the skill of designing curricula.

Subject-oriented learning is positivistic; it falls into Habermas's technical domain of knowledge and Mezirow's instrumental domain of learning. This type of learning has come into and out of fashion in education — a shift to the emphasis on the "three R's" usually indicates a change to subject-oriented learning. In adult education, subject-oriented learning has always had its place; obtaining knowledge and skill related to a learner's discipline, profession, or trade is an essential component of adult learning. In some situations, though, subject-oriented learning predominates simply because it is the educator's preferred model of learning, or it is what the learner expects, or both (Boice, 1991).

Subject-oriented learning most often meets the expectations of the learner and is therefore comfortable. Even though an adult may be filled with worry over whether he or she can still cope with being a student, when the educator assumes the roles of expert and transmitter of knowledge and skill, that role at least seems familiar to learners.

Learning may be passive (listening to a lecture, for example), or it may be active (working in teams to solve content-related problems or working in a shop). The learner may passively receive information, respond to it in some way and integrate those responses and the information into existing memory patterns. The learner observes skills as demonstrated by the expert educator, practices those skills, and achieves some competency in reproducing the behaviors advocated by the educator. Instrumental knowledge is acquired. Subject-oriented learning is valuable and necessary. No one could learn to be a mechanic, electrician, dental hygienist, or teacher without subject-oriented learning. On the other hand, other perspectives on adult learning are equally important, such as the emphasis on critical thinking and liberal learning that Curry, Wergin, and Associates (1993) include in their examination of professional education.

Consumer-Oriented Adult Learning

Consumer-oriented learning takes place when an individual expresses a need to learn, looks to the educator for fulfillment of those needs, and then proceeds to learn under the educator's auspices. Knowles's (1980) conception of self-directed learning is congruent with this perspective. Learners identify their needs, set objectives based on those needs, select materials and resources that are relevant to their learning, choose the strategies by which they will meet their objectives, and evaluate their own progress. The educator becomes a resource person, manager, or facilitator and does not engage in challenging or questioning what learners say about their needs.

The distinction between consumer- and subject-oriented learning may seem to blur when the learner initiates a learning process, for example, by wanting to become more proficient at tuning a motorcycle and then attending a workshop offered by an expert mechanic. However, once that initial choice is made, the learning is subject-oriented. In consumer-oriented learning, the individual is constantly engaged in a series of decisions about what he or she wants, as is the person who goes to the building supply outlet to buy the materials for a house. If this person had decided to turn all decisions over to a contractor and had made only the initial decision to build a house, the process would have looked quite different. In subject-oriented learning, learners turn the decision making over to the expert; in consumer-oriented learning, learners make each decision. In practice, a single learning experience could include a mixture of orientations.

Consumer-oriented learning may come indirectly from misinterpretations of Dewey's (1916) work—particularly misinterpretation of Dewey's (1916) problem-solving model. Consumer-oriented learning is also, and perhaps primarily, a product of the culture in which it was conceived. The North American consumerist value system fostered this approach to learning. McLaren (1991) dramatically describes a society in which the media have reinforced a superficial view of the world and have fostered an expectation that needs will be met immediately by "the system." Learners develop no holistic understanding of either themselves or the system.

It seems difficult to place consumer-oriented learning within the positivist or constructivist paradigms or within the instrumental, practical, and emancipatory domains of learning. However, Habermas's (1971) view that practical knowledge includes a process of negotiation involving an exchange of personally relevant meanings does place consumer-oriented learning in that domain. The learner and the educator meet on some common ground — the learner expresses needs that are based on his or her own construction of those needs, the educator responds to those needs, usually with some negotiation as to what the learning experience will include, and then through collaborative effort, the process is defined. In the contexts of positivism and constructivism, consumer-oriented learning fits most naturally with constructivism for the same reason — the learner makes decisions about learning based on his or her own perception or construction of needs. These perceptions are not viewed as right or wrong but simply as expressions of what a person wants to learn. In practice, consumer-oriented learning can fit into the positivistic paradigm as well (for example, in nursing and medical education), rightly leading to a questioning of its value in that domain (Ash, 1985).

What does consumer-oriented learning look like? In a pure model of self-directed learning as advocated by Knowles, learners are highly motivated, know what they want to learn, and have the skills to set their own objectives, find resources, and evaluate their progress in meeting their objectives. Learners may collaborate with their peers, share experiences and resources, and set up learning networks. Since the learning is based on felt needs, it will be relevant to individuals' goals, whether they are work-related, personal, or based on an intrinsic interest in the subject. For the same reason, learning experiences are unlikely to produce a challenge to learners' assumptions or a questioning of or change in their values. Consumer-oriented learning has been criticized in the literature for that reason (Brookfield, 1986; 1993).

A second version of consumer-oriented learning is found in what Tough (1979) calls individual learning projects. Although these projects may lead a person to enroll in a course or workshop, they are just as likely to be carried out informally through readings, consultation with others, and experiential projects. For example, an adult may be interested in learning to garden, ski, or repair her own car, or in developing a better understanding of the early philosophers. The motivation is high; the individual explores the topic of interest until the desired learning takes place or interest wanes. The learner is a responsible adult who knows what he or she wants to learn and goes about learning it. It is not surprising that this model has inspired educators for several decades.

This idealized process does not always occur. As I have argued elsewhere (Cranton, 1992), although adults may indeed prefer self-directed learning, and although they may be self-directed in every other aspect of their lives, it does not necessarily follow that adult learners have the skills or maturity as learners to be self-directed. Some limited research evidence (Taylor, 1987) supports the notion that becoming self-directed is an emotionally and cognitively taxing process for learners. The extensive literature that provides practitioners with techniques for fostering self-directed learning also supports the notion that individuals must develop the capacity for self-direction (Kirschenbaum and Perri, 1982). Candy (1991) suggests that there are several components to this capacity, including the possession of "deep-level learning," and the ability to ask questions. Also included are the ability to read well, to monitor comprehension, and to think critically. Candy also proposes a more general model for enhancing self-directed learning that includes competence, resources, and rights — that is, learners' personal and socially determined belief in their right to direct their own learning. However, in practice, consumer-oriented learning programs have often been implemented without considering learners' ability to be self-directed (Ferrier, Marrin, and Seidman, 1981; Ash, 1985; Thorne and Marshall, 1984). Learning, then, can become a frustrating experience that leads to hostility toward the educator, to anxiety, and possibly even to withdrawal from the learning experience. Working within a consumer-oriented model does not guarantee learners who are informed consumers.

Finally, consumer-oriented learning is a perspective that includes such approaches as individualized learning packages, competency-based education, and modular instruction. Here we have an application of the consumer orientation that cannot be described as constructivist; the learning is generally instrumental. This is due in part to misinterpretations of Knowles's work—equating self-directed learning with independent or individualized learning. It is also, in part, an attempt to meet the needs of learners efficiently by using a method based on a behavioristic theory of learning.

Individualized learning packages are used in various contexts, including basic academic upgrading and training for the trades. Learners may work through pre-prepared materials in order to master a set of objectives. Learners may make some decisions about the learning process: the decision to enter the program, the sequence of units of instruction, whether they are ready to take a test on a unit, and whether extra assistance is required. The pace of the learning is almost always determined, with some restrictions, by the learner. Learning in such approaches is usually lower-level cognitive learning (rote, comprehension, or routine problem solving). Rarely are critical thinking skills involved, and rarely does the learner cross over into the affective domain. Little or no interaction with others, either peers or educators, is built into the learning, though interaction may occur spontaneously. The learner goes to the educator when in difficulty or for management reasons such as for recording test scores. Individualized learning packages may resemble subject-oriented learning more closely than they do consumer-oriented learning; however, the goal of this approach, the role of the educator, and the perceptions of its users place it within the consumer-oriented perspective.

The consumer-oriented perspective on learning has been severely criticized in the recent adult education literature for some of the reasons already mentioned (Collins, 1991; Griffin, 1987). However, we must understand the place of this type of learning, and perhaps more important, realize how valuable it could be. Brookfield (1993) reminds us of the political dimensions of self-direction: learner control over educational decisions, a concept that is central to emancipatory education; and access to resources, which "can be inherently politicizing as learners come to a critical awareness of the differential distribution of resources . . . " (p. 239). It is equally important to recognize that the process of becoming a self-directed learner often involves critical self-reflection and changes in our assumptions about ourselves as learners, as well as about education in general.

Emancipatory Adult Learning

Emancipation is defined as the process of removing constraints. Emancipatory learning, then, is a process of freeing ourselves from forces that limit our options and our control over our lives, forces that have been taken for granted or seen as beyond our control. Mezirow writes, "Emancipatory learning often is transformative" (p. 88). Mezirow (1991) also describes emancipatory knowledge as that "gained through critical self-reflection, as distinct from the knowledge gained from our 'technical' interest in the objective world or our 'practical' interest in social relationships" (p. 87). This notion is based on Habermas's identification of 'the emancipatory' as the third general area of human interest.

Emancipatory learning has remained a goal of adult education through time and across cultures. For example, in a history of adult education in Britain, Harrison (1961) states that "it has in the main been regarded as a movement for freedom and liberation, both personal . . . and social" (p. xii). In North America, Lindeman (1926) describes ideal adult education as cooperative, nonauthoritarian, informal, and as a quest for the roots of our preconceptions. Freire (1970), in describing his work in literacy education in South America, refers to a "deepening awareness of both the sociocultural reality which shapes [learners'] lives and . . . their capacity to transform that reality through action upon it" (p. 27). Mezirow (1991) writes, "The goal of adult education is to help adult learners become more critically reflective, participate more fully and freely in rational discourse and action, and advance developmentally by moving toward meaning perspectives that are more inclusive, discriminating, permeable, and integrative of experience" (pp. 224–225).

Emancipatory learning is constructivist in nature. Habermas (1970), and then Mezirow (1991), include emancipatory knowledge and learning as separate from instrumental and communicative learning. Mezirow proposes, however, that emancipatory learning may apply to either the instrumental or communicative domains, although it is less likely to apply to the instrumental domain.

Examples of emancipatory learning can be found in diverse contexts. A classic example is the learner who gains literacy skills, sees the world in a new way, and has new power and control in that world. Life changes, such as a change of job or the loss of a spouse, often stimulate an individual to engage in informal or formal learning and to reflect on basic assumptions and beliefs. A college instructor who enrolls in a professional development course may be challenged to view her role as instructor and the educational system itself in a new way. A young man who joins Green Party discussion groups may be stimulated to change his view of political and environmental issues and work toward social change based on a revised perspective. At times, emancipatory learning occurs independently of the educator; at other times it is fostered deliberately. And of course, the educator may try to foster emancipatory learning, but it may not occur; the learner must be, in some way, ready to question assumptions. Adults can be particularly tenacious in holding on to their beliefs (Brookfield, 1990).

I will discuss the nature of emancipatory learning in detail in Chapter Four, and examine how the process varies among individuals of different psychological types in Chapter Five. However, in order to highlight how emancipatory learning is different from subject or consumer-oriented learning, the process will be examined here briefly from the learner's point of view.

Unlike either subject- or consumer-oriented learning, emancipatory learning is a difficult and often painful process. As Brookfield (1990, p. 150) points out, "routine, habit, and familiarity are strongly appealing," and "for some, the conduct of life is a quest for certainty, for a system of beliefs and a set of values — even for a well-defined social structure — that they can adopt and commit to, for life." Adults will resist contradictions to their beliefs and will deny discrepancies between new learning and previous knowledge. In response to a challenge to their assumptions, many learners will entrench themselves even more firmly in their belief system and become hostile or withdrawn in the learning environment. Brookfield (1990, p. 150) again describes this particularly well: "it is as if a perverse psychological law sometimes seems to apply in which the strength of commitment to beliefs and values is inversely correlated with the amount of evidence encountered that contradicts the truth of these. The human capacity for denial knows no limits."

In addition to resisting challenges to their personal beliefs, adult learners will also resist contradictions to their social or cultural value systems. The film *Educating Rita* exemplifies one aspect of this process. Rita, who is engaged in emancipatory learning, must deal with resistance from her husband; she leaves her subculture during the process. Candy (1991, p. 421) writes: "if learning is not part of the cultural norm for a particular group, then the person seeking to emancipate himself or herself through self-education has first of all to transcend the indifference or even antagonism of those with whom she or he is regularly in contact."

If learners overcome the initial personal and social resistance to questioning their assumptions and beliefs and become engaged in critical self-reflection, emancipatory learning does not become any less disquieting. A learner questioning personal psychological beliefs or assumptions related to his or her social context can experience considerable emotional upheaval. Keane (1987, p. 89) describes this experience dramatically: "the most difficult challenges were at the nonrational level . . . . Immersed in pain and confusion of my own and others' doubts I tried to understand what was happening within myself while cognitively searching for patterns and relationships. Vague, confused and varied feelings, ranging from shame to anger, surfaced . . . . Loneliness was enormous . . . . I became a powerful learner in this nonrational world. Images, feelings, intuitions, dreams and bodily sensings led me to a knowing which went beyond a factual knowing and which I increasingly trusted and came to value."

In his earlier work, Mezirow (1978) describes how this sense of alienation can lead a person to seek out others in similar situations. Taylor (1987) substantiates this with evidence from a qualitative study of a group of learners becoming self-directed. She found that collaboration and "sharing the discovery" took place in two stages of the learning cycle. This, of course, is not unique to emancipatory learning. Adult learners are often described as preferring collaborative learning.

Finally, emancipatory learning is usually described as including some behavior or action based on the changes that have taken place in the learner. The learner is described as experiencing a "reintegration into society" (Mezirow, 1978) or "equilibrium" (Taylor, 1987, p. 183). Although learning of any type (subject- or consumer-oriented) is expected to yield visible changes in the behavior of the learner (hence the emphasis on behavioral objectives in the instructional design literature), it is only with emancipatory learning that terms such as *reintegration, reorientation,* and *equilibrium* are used. This distinction underlines the significance of the upheaval experienced in emancipatory learning.

Clearly, emancipatory learning cannot be the single or even the most common objective of adult education. Little of what adults want to and need to learn involves revisions to basic assumptions and beliefs or transformations of perspective. Mezirow (1991) clarifies this: "not all learning is transformative. We can learn simply by adding knowledge to our meaning schemes or learning new meaning schemes . . . and it can be a crucially important experience for the learner" (p. 223). On the other hand, if we view education as the means by which individuals and societies are shaped and changed, fostering emancipatory learning is the central goal of adult education. That there is a substantial qualitative difference between emancipatory learning and other types of learning will already be evident.

Summary

The adult education literature contains many descriptions of the nature of adult learning and attempts to define the uniqueness of adult learners. These descriptions have evolved into numerous lists of characteristics of adult learners and, for the practitioner, lists of principles of adult education based on such characteristics. This endeavor seems rather futile, somewhat akin to attempting to describe human nature by drawing up a list of human characteristics. The more specific the characteristics are, the less likely they are to apply to all individuals; the more general they are, the less likely they are to be useful to the educator. Nevertheless, some examples of such descriptors of adult learning are discussed in this chapter.

The aim of this book is to describe the nature of adult learning by placing it within larger systems for the classification of knowledge, such as positivism, constructivism, or Habermas's (1970) technical, practical, and emancipatory knowledge. At the same time, it is important to maintain a sense of the development of adult education as a field of practice and thought and to appreciate the diversity of adult education practices across contexts and cultures. One downfall of education has been the tendency of practitioners to fall into fads and fashions and lose overall perspective. Adult education has been no less susceptible to this trap than other areas of education.

In an attempt to maintain an overall perspective, I have described adult learning here as *subject-oriented learning* (acquiring knowledge and skills), which can also be described as positivistic or related to the technical domain of knowledge; *consumer-oriented learning* (directly meeting the needs of the learner), which could be positivistic but is most likely to be constructivistic and related to practical knowledge; and *emancipatory learning* (engaging in critical self-reflection), which is constructivist and also called emancipatory knowledge by Habermas.

Adult learning in each of these categories has its important place in different settings and contexts. Emancipatory learning, however, is probably the most complex and difficult experience from the learner's point of view and the most challenging for the educator. Emancipatory learning is also a fundamental goal of education and in large part defines the role that education is seen to play in society.

TWO

Understanding
Transformative Learning

By the time they reach adulthood, people have acquired a way of seeing the world, a way of interpreting their experiences, and a set of values. Although adults continue to acquire new knowledge and skills, they often must integrate new experiences with prior learning. When this integration does not occur easily and contradictions or dilemmas result, the prior learning must be examined and some adjustments made. Individuals can reject the contradictory new information or revise their previous views. This, simply stated, is the process of reflection and transformative learning.

Mezirow's (1991) theory of transformative learning has developed over nearly two decades into a comprehensive and complex description of how learners construe, validate, and reformulate the meaning of their experiences. He has drawn from developmental and cognitive psychology, psychotherapy, sociology, and philosophy to come to an understanding of how adults learn, transform, and develop; the roots of his theory lie in humanism and critical social theory. However, Mezirow (1991, p. xiv) states that transformative theory "does not derive from a systematic extension of an existing intellectual theory or tradition. . . ."

This chapter includes a brief description of the development of transformative learning theory, an overview of the

22

theory, an examination of the different perspectives through which individuals see the world, and an analysis of how those perspectives can be distorted.

Development of Transformative Learning Theory

Why discuss the development of a theory? Simply because by understanding the basis of a theory, we can be better informed when questioning and challenging the applicability of the theory to our own practice; this is crucial to developing a perspective on practice.

Based on a study of eighty-three women returning to college in twelve different reentry programs, Mezirow (1975) initially described a process of *personal transformation* that included ten phases:

- Experiencing a disorienting dilemma
- Undergoing self-examination
- Conducting a critical assessment of internalized role assumptions and feeling a sense of alienation from traditional social expectations
- Relating one's discontent to similar experiences of others or to public issues — recognizing that one's problem is shared and not exclusively a private matter
- Exploring options for new ways of acting
- Building competence and self-confidence in new roles
- Planning a course of action
- Acquiring knowledge and skills for implementing one's plans
- Making provisional efforts to try new roles and to assess feedback
- Reintegrating into society on the basis of conditions dictated by the new perspective

The results of this research led to the "outline of a theory of adult development and a derivative concept of adult education . . . " (Mezirow, 1978, p. 153). Here, Mezirow discussed learning that is "cardinal for adult development," that is, how we are caught in our own history and are reliving it. He described

Freire's (1970) work as parallel to perspective transformation, and saw this process as "a structural reorganization in the way that a person looks at himself and his relationship" (Mezirow, 1978, p. 162).

In 1981, Mezirow presented what he called a critical theory of adult learning and education. He grounded this work in Habermas's (1971) three domains of learning: the technical (empirical knowledge governed by technical rules), the practical (social norms), and the emancipatory (self-knowledge and self-reflection). Although the application of this framework to transformative learning was not completely clear then, Mezirow (1981, p. 6) wrote, "The intent of education for emancipatory action — or . . . perspective transformation — would be seen by Habermas as the providing of the learner with an accurate in-depth understanding of his or her historical situation." He described perspective transformation as "the emancipatory process of becoming critically aware of how and why the structure of psycho-cultural assumptions has come to constrain the way we see ourselves and our relationships, reconstituting this structure to permit a more inclusive and discriminating integration of experience and acting upon these new understandings" (Mezirow, 1981, p. 6). At that time, Mezirow was primarily interested in *personal* transformation — how people change their view of themselves as a result of new experiences.

By drawing further on the work of Habermas (1971), Mezirow (1985a) elaborated on perspective transformation and related the process to self-directed learning. He described learning as the extension of one's ability to make assumptions explicit, contextualize them, validate them, and act on them. He saw education, then, as the process of fostering this effort and self-directedness as the ability to "spell out the specifics of our experience" (Mezirow, 1985a, p. 142). Mezirow defined a *meaning perspective* as "the structure of cultural and psychological assumptions within which new experience is assimilated and transformed by one's past experience" (p. 144). *Meaning schemes* were defined as rules, roles, and expectations that govern the way we see, feel, think, and act. *Psychological assumptions* support meaning schemes. Mezirow discussed three types of distortions, which he called false consciousness, in meaning perspectives: errors of knowledge, errors in understanding social functions, and errors in understanding one's own true motives. The distinction between psychological and cultural meaning perspectives became sharper than in his earlier work, but Mezirow's concepts remained interrelated.

In 1985, Mezirow presented a "critical theory of self-directed learning" (Mezirow, 1985b). Basing his ideas on Habermas (1971), he described instrumental learning (learning to control the environment), dialogic learning (understanding what others mean in communication), and self-reflective learning (understanding ourselves). In this work he included meaning schemes (to be discussed later in this chapter) as the basic assumptions from which meaning perspectives are derived. He defined perspective transformation as he had in 1981 and described three learning processes, one from each of Habermas's three domains of learning. In examining this integration of perspective transformation and self-directed learning, he stated that "there is probably no such thing as a self-directed learner, except in the sense that there is a learner who can participate fully and freely in the dialogue through which we test our interests and perspectives against those of others and accordingly modify them and our learning goals" (Mezirow, 1985b, p. 27).

In response to a criticism of his work, Mezirow (1989) suggested that emancipatory learning is not a third domain, rather, it is applicable to both instrumental and dialogic learning. We now have the foundations for the theory Mezirow presented in 1991.

Overview of Transformative Learning

Transformative learning theory is based on constructivist assumptions as I mentioned in Chapter One. Mezirow (1991, p. xiv) describes the constructivist assumptions that underlie his theory as including "a conviction that meaning exists within ourselves rather than in external forms such as books and that personal meanings that we attribute to our experience are acquired and validated through human interaction and communication."

We interpret our experiences and the things we encounter in our own way; what we make of the world is a result of our perceptions of our experiences. Transformative learning, then, is a process of examining, questioning, validating, and revising these perceptions. If we were to claim the existence of absolute truths or universal constructs that are independent of our knowledge of them, the goal of learning would be to discover right answers rather than to reflect on our perspectives of the world.

Given this, Mezirow (1991) describes adults as having *meaning perspectives,* or "sets of habitual expectation" (p. 4). We expect to see things in a certain way because of our past experiences. We have a frame of reference for interpreting what happens to us, what we read, what we see, and what others say. This frame of reference comes from the way we grew up, the culture in which we live, and what we have previously learned.

To illustrate how meaning perspectives act as a frame of reference, consider Brigitte and Hui-e, who work side-by-side on an assembly line in a factory that produces prefabricated homes. Hui-e grew up in an environment in which education was valued as was having a professional career; however, a series of changes in her life have led her to this position and she cannot see a way to improve herself. Brigitte grew up in a family in which unemployment was the norm and office workers and others considered to be "brains" were laughed at. She is pleased with this position; it pays well, and she is proud of being hard-working. The manager announces layoffs but indicates the possibility of a ten-month retraining position for those interested in operating the computerized portion of the assembly process. These two individuals have quite different perspectives on retraining. In Hui-e's perspective, it is an opportunity to learn something new and perhaps obtain a better position. Brigitte thinks of how her friends will laugh at her if she tells them she is taking a computer course. If retraining were to become the only option available for maintaining employment, these two adult learners would view the experience in different ways; Hui-e's perspective would lead her to obtain new knowledge and skills, but Brigitte's perspective could lead to critical self-reflection.

Our experiences are filtered through our meaning perspectives, which for most of us are uncritically assimilated ways of knowing, believing, and feeling. They include distortions, prejudices, stereotypes, social context, and lack of knowledge. Staying within a meaning perspective is safe — although awareness is diminished, anxiety and loss of self-confidence are avoided. The assembly-line worker who laughs at office workers could experience a considerable loss of face in her culture by entering the retraining program.

Learning occurs when an individual enters a process of reconciling newly communicated ideas with the presuppositions of prior learning. To return to our factory worker: if Brigitte were to begin examining the discrepancies between the new idea of retraining as valuable and her old negative view of office workers, she would have begun a learning process. "Reflective learning involves assessment or reassessment of assumptions," and "reflective learning becomes transformative whenever assumptions or premises are found to be distorting, inauthentic, or otherwise invalid" (Mezirow, 1991, p. 6).

Under this model, the ideal conditions for learning are those that allow full participation in reflective discourse. In other words, when a person is interpreting the meaning of a new experience and examining the validity of prior learning, discussion with others provides a vehicle for learning. Under optimal conditions, participants in rational discourse will:

- Have accurate and complete information
- Be free from coercion and distorting self-perception
- Be able to weigh evidence and assess arguments objectively
- Be open to alternative perspectives
- Be able to reflect critically on presuppositions and their consequences
- Have equal opportunity to participate (including the chance to challenge, question, refute, and reflect, and to hear others do the same)
- Be able to accept an informed, objective, and rational consensus as a legitimate test of validity (Mezirow, 1991, p. 78)

In transformative learning theory, an adult's psychological and cognitive development is marked by an increased ability to validate prior learning through reflection and to act on the insights obtained. The person moves toward more inclusive, differentiated, open, and integrated meaning perspectives.

Types of Meaning Perspectives

A meaning perspective is a frame of reference or a set of expectations that is based on past experience. Mezirow (1991) distinguishes three types of meaning perspectives: *epistemic, sociolinguistic,* and *psychological.*

Epistemic meaning perspectives are those related to knowledge and the way we use knowledge. For example, if an educator has studied education primarily through the disciplines of instructional design and educational technology, she would believe that her job is to design sequential hierarchical learning activities and evaluate learner mastery of each step. This epistemic perspective would be based on her knowledge of education. Similarly, a manager who has no knowledge of teambuilding will have an epistemic perspective on leadership that is influenced by a limited scope of awareness. Epistemic perspectives also pertain to the uses of knowledge, and they may be influenced by learning style or preferences, that is, whether a person thinks concretely or abstractly, or globally or in detail. A learner, for example, who likes to classify materials and focus quickly on organizational thinking will have epistemic perspectives that are influenced by that preference. That person may have great difficulty in dealing with either abstract and theoretical or global and future-oriented issues. In other words, how people learn is related to their epistemic meaning perspectives.

Sociolinguistic meaning perspectives are based on people's social norms, cultural expectations, socialization, and language codes, that is, their cultural background, spoken language, religious beliefs, family and upbringing, and interactions with others. For example, the child who watches inordinate numbers of violent television programs may come to think violence is acceptable, that is, to develop a sociolinguistic perspective in which violence is acceptable. A woman who lives in a culture in which women's roles are clearly defined as submissive will have a sociolinguistic perspective that delineates a code of behavior for women, and she will act accordingly. An individual who has limited exposure to cultural differences may believe in the superiority of Eurocentric ways of living. A worker who has had no opportunity to participate in company decision making will have a perspective that describes the role of the worker in that way.

Psychological meaning perspectives pertain to the way people see themselves as individuals — their self-concept, needs, inhibitions, anxieties, and personality-based preferences. A person who felt unloved as a child may develop a psychological perspective that includes lack of self-worth. Someone whose parents had very high expectations of achievement in school may develop a perspective that includes great motivation to achieve or possibly a sense of guilt at not having achieved enough. A woman who was abused by her spouse may see herself as blameworthy and expect others to treat her that way. The sources of psychological meaning perspectives are often buried in childhood experiences (including trauma) and may not be easily accessible to the conscious self. Mezirow (1991, p. 43) lists self-concept, inhibitions, psychological defense mechanisms, neurotic needs, and approach/avoidance as being among the factors shaping psychological meaning perspectives. Here, the influence of Mezirow's early interest in personal transformation is apparent.

Distortions in Meaning Perspectives

The way we see the world, then, is a product of our knowledge about the world, our cultural background and language, and our human nature. Each meaning perspective is made up of sets of meaning schemes: specific knowledge, beliefs, value judgments, feelings, and assumptions. For example, the person who has grown up in and continues to live in a conservative working-class community will have sociolinguistic meaning perspectives that act as filters through which ideas about political, social, and economic issues must pass. Meaning perspectives can consist of sets of specific assumptions and beliefs about, for example, the value of education, socialized medical care, or the role of government in society.

Most of us have not examined our meaning perspectives critically. Nor is it likely that anyone has examined all of his or her meaning perspectives. Our meaning perspectives are a product of what we have learned, how and where we grew up, and how we see ourselves. Consequently, meaning perspectives and the meaning schemes of which they are composed can be distorted.

Mezirow (1991, p. 118) defines a distorted assumption or premise as one "that leads the learner to view reality in a way that arbitrarily limits what is included, impedes differentiation, lacks permeability or openness to other ways of seeing, or does not facilitate an integration of experience." In one way, a distorted assumption can be seen as an error in learning; however it is more useful for the educator to think of a distortion as an unquestioned, unexamined, perhaps even unconscious assumption that limits the learner's openness to change, growth, and personal development.

Distorted Assumptions in Epistemic Meaning Perspectives

In epistemic meaning perspectives, assumptions about the nature and use of knowledge can be distorted. The word *epistemic* is in fact derived from *epistemology,* a term for the branch of philosophy concerned with the justification of knowledge claims in the face of scepticism and hence with the nature of knowledge. If it seems confusing to think of distortions of things known, it may be useful to consider the relationship between *knowing* and *believing.* Philosophers agree that knowledge can be distinguished from belief, although they do not agree on exactly how the concepts are different (Vesey and Foulkes, 1990). Generally, though, if a person believes she knows something, it is possible that she is wrong; whereas if she thinks she knows something and says so, and it turns out that she does not, the word *know* was misused by that person. An assumption is a supposition, a postulate, or something claimed or taken for granted. In other words, holding an epistemic assumption is equivalent to saying, I believe I know. . . .

Mezirow (1991) relates distorted assumptions in epistemic meaning perspectives to stages in the development of reflective judgment and to Knox's (1977) dimensions of cognitive style — which can also be seen as describing a developmental progression. This approach is useful in that it emphasizes the notion of distorted assumptions as limiting factors in a learner's development; however, it may not be the only way in which this form of distortion is acquired and expressed. Examples of a different nature will be presented after a discussion of distorted assumptions from the developmental perspective.

Mezirow relies on Kitchener's (1983; Kitchener and King, 1990) seven stages in the development of reflective judgment, although other theorists (Perry, 1970, for example) provide a similar framework. Developmental theorists usually portray individuals as moving from a black-and-white (true versus false) perception of the world to a relativistic perception of it. At the earlier stages, reflective thinking or questioning of assumptions does not occur. A child may accept her parents' statements as absolute truth requiring no justification. Because Mommy said so! is the only reason a young child needs to hear. Some adults may also display this characteristic. For example, they may accept information as absolute truth because it is printed in a textbook or stated by a person in a position of power. At the other end of the continuum, the individual whose reflective judgment is developed perceives knowledge to be the product of inquiry and reflection. The process of inquiry is seen to be, in itself, fallible; justification is based on a rational evaluation of the evidence. The epistemic assumptions of Kitchener's (1983) seven stages include:

- Beliefs need no justification; what is believed is true.
- Knowledge is absolutely certain but may not be immediately available.
- Knowledge is absolutely certain or temporarily uncertain.
- Knowledge is idiosyncratic; some information may be in error or lost, therefore one cannot know with certainty.
- Knowledge is contextual and subjective; it is available through interpretation.
- Knowledge is constructed by each person and is based on the evaluation of evidence and argument.
- Knowledge is the product of rational inquiry, which is fallible.

Clearly, individuals at the earlier stages in the development of reflective judgment are more likely to have distorted epistemic meaning perspectives. In one way, progression through these developmental stages strongly resembles the overall process of working toward transformative learning. From this perspective, fostering transformative learning is a means of facilitating the development of reflective judgment in the learner. This view of learning will be emphasized in Chapters Four and Seven. Meanwhile, some examples generated from Mezirow's use of developmental theory to define epistemic distortions will be suggested.

Every educator will have encountered learners who held assumptions — not always explicitly — similar to those apparent in the statements below:

- I know the correct procedure for implementing a quality control program because I learned it from the manual I received at a workshop last spring.
- Behavioristic psychology has been proven to be wrong.
- Good teachers are those who clearly state what they expect of students and present information in a well-organized manner.
- In order to get a job as a welder, I must perfect each of the skills on this checklist.
- Modularized instruction is most effective for academic upgrading; the curriculum director decided this after doing a lot of research on it.
- The recession is over — I heard it on the news last night.
- If I can't solve the problem it's only because I didn't listen carefully enough; every problem has a solution.
- My teacher gave me an A on my practicum so I know that I can wire a house.

Epistemic assumptions of this nature result when knowledge or beliefs are not questioned or reflected upon, particularly when the knowledge is obtained from someone who appears to be an expert (the author of a book or a teacher) or a person in a position of authority (a leader or a supervisor). In-

dividuals who are at the early stages in the development of reflective judgment would be most likely to hold such assumptions.

However, a learner can be advanced in the development
of reflective judgment or the intellect and still hold distorted
epistemic assumptions. Mezirow (1991) does not deny this. In
fact, he lists factors such as *scope of awareness* and *learning styles*
as important in shaping the epistemic meaning perspective (p.
43). He simply does not discuss the nature of distorted assumptions based on such factors. Examples will facilitate the discussion.

Professor Jones is an instructor of economics. In his field
as well as in other aspects of his life he is a critical thinker and
clearly at a high level of intellectual development. He questions
the theoretical models in economics and hopes that his students
also obtain critical questioning skills. He has not encountered
any method of instruction other than an instructor-centered
didactic approach. As a student of economics, he was taught
in this way; his colleagues teach in this way; he is unaware of
educational literature; he assumes that with the large classes in
the department he cannot hold discussions with his student
group. In other words, Professor Jones holds distorted epistemic
assumptions related to his practice as an educator. When he
consults with an instructional development office for the purpose of understanding his low student ratings, he is an adult
learner who is at a high stage in the development of reflective
judgment but who has a limited scope of awareness in what forms
a large component of his professional practice.

Valerie is a student in a steel fabrication program at a
technical college. She has never accepted others' ideas of what
she could do or learn; she has critically questioned the social
norms that keep women out of the trades; she has challenged
authority figures and experts in many areas. One of the reasons Valerie has chosen to go into a trade is that she knows herself as a learner — she enjoys working with her hands, learns by
doing, views learning as an accumulation of experiences, is interested in the concrete and the practical, does not care much about
how others feel, and she clearly states, "I am not a people person."
In an orientation to a welding course, Valerie encounters an
instructor who emphasizes relations with an employer, depend-

ability, consideration of co-workers, and a global view of the trade more heavily than the actual skills of welding. The instructor even quotes the results of a survey of employers that suggest that employers value these traits more than specific skills. In other words, Valerie's learning style has led her to distortions of epistemic assumptions about her chosen trade.

If epistemic meaning perspectives refer to the nature and use of knowledge, we should find distortions that are related to the nature or scope of knowledge (such as for Professor Jones) as well as distortions due to how knowledge is obtained (such as for Valerie).

Distorted Assumptions in
Sociolinguistic Meaning Perspectives

Mezirow (1991) describes the factors that lead to distorted assumptions in sociolinguistic meaning perspectives as including "all the mechanisms by which society and language arbitrarily shape and limit our perception and understanding, such as implicit ideologies; language games; cultural codes; social norms, roles and practices; and underdeveloped levels of consciousness, as well as theories and philosophies" (pp. 130–131). This list leaves no individual free from distorted sociolinguistic assumptions. The culture in which we grew up, the society in which we currently live, and the language we speak all serve to determine our meaning perspectives — the way we see the world, and the way we interpret our experiences.

Habermas (1984), whose writings strongly influenced Mezirow's theory, describes a *system world*. Habermas sees one system as evolving from status and power and leading to the authority of a legal state — its legal system. He sees a second system as evolving from ownership and exchange of possession and products and leading to the establishment of a monetary system. These systems have been removed from the realm of individuals' control; that is, they are no longer questioned or seen as questionable. It can be argued, then, that distorted sociolinguistic assumptions become embedded in our society as it evolves and are virtually inaccessible to most members of our society. Rarely do we overhear a critical discussion of the value of having a legal system, or the necessity for using money as a means of exchange of property, or whether or not educational institutions should exist, or whether it is better to be rich than poor. Mezirow (1991, p. 131) describes it this way: "For the most part we take for granted and are unaware of these social norms and cultural codes, which distribute power and privilege. Our meaning perspectives mirror the way our culture and those individuals responsible for our socialization happen to have defined various situations." He then discusses four types of sociolinguistic distortions. Of those, the ones that are language-based are the most insidious and most commonly encountered by practitioners in all fields.

Many distorted assumptions are *language-based*. Since language, either spoken or written, is the primary method of communication among human beings, the use of language touches on all aspects of education and learning. Ewert (1991), in an analysis of Habermas's influence on education, writes that "the central core of practical knowledge is the understanding of the subjective meaning of language . . . " (p. 351). And language can be described as "the use of inter-subjectively understood symbols within the context of rule-governed institutions" (Hoffman, 1987, p. 235). Habermas (1984) focuses on the use of language in his theory of communicative action—language is the means we have for reaching understanding. Reaching understanding, however, implies that the "rightness, truthfulness, or sincerity of a speech act . . . can be raised and responded to in discourse" (Ewert, 1991, p. 359).

The intent of this preamble is to underline the power and pervasiveness of language-based distortions in assumptions. We are now becoming aware of the assumptions underlying sexist language in our culture, for example. The use of the pronoun "he" throughout an article on management implies underlying assumptions about women's capabilities, their role in organizations, and their role in society. By labeling something or someone through language, we attach the characteristics of the label to the person or thing we have labeled. This is fine except when the label has associations that are uncharacteristic of the object.

When that label has been uncritically assimilated, we find language-based distortions in assumptions. Many examples of such labeling can be found in advertising and in the naming of products. Cars can be, for example, cougars, jaguars, colts, mustangs, rabbits, cobras, and foxes.

Our use of metaphors quickly reveals language-based distortions in our assumptions. When asked to complete the metaphor, Students are . . . , a group of college instructors might generate responses such as: blank pages, sponges, burdens, empty vessels, and puzzles — without even being aware of the assumptions underlying their choice of words, let alone being critical of those assumptions.

Mezirow (1991) also describes *distortion through selective perception* — seeing only what we want to see. Racist meaning perspectives could be products of selective perception. An individual who assumes that Canadian Indians are happy on their reservations and like being taken care of by a white government, for example, has probably chosen not to see the anger and violence of Oka, Quebec, or the issues involved in native people's land claims. Many people prefer not to see the statistics on the frequency of spousal abuse or child abuse.

Level of consciousness is another source of distorted sociolinguistic assumptions. Mezirow cites Freire's (1970) four levels of consciousness: the first (lowest) level in which people are preoccupied with survival needs, the second level in which the oppressed internalize the values of their oppressors, the third level in which people engage in questioning but are easily impressed by populist leaders, and the highest level in which learners engage in action to bring about social change. Although Freire works in and writes about developing countries, there are many examples of low levels of consciousness in North American society. The learner who enters an academic upgrading program or a retraining program may well be preoccupied with survival needs or see himself as a victim of an oppressive bureaucracy but be unable to question the authority of that bureaucracy. Level of consciousness, here, leads not only to distortions in the sociolinguistic meaning perspective but in the psychological perspective as well.

People can be described as having *constrained or unconstrained visions* of humanity. In the constrained vision, humanity is seen as flawed; reason, effort, or action cannot make the world better. In the unconstrained vision, humanity is seen as being able to perfect itself, and social change is possible. The person who believes that nothing can be done will have unquestioned sociolinguistic assumptions. For example, when instructors believe that students today are just not motivated, and there is nothing much an instructor can do to get them to learn, they demonstrate a constrained vision of learners. This type of assumption can also be found among managers who believe that workers will never care about their jobs, political leaders who view the public as stupid or naive, health professionals who do not see the point in trying to educate patients, and lawyers who do not inform their clients.

In addition to these sociolinguistic distortions, other factors influence individuals' assumptions. A person's *cultural and socioeconomic background* provides an obvious source of potential distortion (although to some extent, this factor overlaps with language-based distortions and levels of consciousness). The learner who grew up in an isolated rural environment where cultural activities were not available or where education was not valued may retain distorted assumptions about what constitutes culture and education throughout adulthood. The learner who is from a ghetto in a large city may have quite different meaning perspectives from those of the learner from a suburb of the same city that is made up of single-family dwellings. The person whose parents were farmers may see the world differently from the way a person whose parents were lawyers sees it. The learner who comes from a Jewish family may have different assumptions from those of the learner who comes from a Protestant family. Most of these assumptions will have been uncritically assimilated, and often learners will not even be conscious that assumptions from their upbringing remain intact.

The *current society or culture* in which people live also influences their sociolinguistic meaning perspectives. To varying degrees, people become resocialized when they move from rural to urban areas, from one country to another, or from one socioeconomic class to another. They retain some assumptions that are derived from their background (although these may be unconscious), but revise others to match the change in context. If this is a conscious process based on critical reflection, then transformative learning has taken place; however, it may be a simple adaptation to a new environment — an uncritical response to change. The learner who moves to the city from the farm to attend the university may adopt the values of her peers in order to survive in her new context. The individual who enters into a profession may accept the social norms of his peers in order to have good interpersonal relationships in the workplace. The new values or assumptions, then, form the uncritically assimilated meaning perspective of that environment. A new doctor, a new faculty member, a new farmer, or a new citizen must fit into the social context that accompanies that position. These are but two more examples of the many factors that influence our sociolinguistic meaning perspectives. While no one is free of these influences, educators can foster in learners an awareness of how everyone is affected by social, cultural, and linguistic contexts (see Chapter Eight).

Distorted Assumptions in Psychological Meaning Perspectives

Distorted psychological assumptions "produce ways of feeling and acting that cause us pain because they are inconsistent with our self-concept or sense of how we want to be as adults. They are artifacts of our earlier experience — ways we have learned to defend ourselves after childhood traumas — that have become dysfunctional in adulthood" (Mezirow, 1991, p. 138). To elaborate on this definition, Mezirow cites the psychiatrist Gould (1989) who describes psychological blocks based on hidden prohibitions developed in childhood: for example, an individual who is unable to confront people on behalf of his own interests because of a trauma experienced in confronting his father or a writer who is blocked because of her abusive father's expectation that she perform perfectly. Distorted psychological assumptions are often related to such childhood trauma. The ethical issues this raises — for example, to what extent can the educator be a counselor? — are discussed in Chapter Nine. However, psychological assumptions may also be of a less dramatic nature and fall more readily into the responsibilities of the adult educator.

A learner may lack self-confidence in her ability to succeed as a result of *past educational experiences.* Perhaps she failed courses, was criticized extensively by a teacher, or was simply studying a subject that was inappropriate for her abilities or nature. This learner will have distorted assumptions about her ability to succeed as a learner.

From *past life experience,* a learner may not feel like a real learner. The man who has been a fishing captain for twelve years and is now training to be an instructor in the fisherman certification program may not describe himself as a learner or think he can comprehend theories of instruction. The woman who has not been employed outside the home for several years may have a self-concept that does not include the role of learner. Again, these distorted psychological assumptions will inhibit learning.

Mezirow (1991, p. 43) also lists some *personality variables* (preferred locus of control, characterological preferences) that shape psychological meaning perspectives. If a person believes that other people and situations are primarily responsible for what happens to him (external locus of control), this will influence his psychological assumptions. For example, the educator who says, "The students just have a poor attitude, and I have high standards; therefore I cannot do anything with these students; in fact, they should not be in the program at all," is exhibiting an external locus of control with regard to his practice. As a learner, this individual must question the validity of such an assumption before any change in practice can take place.

As I will discuss in Chapter Five, an individual's *psychological type* shapes psychological meaning perspectives. A person who prefers studying logic and discovering meaning and who believes in truth and justice (the thinking type under Jung's [1971] classification) will have psychological assumptions that reflect those preferences. That person might, for example, have little tolerance for someone who seems to shift with the wind or have little interest in seeing the many alternatives in a situation. Preferences related to psychological type can limit a learner. Jung (1971) would have argued that these assumptions cannot be transformed; however, making them conscious and reflecting on them would constitute growth and development for the learner. Boyd (1989), for example, describes a method based on Jung's work that facilitates personal transformation in a small-group setting. Boyd states that "in developing a resolution to a personal dilemma the individual must first come to know the nature of this dilemma. This is achieved through the expansion of consciousness" (p. 470).

Self-concept, or self-esteem, may be the most common source of psychologically distorted assumptions that the adult educator encounters. This factor, of course, overlaps with each of the other influences listed above — learners have poor self-concepts because of previous educational experiences, previous life experiences, and childhood traumas. For example, learners may say:

- I can't see how I can ever really write a thesis.
- I know I can't understand that theoretical reading.
- I can't see myself as a real academic.
- I just forgot how to study; I know I won't do well.
- I'll never be able to remember all that material.

Psychologically distorted assumptions are shaped by many factors, including dramatic and traumatic childhood events, personality or character traits, past experiences, and possibly the context or environment in which we live. These factors could be categorized in several different ways. It is important, however, that the educator perceive the range, depth, and complexity of the nature of psychologically distorted assumptions as well as the power of these assumptions over learners' behavior and their approach to learning.

Interrelated Meaning Perspectives

In working with a theory based on constructivist assumptions, we should resist the temptation to rigidly compartmentalize our understanding of that theory. The three types of meaning perspectives that I have discussed are not distinct systems of construing meaning. Classification systems do help us make meaning out of chaos, but we also must question our systems. To what extent, for example, are Mezirow's three meaning perspectives discrete? There are various ways of classifying learning and knowledge into domains, and maintaining an awareness of alternate systems helps us continue to question a system.

For example, in the instructional design literature, learning is classified as cognitive, affective, and psychomotor. Cognitive learning would be called epistemic by Mezirow; affective learning would be a combination of the sociolinguistic and psychological meaning perspectives; psychomotor learning would be a combination of the epistemic and the psychological (nonverbal communication, mental set) meaning perspectives. Philosophers have other ways of classifying both knowledge and learning. They ask whether the knowledge is knowing that something is the case (empirically verifiable), knowing some person or place (acquainted with), or knowing how to do something (skill) (Vesey and Foulkes, 1990). As I mentioned previously, Habermas (1971) describes human interests that generate knowledge as belonging to three discrete but broad areas: technical (empirically verifiable), practical (an understanding of social norms), or emancipatory (self-knowledge).

Any classification system is arbitrary and open to question. Even the classification of plant and animal life into taxonomies can be disputed by scientists. We cannot neatly classify human beings' ways of seeing the world into three discrete categories. My way of seeing myself (psychological meaning perspective) will be influenced by my cultural background and family upbringing. Self-concept, which in this discussion belongs to the psychological perspective, can be shaped by factors from the sociolinguistic perspective. The epistemic meaning perspectives overlap both the sociolinguistic and the psychological perspectives. A person growing up in an isolated community may have no exposure to certain forms of knowledge or ways of using knowledge. This is sociolinguistic in origin, but leads to distorted epistemic assumptions. A person who does not believe that she can learn something new (psychological meaning perspective) may not gain the knowledge that is available and thus may have a distorted epistemic meaning perspective. These three perspectives are not easy to sort out, especially when a particular learner is being considered. As with any classification system, this one is best used as a guide for understanding the nature of the phenomenon rather than an absolute way of describing that system.

Summary

Over the years, Mezirow (1975) developed his early interest in the personal transformation undergone by women returning to college into a comprehensive description of how adult learners see the world, question the meaning of what they see, and develop through critical self-reflection (Mezirow, 1991).

A meaning perspective is a way of seeing the world, that is, the perspective or view through which meaning emerges from experience. Since there are different aspects of the world, there are different types of meaning perspectives. Epistemic perspectives are views about knowledge and the way knowledge is used. Sociolinguistic perspectives are views about social norms, culture, and language. Psychological perspectives are views about personal selves.

A person's perspectives are made up of specific values, assumptions, and beliefs, that Mezirow called meaning schemes. A man whose psychological perspective classifies him as introverted may believe he is happier when he is alone, may not think he needs other people, may value peace and quiet, and his inner world may be more important to him than the outside world.

Values, assumptions, and beliefs can be distorted or invalid. Individuals are products of their knowledge (epistemic meaning perspective), their upbringing and background (sociolinguistic perspective), and their psychological development (psychological perspective). Few people question their basic assumptions about the world or are even aware of them. Distortions in underlying assumptions lead, naturally, to distortions in the perspectives they have on the world.

THREE

The Theoretical
Context of
Transformative Learning

Transformative learning theory is not an independent or isolated explanation of a specific learning process. The initial model of perspective transformation (Mezirow, 1978) could perhaps be described in that way; however as I mentioned at the outset of Chapter Two, Mezirow has since drawn on extensive research and related theory in order to provide a fuller description of adult learning and development. He has also worked to place his theory in a broader social context.

Types of meaning perspectives and distorted assumptions within those meaning perspectives have been analyzed. But what about the nature of the learning or change that can take place? How is technical knowledge different from practical understanding? What is emancipatory learning and how is this related to ordinary learning? When a learner engages in reflection, he or she might ask, for example, What do I believe? How have I come to hold this belief? Why is this important? In order to stimulate and support learner reflection, the educator should understand the different types of reflection and know how they relate to different types of learning.

Critically reflective educators continually question their theories as a part of developing their theories of practice. Some critical responses to transformative learning theory have been presented in the literature; many other aspects of the theory yield provocative questions for reflection.

The educator who is working toward transformative learning should be familiar not only with the process of making assumptions explicit by questioning and possibly even revising them but also should understand such intertwined concepts as self-directed learning, autonomy, and critical thinking. Can a learner become more self-directed by working toward transformative learning? Is learner autonomy a prerequisite of transformative learning?

This chapter contains a discussion of the different types of learning and reflection in which adults engage. Some critical responses of other researchers and theorists will be examined. Finally, I will relate the process of transformative learning to three concepts in adult education: self-directed learning, autonomy, and critical thinking.

Types of Learning

Meaning perspectives describe a worldview; learning, whether it is related to psychological, sociolinguistic, or epistemic perspectives has different goals or ends. Learning how to repair a car is quite different from understanding the social norms portrayed on television—which is yet different from working toward individual or societal equality and freedom. This is not to say that learners and educators should simply select whatever form of learning suits their objectives; the overall goal of education exists within a broader cultural context. To this end, Mezirow chooses to embed his theory of adult learning in the cultural context described in Habermas's (1984) theory of communicative competence. If educators are to understand Mezirow's types of learning, some awareness of this context is useful.

Habermas is a powerful and prolific critical social theorist and philosopher who has, in numerous books, presented a comprehensive theory of knowledge, human interest, and communication. Mezirow comments that his work "suggests a new foundation for understanding adult learning and the function and goals of adult education" (1991, p. 65). Ewert (1991), in a review of Habermas's influence on education, found more than 3,200 published articles that made reference to Habermas. The variety of the topics of these articles — sociology of education, teacher education, international education, higher education, program evaluation, adult education — serves to underline the scope of Habermas's work.

Although he has been criticized for his interpretation of Habermas, Mezirow (1991, p. xiv) notes that he has not "attempted to interpret systematically what Habermas or any other single theorist has to say about adult learning." As I mentioned earlier, Mezirow's original model was derived from his observations of women returning to college. Only as he elaborated on and expanded this model into a theory did he begin to relate his work to that of other theorists, including Habermas.

In this section, therefore, I will not survey Habermas's theories of knowledge and communicative action but will present some concepts that may be useful in informing adult educators' theories of practice. These concepts will constitute a framework for understanding transformative learning.

Since the terminology used here can be confusing, I will show how Habermas's *interests* and *learning domains,* and Mezirow's types of *meaning perspectives* are related to each other. Table 3.1 summarizes the terms used by Habermas and Mezirow's subsequent learning domains.

As I have mentioned, Habermas classified people's interests into three broad areas: technical, practical, and emancipatory. Technical interests are based on "the need to control and to manipulate the external environment . . . and are ex-

Table 3.1. Interests, Knowledge, and Learning Domains.

Interests: (Habermas)	Technical (work)	Practical (language)	Emancipatory (power)
Knowledge: (Habermas)	Instrumental (causal explanation)	Practical (understanding)	Emancipation (reflection)
Learning Domain: (Mezirow)	Instrumental	Communicative	Emancipatory

pressed through the medium of work . . . (Bullough and Goldstein, 1984, p. 144). Practical interests are reflected in people's use of language to "further mutual understanding of individual interests and needs and to coordinate social action to satisfy mutual interests and needs" (Ewert, 1991, p. 351). People's emancipatory interests are reflected in their "drive to transcend, to grow and to develop" (Bullough and Goldstein, 1984, p. 144) both as individuals and in relation to groups or societies.

Habermas (1984) states that different human interests require different forms of knowledge; that is, a natural science orientation (positivism) does not apply to understanding or validating subjective knowledge. An interest in controlling and manipulating the external environment requires knowledge about causal relationships between events; Habermas (1971) calls this *instrumental knowledge*. An interest in understanding each other through language leads to knowledge about social norms, cultural values, and the traditions underlying the society we live in — Habermas's *practical knowledge*. An interest in understanding ourselves, maintaining our freedom, and developing relational autonomy leads to self-knowledge. This includes a knowledge of the influence of past experience and social context — Habermas's *emancipatory knowledge*.

Mezirow (1991) describes three *learning domains* based on Habermas's classification of interests and knowledge. The domain of *instrumental learning* "centrally involves determining cause-effect relationships and learning through task-oriented problem solving" (p. 73). Instrumental learning involves forming hypotheses about observable events, making predictions based on these hypotheses, and evaluating the outcome. For example, a person who wants to learn how to care for fruit trees organically might read several books on the topic, consult a fruit farmer, then develop plans (hypotheses) for controlling insects and disease, for pruning, and for fertilizing the trees. These hypotheses could then be tested by implementing the plans for one season. A good crop of disease-free fruit would validate the hypotheses. Truth is determined and instrumental learning takes place through empirical inquiry.

Mezirow's domain of *communicative learning* includes "learning to understand what others mean and to make ourselves understood as we attempt to share ideas through speech, the written word, plays, moving pictures, television, and art" (1991, p. 75). Mezirow sees this domain as encompassing most of the learning in adulthood, including "understanding, describing, and explaining intentions; values; ideals; moral issues; social, political, philosophical, or educational concepts; feelings and reasons" (1991, p. 75). Although problem solving may be involved, the process is quite different from instrumental learning. The learner interacts with others using language and nonverbal communication and attempts to anticipate the actions of others. The process is influenced by social norms. For example, a manager may wish to learn how to increase participative decision making and teamwork among his staff. He enrolls in a workshop series in which this is among the stated goals of learning. In their first discussion, the group tries to arrive at a consensus on the meaning of participative decision making and the reasons for using it in an organization. Participants then imagine ways to implement it in their work contexts. Following this session, the managers meet with their staff members to discuss the possibilities for implementation arising from the workshop and then share the results of this experience in the next workshop. Communicative learning takes place as the managers develop an understanding of others' perceptions and try to make themselves understood.

Mezirow defines *emancipatory learning* as "emancipation from libidinal, linguistic, epistemic, institutional or environmental forces that limit our options and our rational control over our lives but have been taken for granted or seen as beyond human control" (1991, p. 87). Emancipatory learning takes place through critical self-reflection, including reflection on the instrumental and communicative learning domains as well as on self-knowledge. Mezirow states that "critical reflection clearly constitutes an integral element in the process involved in validating learning about the environment and other people as well as ourselves; that is, in both instrumental and communicative learning" (1991, p. 87). Consequently, "emancipatory learning often is transformative" (p. 88). If the manager in the example had been an autocratic leader with a firm belief in the necessity of telling subordinates how to do their jobs, emancipatory learning could still have taken place as employees tried alternative ways of interpreting his actions. Personal and social (and in this case, organizational) change could become possible through awareness of the psychological and cultural assumptions inherent in the autocratic leadership style.

What type of learning occurs within the different meaning perspectives? Emancipatory learning can occur in each of the three meaning perspectives, which makes it almost equivalent to transformative learning. Communicative learning does appear to be primarily within the sociolinguistic perspective; however, communicative learning can lead to changes in the psychological or epistemic perspectives. If this is the case, does the learning then become emancipatory? Instrumental learning primarily occurs in relation to the epistemic meaning perspective but is only one component of knowledge and the use of knowledge. Mezirow comments that communicative and instrumental learning are "two interacting" domains of learning, while emancipatory (or reflective) learning is a process that affects each of the other two domains (Mezirow, 1991, p. 64). In Chapter Two, the three meaning perspectives were not treated as separate from or unrelated to each other. Now, it also becomes apparent that learning is multidimensional and can influence meaning perspectives in a variety of ways and at different levels. In Chapter Four, I will propose a taxonomy of transformative learning in order to clarify some of these interrelationships among concepts.

Types of Reflection

Traditionally, learning has been defined as the acquisition of any relatively permanent change in behavior as a result of practice or experience. The concept of reflection, or critically assessing our interpretations of experience, has often been neglected in psychological theories of learning.

Reflection is a key concept in transformative learning theory. Indeed, reflective thinking has become a goal of education and a topic of extensive research and writing. Educators are no longer interested in seeing learners memorize content but rather in teaching learners how to think. This transition in educational theory and practice can be traced to Dewey (1933), who defined reflection as "active, persistent and careful consideration of any belief or supposed form of knowledge in the light of the grounds that support it and the further conclusion to which it tends" (p. 9). Definitions in the recent literature do not deviate conceptually from Dewey's understanding. Boyd and Fales (1983, p. 100) define reflection as "the process of internally examining and exploring an issue of concern, triggered by an experience, which creates and clarifies meaning in terms of self, and which results in a changed conceptual perspective." Boud, Keogh, and Walker (1985, p. 3) see reflection as "a generic term for those intellectual and affective activities in which individuals engage to explore their experiences in order to lead to new understandings and appreciation." Mezirow (1991, p. 104) writes that "reflection is the process of critically assessing the content, process, or premise(s) of our efforts to interpret and give meaning to an experience." This definition leads him to distinguish among three types of reflection.

Content reflection is an examination of the content or description of a problem. If a learner of automobile mechanics encountered a new piece of equipment for diagnosing fuel injection problems, he probably would ask, What is this equipment? He might try to determine the characteristics of the equipment, observe someone else using it, or read the manual. An older adult learner attending an adult education center in an effort to upgrade her high school skills might feel uncomfortable and out of place and ask herself, What is the problem here? She could examine her feelings, that is, question whether she feels intellectually inferior, or socially out of place, or worried about her study habits. The *content* of the problem is examined.

Process reflection involves checking on the problem-solving strategies that are being used. The student of mechanics would ask how he tried to identify the equipment. Did he miss key characteristics? Did he neglect to consider a similar piece of equipment he had observed while in the shop? Did he not understand the manual? The older learner might ask, How have I understood this problem? Did I overlook any clues? Have I considered my own nature in interacting with others? The *process* of problem solving is examined; the learner stops to think.

Premise reflection takes place when the problem itself is questioned. The apprentice mechanic would ask, Why do I need to learn to operate this equipment? What is the basis of my belief that I need to learn it? Is it valid? The older student might ask, What is the basis for my belief that I am uncomfortable? Is this just a natural reaction to an unfamiliar setting? The basic premise underlying the posing of the problem is questioned.

Premise reflection leads the individual to a transformation of meaning perspectives. Mezirow (1991, p. 111) writes that "content and process reflection are the dynamics by which our beliefs — meaning schemes — are changed, that is, become reinforced, elaborated, created, negated, confirmed, or identified as problems. . . . Premise reflection is the dynamic by which our belief systems — meaning perspectives — become transformed." When people engage in content or process reflection, their meaning schemes may be transformed; when they engage in premise reflection, their meaning perspectives may be transformed.

Each type of reflection can take place in each of the learning domains and with regard to each of the meaning perspectives. Table 3.2 contains examples of the types of questions that a learner engaged in content, process, or premise reflection might ask and shows how the questions relate to each meaning perspective.

My intent is not to oversimplify Mezirow's complex discussion of reflection but to differentiate clearly among the three types of reflection so that we can design educational strategies to foster each type.

Similarly, Table 3.3 provides examples of the kinds of questions that an individual engaged in instrumental, communicative, or emancipatory learning might ask. Again, care must be taken not to use such examples to oversimplify the underlying concepts. Awareness of the questions simply facilitates the development of strategies to encourage content, process, and

Table 3.2. Types of Reflection and Meaning Perspectives.

Reflection	Perspective		
	Psychological	Sociolinguistic	Epistemic
Content	What do I believe about myself?	What are the social norms?	What knowledge do I have?
Process	How have I come to have this perception of myself?	How have these social norms been influential?	How did I obtain this knowledge?
Premise	Why should I question this perception?	Why are these norms important?	Why do I need/not need this knowledge?

Table 3.3. Types of Reflection and Learning Domains.

Reflection	Learning		
	Instrumental	Communicative	Emancipatory
Content	What is the causal relationship between events?	What do others say about this issue?	What are my assumptions?
Process	How did I empirically validate the causal relationship?	How did I obtain consensual validation on this issue?	How do I know my assumptions are valid?
Premise	Why is this knowledge important to me?	Why should I believe in this conclusion?	Why should I revise/not revise my perspective?

premise reflection. Emancipatory learning should not be seen as a discrete category; therefore the assumptions being reflected on could be related to either the instrumental or communicative domains of learning as well as to self-knowledge.

Critical Responses to Transformative Theory

It was not until eleven years after Mezirow (1978) first proposed transformative learning as a goal of adult education that the first critique of his work appeared (Collard and Law, 1989). Since that time, there has been surprisingly little critical response to Mezirow's theorizing. Educators should be aware of the areas in which Mezirow has been questioned, however, and should continue to reflect on this theory and the extent to which it influences their own theory of practice. To aid in the process, I will describe four types of criticism in the literature and pose some questions for critical reflection.

Social Change

Collard and Law (1989, p. 102) suggest that "the fundamental problem in Mezirow's work" is "the lack of a coherent, comprehensive theory of social change . . . evident in his selective interpretation and adaptation of Habermas, and partially dependent on problems within Habermas's own work." The main thesis of the essay is that Mezirow emphasizes the individual perspective transformation and fails to acknowledge the "social environment in which structural inequalities are entrenched" (p. 105). The authors suggest that social action is a necessary *prerequisite* for "emancipatory discourse." They trace the problem with transformative learning theory to Mezirow's use of Habermas's work but attribute some of the difficulty to a flaw in Habermas's concept of self-reflection. They also note Mezirow's difficulty in incorporating a shift in Habermas's thinking into his own work. Mezirow is described as having "painted himself into a Habermasian corner" (p. 101). Collard and Law (1989, p. 104) point out that Habermas's ideal conditions for discourse require a relationship of equality among all participants, yet the adult educator's role is clearly not one of equality; the educator is more like an organizer of enlightenment.

Mezirow (1989) responds to Collard and Law by clarifying the point that he sees perspective transformation as individual, group, or collective. He describes social action as crucial, but not as the only goal of adult education, emphasizing that the learner must decide to take social action; the educator cannot make such decisions. For the educator to set out to effect a certain political action would be indoctrination, Mezirow argues (p. 172). Finally, Mezirow points out that his shift in view — seeing critical reflection as applicable to both instrumental and communicative learning — had "nothing to do with Habermas" (p. 175).

The social context is also of concern to Tennant (1993) who examines the developmental process inherent in transformative learning. He argues that "what is, and what is not, more integrative of experience depends on the social and historical context in which experience occurs" (p. 37). He sees adult development as both social and psychological, and describes a person's life course as socially constructed. As do Collard and Law, Tennant sees a danger in omitting a social critique because conventional views of what it means to learn and develop might dominate the process.

Power

Hart (1990a) enters into the debate but chooses to discuss the dimension of social action in slightly different terms. She criticizes Mezirow's interpretation of Habermas's theory of communicative action on the grounds that it is severed from a critique of power.

Hart (1990a) points out an implicit claim in Mezirow's work that the educator can be outside a power-bound and therefore distorted context. She argues that the role of the educator cannot be that clear-cut, "particularly not when power, and distorted forms of interaction and communication are placed at the center of one's educational program" (p. 136). Further, in Hart's view, "to espouse a concept of emancipatory education binds one to the full range of its practical implications. It therefore signifies a fundamental commitment to struggle against the blinding and distorting effects of power in as many ways as are appropriate or possible, and a commitment to help create non-oppressive communities" (p. 136).

Underlying Habermas's writing is a concern for dominance-free forms of social relations. The educator must understand the nature of such distortions and incorporate that understanding into their work with learners. Hart argues that by placing the issue of power at the center of the analysis, the list of distortions relevant to transformative learning is closely associated with the three dimensions of communicative action and therefore differs from Mezirow's list of distortions in meaning perspectives. Similarly, Hart argues that communicative action is the center of transformative learning — the concept of power underlies communicative theory — and that "instrumental learning is *always* embedded in a communicative or normative context" (p. 129).

Hart raises interesting points. I will discuss the concept of power in Chapter Six as central to learner empowerment through transformative learning, and I have already mentioned the confusion between Habermas's domains of knowledge and Mezirow's meaning perspectives. Whether or not Mezirow neglects the issue of power, however, is questionable. Although he does not explicitly define or discuss types of power, an awareness of power seems to underlie his theory. In fact, Mezirow's reluctance to suggest that the educator deliberately influence learners' decisions to engage in social change shows his sensitivity to the power inherent in the educator's role.

Context

Clark and Wilson (1991) present a critical response to Mezirow in which they argue that he fails to account for the cultural context of learning; he limits himself to masculine, white, middle-class values and fails to reflect the values he holds. "What he fails to do . . . is to maintain the essential link between the meaning of experience and the context in which it arises and by which it is interpreted" (p. 76). Turning Mezirow's theory on itself, they argue that the fundamental assumptions underlying Mezirow's theory reflect "the hegemonic American values of individualism, rationality, and autonomy" and that these values have been incorporated "uncritically within his theory" (p. 80).

Mezirow, however, has from the beginning described individuals' distorted assumptions as products of their cultural context. He responds by saying "the cultural context is literally embodied and gives meaning to the symbolic models and meaning perspectives central to my argument. Both are learned in a social context and are, for the most part, uncritically assimilated . . ." (Mezirow, 1991b, p. 190). He agrees that his 1970s work does not include an analysis of social trends and that his original study was of white middle-class women returning to college. But he describes this as "my historic insensitivity to the cultural context" rather than a "challenge to the findings regarding perspective transformation" (p. 192).

Rationality

Although Mezirow sees transformative theory as having as its context constructivism, critical theory, and deconstructivism, he describes the process of critical self-reflection leading potentially to transformation as conscious and rational. Boyd and Myers (1988; Boyd, 1985; Boyd, 1989) define personal transformation within a framework of analytical psychology (Jung, 1969a; 1969b) and suggest that transformation is not entirely rational. They describe the process of discernment in which symbols, images, and archetypes play a role in personal illumination. Boyd (1989) reports on a method of working in small groups in which individuals struggle to deal with unconscious content. The group itself affects the way individual members create images, identify personal dilemmas, and relate developmental phases to personal stages. Boyd defines personal transformation as "a fundamental change in one's personality involving conjointly the resolution of a personal dilemma and the expansion of consciousness resulting in greater personality integration" (Boyd, 1989, p. 459).

   Arguments against the solely rational approach to transformation have also been made on philosophical grounds. Stanage (1989), for example, suggests that meaning transformations can be interpreted through a postmodern perspective in which change is not linear, determinable, or predictable.

Questions for Critical Reflection

I do not intend to further develop or expand Mezirow's work but rather to stimulate educators' questioning of the theoretical perspectives within which they may be working. I will raise questions related to social change, power (Chapter Six), context, and rationality (Chapter Five.)

The educator can and should question several aspects of transformative learning theory, particularly in relation to his or her own practice. Any theory of practice must be informed through an understanding of what others write and say, but it also must be freely chosen on the basis of experience. The educator should be particularly aware of his or her own content (What is the theory?), process (How do I validate this?), and premise reflection (Why does this matter?).

With regard to the content and structure of the theory, the educator could reflect on questions such as:

- Can the three meaning perspectives (psychological, sociolinguistic, and epistemic) be clearly distinguished from each other? Does it matter if they cannot be?
- Can the relationships among the three domains of learning (instrumental, communicative, and emancipatory) be clearly described? Does it matter if they cannot be?
- How can one describe types of learning within each meaning perspective? Of what advantage is it to describe types of learning in this way?

With regard to the process of transformative learning in practice, the educator may consider questions such as:

- Is transformation of an epistemic meaning perspective emancipatory learning? Is transformation of an epistemic meaning scheme emancipatory learning?
- Can only premise reflection lead to transformative learning? How do we know when learners engage in premise reflection? Why should we foster it?
- Can transformative learning occur that does not lead to social change? How? Why should we foster it?
- Is social change a prerequisite to emancipatory learning? How? Why should an educator promote social change?
- Can we come close to the ideal conditions for critical discourse? How? Why should we?

- What effect does educator power have on critical discourse? How can we know about this effect?
- Can or should the educator be an equal participant in discourse? Why?
- How can the educator participate in critical discourse while still fostering learners' examination of their assumptions? Should the educator do this?
- Can an educator be free from his or her own cultural context? Should the educator work toward this? Why?

These are only examples of questions that might have already occurred to educators. I will discuss the process of transformative learning in practice in Chapter Four and explore the fostering of critical reflection and transformative learning in practical detail in Chapters Seven through Nine. Other questions and issues will arise as these discussions proceed. Chapter Ten is dedicated to the educator as learner, including reflection on practice and the educator's development of an informed theory of practice.

Transformative Learning in Adult Education Literature

I described three types of adult learning in Chapter One: subject-oriented, consumer-oriented, and emancipatory learning. Transformative learning can be stimulated by participation in subject or consumer-oriented learning, but transformation is most likely to occur in emancipatory learning. Although this categorization places transformative theory within the context of adult education theory and practice, it does not address the interrelationships among popular concepts in the literature. For example, must a person be self-directed in order to engage in transformative learning? Or does the process of transformative learning foster self-directed learning? Can critical thinking be developed that is independent of the transformative learning process? Does transformative learning increase learner autonomy? Of the popular concepts in the literature, self-directed learning, critical thinking, and autonomy have the closest connections with transformative learning theory.

Self-Directed Learning and Transformative Learning

The literature on self-directed learning contains a confusing array of definitions. As I mentioned in Chapter One, Knowles's (revised, 1984) concept was one of learner involvement in the decisions of instructional design. Researchers have also extensively examined the supposed self-directedness of learners (see Guglielmino, 1977), thus treating the concept as a characteristic of people rather than as a learning process. Brookfield (1986) distinguishes between two forms: the techniques of self-directed learning I listed earlier and an internal change of consciousness that occurs "when learners come to regard knowledge as relative and contextual, to view the value frameworks and moral codes informing their behaviors as cultural constructs, and to use this altered perspective to contemplate ways in which they can transform their personal and social worlds" (p. 47). Candy (1991) argues that the concept is actually several concepts incorporating both process and product. He describes four distinct but related phenomena: "'self-direction' as a personal attribute (personal autonomy); 'self-direction' as the willingness and capacity to conduct one's own education (self-management); 'self-direction' as a mode of organizing instruction in formal settings (learner-control) and 'self-direction' as the individual, noninstitutional pursuit of learning opportunities in the 'natural societal setting' (autodidaxy)" (Candy, 1991, p. 23). Most recently, Brookfield (1993) discusses the political dimensions of self-directed learning; that is learner control over decision making, and learner access to resources for learning.

Brookfield's (1986) characterization of self-directed learning is similar to the transformative learning process. In 1993, he moves his perspective on self-directed learning even closer to transformation by emphasizing the importance of control, by questioning who decides what is right or good, and by suggesting that these processes are also central to emancipatory adult education. Brookfield is clear that implementing self-directed learning does not require an educator to abandon his or her own goals and act in a purely accommodative fashion. When he states that "a fully adult form of self-direction exists only when we examine our definitions of what we think it is important for us to learn and the extent to which these definitions serve repressive interests" (p. 234), he is describing critical self-reflection, a process that lies at the heart of transformative learning.

Candy's (1991) constructivist interpretation of self-directed learning also falls within transformative theory, especially his emphasis on learning as a social activity and the attainment of personal autonomy through interdependence. Candy sees the learner's social background as a possible constraint to self-direction, as do Brockett and Hiemstra (1991). But becoming more self-directed could be, in some circumstances, a transformative learning process.

Self-directed learning is interwoven with transformative learning. The nature of the relationship varies with the definition of self-directed learning and the component of it that is being considered. To some extent, an individual must either already be self-directed or have the skills to engage in self-directed learning if transformative learning is to be possible. Self-directed learning can also be described as the process by which learners question their assumptions and contemplate ways in which they can change their worlds. And, finally, increased self-directedness is likely to be a product of the transformative learning process.

Autonomy and Transformative Learning

'Autonomy' has been of interest to philosophers and educators for centuries. In 1762, Rousseau described an autonomous person as one who "is obedient to a law that he prescribes to himself." The diversity of definitions of autonomy reflects the attention that has been paid to this concept. Generally, autonomy is described as having three dimensions: intellectual, moral, and emotional (Plato's three cardinal virtues were intellectual self-determination, fortitude, and temperance); however, such simplicity is misleading. Autonomy has also been described as an innate disposition (Rogers, 1969), a characteristic that develops as a person matures (Strike, 1982), and a characteristic acquired through learning. Brookfield (1986) sees autonomy (defined as the possession of an understanding and awareness of a range of alternative possibilities) as being at the heart of self-directed learning. He proposes a philosophy of practice that centers on the adult's developing sense of control and autonomy, the purpose of which is "to assist individuals to begin to exercise control over their own lives, their interpersonal relationships, and the social forms and structures within which they live" (Brookfield, 1986, p. 291).

Candy (1991) argues that autonomy is a process rather than a product and that "one does not 'become' autonomous in any final or absolute sense; rather one is able to think and act autonomously in certain circumstances" (p. 114). After reviewing the literature on personal autonomy, he concludes that "a person is autonomous to the extent that he or she: conceives of goals and plans; exercises freedom of choice; uses the capacity for rational reflection; has will power to follow through; exercises self-restraint and self-discipline; and views himself or herself as autonomous" (Candy, 1991, p. 125). Jarvis (1992) discusses autonomy as free will, emphasizing both interior and exterior freedom. Previous experiences, socialization, and the resulting habitualized thought process inhibit autonomy.

According to Brookfield's, Candy's, and Jarvis's characterizations of autonomy, becoming autonomous is a transformative process, that is, becoming free of the constraints of unarticulated or distorted meaning perspectives. Full autonomy is an ideal, as is being completely conscious of the sources and consequences of meaning perspectives and being free from coercion, constraints, and distortions in those perspectives. Transformative learning theory articulates the process of becoming autonomous. The more autonomous a learner is, the more likely he or she would be to engage in transformative learning. Likewise, participation in the process of transformative learning further increases autonomy. In describing the process of questioning and possibly revising assumptions in the transformative learning process, Candy writes, "an autonomous person is able to assent to rules, or modify or reject them, if they are found wanting" (1991, p. 113).

Critical Thinking and Transformative Learning

Critical thinking has recently come to resemble a slogan adorning a bandwagon in North American education. Conferences on critical thinking, funding for research on critical thinking, and media attention have served to encourage educators at all levels to espouse the importance of teaching students how to think critically. As a concept in the literature, critical thinking has been described in several ways. For example, it has been called logical reasoning (Hallet, 1984), rational reflection on experience (Jarvis, 1987), an act of enquiry to settle a doubt (Dewey, 1933), and scepticism toward a given statement or established norm (McPeck, 1981).

Garrison (1991) proposes a five-stage cycle of critical thinking (problem identification, problem definition, exploration, applicability, and integration), which he describes as indistinguishable from Mezirow's (1981) process of perspective transformation.

In spite of Garrison's claim, Brookfield's (1987) four components of critical thinking show an even clearer connection to transformative learning. In fact, Brookfield writes, "one alternative interpretation of the concept of critical thinking is that of *emancipatory learning*" (p. 12). He describes critical thinking as including: identifying and challenging assumptions, challenging the importance of the context that has influenced our assumptions, imagining and exploring alternatives, and exhibiting reflective scepticism. Brookfield emphasizes that critical thinking involves more than logical reasoning or "scrutinizing arguments for assertions unsupported by empirical evidence" (p. 13). He sees the phases of becoming a critical thinker as including:

- The occurrence of a trigger event that prompts inner discomfort and perplexity
- An appraisal of oneself or self-scrutiny
- An exploration of ways to either explain discrepancies or to live with them

- The development of alternative perspectives or new ways of thinking and acting
- The integration of new perspectives into one's life

"Sometimes," writes Brookfield (1987, p. 27) "this integration involves transforming attitudes and assumptions. At other times it entails confirming, with a renewed sense of conviction, existing stances."

Brookfield's conceptualization of critical thinking is analogous to Mezirow's description of transformative learning in its skeletal form. Other interpretations of critical thinking in the literature tend to be parallel to transformative learning in one meaning perspective or another (epistemic for Garrison and sociolinguistic for Jarvis, for example). This is not surprising, given that Mezirow calls critical reflection the key concept in transformative learning.

Summary

Transformative learning theory is embedded in the broader context of Habermas's theory of communicative competence, particularly the concepts of instrumental, practical, and emancipatory knowledge. Mezirow describes instrumental learning as understanding cause and effect relationships through problem solving, communicative learning as understanding what others mean, and emancipatory learning as becoming free from restraints through critical self-reflection. Both *learning* and *reflection* are multidimensional processes. A person can engage in *content reflection* (describing what the problem is), in *process reflection* (checking on the strategies being used to address a problem), or in *premise reflection* (questioning the problem itself). Each type of reflection can take place within each domain of learning. Also, each type of reflection can be placed within the psychological, sociolinguistic, and epistemic meaning perspectives.

Few critical responses to transformative learning theory have appeared in the literature. The underemphasis on social action and on the concept of power have been mentioned critically; also, Mezirow's understanding of the cultural context of learning has been questioned. An alternate nonrational view of personal transformation can be seen as complementary to transformative theory. It is equally interesting to raise our own questions for critical reflection. I provided some examples to stimulate such thinking.

Finally, transformative learning theory can be related to other perspectives in adult education theory and practice, including self-directed learning, autonomy, and critical thinking.

What does the process of transformative learning look like from the learner's perspective? Are there different types or degrees of transformative learning? Although Mezirow (1975) based his original ideas on observations of learners, he has not yet examined his more comprehensive theory from the learner's perspective. The educator who is interested in fostering transformative learning in practice should consider learners' perspectives and reflect on his or her own experiences with learners. In the next chapter, I will discuss how learners engage in transformative learning and propose different levels or types of transformative learning.

FOUR

How Transformative
Learning Occurs

In this chapter, I will examine the process of transformative learning from the learner's point of view. We might want to know, for example, whether there are stages in the process. Are these stages necessarily consistent across learners? Must a learner feel empowered before transformative learning can begin? Or is empowerment a consequence of transformative learning? Or both? What triggers transformative learning? How can learners go about questioning their own assumptions? How do learners see the role of others — fellow learners, family, friends, educator, co-workers — in the process?

First, note that there are different types or levels of transformative learning. To understand what transformative learning looks and feels like from the learner's perspective, the possible variations in the nature of the process must be clarified. As I discussed in Chapter Two, learners can engage in content, process, or premise reflection within the psychological, sociolinguistic, and epistemic meaning perspectives. Each type of reflection can also occur as a component of instrumental, communicative, or emancipatory learning. Emancipatory learning can apply to each meaning perspective. The process of reflection and hence of transformative learning will be different across perspectives and across learning domains. To clarify these differences, I propose a taxonomy of processes for working toward transformative learning.

Taxonomy of Processes for
Working Toward Transformative Learning

When does reflection become critical reflection? When does critical reflection become critical self-reflection? When does critical self-reflection lead to transformative learning? Is transformative learning always emancipatory? These are some of the questions that can be addressed through a classification system. I have deliberately chosen the phrase *working toward transformative learning* rather than simply *transformative learning* so I can include reflection that does not necessarily lead to transformation. Mezirow (1991, p. 111) writes that "reflective learning can be either confirmative or transformative. It becomes transformative when assumptions are found to be distorting, inauthentic, or otherwise unjustified. Transformative learning results in new or transformed meaning schemes, or when reflection focuses on premises, new or transformed meaning perspectives—that is, in perspective transformation." He suggests that only premise reflection leads to transformation of meaning perspectives. However, content and process reflection may lead to changes in meaning schemes: "transformative learning here may refer to content and process reflection, which can lead to transformation in meaning schemes . . . " (p. 108). This would hold true for the psychological, sociolinguistic, and epistemic meaning perspectives.

In relating transformative learning to the domains of learning, Mezirow (1991, p. 87) argues that "emancipatory knowledge is knowledge gained through critical self-reflection as distinct from the knowledge gained from our 'technical' interest in the objective world or our 'practical' interest in social relationships." Habermas (1971) describes instrumental, communicative, and emancipatory knowledge as different kinds of knowledge based on "our discrete cognitive interests in controlling nature, social harmony, and individual growth" (Ewert, 1991, p. 347). However, Mezirow suggests that the emancipatory interest has implications for both instrumental and communicative learning.

In Table 4.1, a classification system that incorporates

Table 4.1. A Taxonomy of Processes
for Working Toward Transformative Learning.

| | Domain of Learning | |
Instrumental	Communicative	Emancipatory
Least complex learning (complexity increases down column)	More complex learning (complexity increases down column)	Most complex learning (complexity increases down column)
Positivism	Constructivism	Constructivism
Content reflection on epistemic meaning schemes	Content reflection on epistemic, psychological, and sociolinguistic meaning schemes	Content and process reflection on epistemic, psychological, and sociolinguistic meaning schemes leading to transformed meaning schemes
Process reflection on epistemic meaning schemes	Process reflection on epistemic, psychological, and sociolinguistic meaning schemes	
Premise reflection on epistemic meaning perspectives	Premise reflection on epistemic, psychological, and sociolinguistic meaning perspectives	Premise reflection on epistemic, psychological, and sociolinguistic meaning perspectives leading to transformed meaning perspectives

domains of learning, types of reflection, and domains of meaning perspectives is shown. Content reflection and process reflection are depicted as components of instrumental learning and are the least complex processes. Premise reflection (emancipatory domain of learning) on meaning perspectives is the most complex process. Within this cell of the taxonomy, it may be that for some learners premise reflection on the sociolinguistic meaning perspective is more complex than on the psychological perspective — which is in turn more complex than premise reflection on the epistemic meaning perspective. Similarly, within each cell, content reflection is probably less complex than process reflection. Premise reflection, which occurs only in the emancipatory domain of learning, is more complex.

Note that the elements of the taxonomy represent processes, not educational aims, and the degree of complexity described refers to those processes. From a constructivist perspective, educational aims are not end states but criteria for the process of education. "Educational ends are not clear or definitive" (Ewert, 1991, p. 351).

Instrumental learning can also be classified as positivistic (Ewert, 1991, p. 348) and communicative learning and emancipatory learning as constructivistic (Mezirow, 1991). However, Mezirow is careful to state that such a differentiation should not be understood as a dichotomy; he sees most learning as involving both instrumental and communicative learning. Consequently, the taxonomy implies that we can move freely between different learning processes.

What would the learning process in each of these cells look like? Some examples will clarify the terminology used in this classification system. In the first cell (instrumental learning), an individual may consider whether changing the grip she uses on her squash racquet will improve her backhand swing (content reflection). Further, she may question how this would have an effect (process reflection), formulate a hypothesis, and then experiment with a variety of grips in an effort to support the hypothesis. She could question why this matters at all since she plays squash for fun rather than to win (premise reflection). As soon as the learner asks *why,* her reflection begins taking place on the level of a meaning perspective rather than a meaning scheme. Asking why takes account of the larger framework within which an assumption exists.

In the second cell (communicative domain of learning), several kinds of reflection are included. A learner may question what the neo-Nazis in Germany are doing (content reflection, epistemic meaning scheme). He then may discuss this issue with others to determine how others view it (process reflection, epistemic meaning scheme) and ask why he should believe what others say (premise reflection, epistemic meaning perspective). The same learner may ask, What are my beliefs about the behavior of the neo-Nazis? (content reflection, psychological meaning scheme). Going a step further, he may ask, How do I know my beliefs are valid? How do I know that I am not making unwarranted assumptions about this issue? (process reflection, psychological domain) or Why should I question my beliefs; I've always held these beliefs so why should I examine them now? (premise reflection, psychological meaning perspective). And finally, the learner may examine media reports and the social context of the issue. He may ask such questions as What language are the media using? What is the social relevance or historical context of this issue? (content reflection, sociolinguistic perspective). This could lead to reflection on how media language influences people's perceptions and how the history of Germany relates to the way the neo-Nazi behavior is currently discussed (process reflection, sociolinguistic meaning perspective). Reflection on why this is important or why the conclusions reached are valid (premise reflection, sociolinguistic meaning perspective) could follow.

Emancipatory learning is divided into two parts: critical reflection on meaning schemes and critical reflection on meaning perspectives. The first part — reflection on epistemic, psychological, or sociolinguistic meaning schemes — is similar to what happens in communicative learning. But this reflection becomes emancipatory learning when meaning schemes are transformed as a result of the reflection. In the example given earlier, if as a result of his reflection the learner realizes that his beliefs about neo-Nazi behavior reflect misconceptions or distortions and subsequently changes those beliefs, his learning moves into the emancipatory domain.

Premise reflection on meaning perspectives, the most complex type of learning in the taxonomy, can lead to transformative learning. When it does, it comes under the emancipatory domain of learning. If, for example, a college instructor enrolls in a certificate course entitled "Curriculum Development" and finds that the course is intended to foster self-directed learning and reflection on practice as well as to encourage an increased understanding of curriculum development, she may engage in premise reflection on several meaning perspectives. The learner could question the validity of self-directed learning as a model for certificate level courses (epistemic meaning perspective). She could critically reflect on her own role as an educator (psychological meaning perspective). She could ask how this approach fits in with the constraints of the college system and the beliefs of her peers (sociolinguistic meaning perspective). If such reflection leads to a change in meaning perspective and in the direction of differentiation and integration, transformative learning will have occurred.

These examples emphasize two important points: domains of learning and types of meaning perspectives do not fall into neat categories, and there are clearly qualitative differences among types of reflection and types of learning on some continuum of complexity, although this continuum is not rigidly hierarchical.

Stages in Working Toward Transformative Learning

There is some danger in searching for generic stages in a learning process, particularly given the variations and complexities in the process just discussed. I will use the term *stage* here to mean a period in a process, with no intention of implying a linear or hierarchical sequence. All learners do not go through the same stages at the same time. Also, learners do not necessarily complete one stage and then move on to the next; rather, in practice, the distinctions between the stages are likely to be blurred, and learners are likely to move back and forth between stages or experience more than one stage at the same time.

At the most general level, Brookfield (1987, pp. 26–28) describes five phases of critical thinking, basing these phases on an integration of literature from several sources. As I mentioned in Chapter Three, Brookfield's characterization of critical thinking is parallel to the tansformative learning process. He describes a *trigger event* as an unexpected event that leads to discomfort or perplexity in the learner. A trigger event can be a trauma such as the loss of a job or a positive event such as succeeding at a difficult task. After the trigger event comes a phase of *appraisal,* that is, a self-examination, or identification and clarification of the concern. In relation to the taxonomy presented earlier, this phase could include content reflection on epistemic, psychological, or sociolinguistic meaning perspectives. The individual asks, What is going on here?

The third phase is labeled *exploration;* the person tries to explain discrepancies found in the appraisal phase or investigates new ways of thinking or behaving. The individual is open to new ideas and is searching for new ways of doing things. To some extent, this phase may be equivalent to process reflection on meaning perspectives — the person asks How do I know this? How can I validate this? How do others think? *Developing alternative perspectives,* the next phase, includes trying out the new ways of thinking or acting. It is quite possible that the learner will now choose to retain his or her original beliefs or assumptions or modify them slightly to fit a new situation. On the other hand, changes in meaning schemes can take place here. Finally, *integration* will occur. Brookfield (1987, p. 27) writes that, "having decided on the worth, accuracy, and validity of new ways of thinking or living, we begin to find ways to integrate these into the fabric of our lives." He sees this integration as involving the transformation of beliefs and assumptions. The learner comes to a sense of closure; there may be visible actions as a result of the integration, or the process may be completely internal. If several meaning schemes have been revised, it is likely that this final phase would involve transformation of a meaning perspective.

Mezirow's (1975) original conception of transformation theory includes ten phases, as I mentioned in Chapter Two. As Brookfield did in his phases of critical thinking, Mezirow saw a *disorienting dilemma* as provoking the process followed by a *self-examination.* He then described the learner as engaging in a *critical assessment* of internal assumptions accompanied by some sense of alienation from his or her usual social context. *Relating to others' experiences* and recognizing that others have gone through a similar process was described as a separate phase in Mezirow's model. The learner then *explores options* for new behaviors and *builds competence* in new roles. A *plan of action* is developed, and the learner *acquires knowledge and skills* for implementing the plan. *Provisional efforts* are made to try out the new roles and obtain feedback. Finally, as in Brookfield's proposed phases, a *reintegration* into society takes place. The notion that a disorienting dilemma might stimulate reflection may describe personal or psychological reflection; Brookfield (1987) rightly points out that positive events stimulate reflection. I will discuss this issue in more detail later in this chapter.

Mezirow (1991) quotes the results of research conducted by several graduate students in which phases of transformative learning specific to different settings or contexts were described. These included commitment to religious life, response to changes in a workplace setting, participation in postpartum classes, participation in Alcoholics Anonymous, and commitment to an ecological worldview. Although the terminology and number of phases varies in these studies, the pattern of phases is essentially the same. Keane (1985, cited in Mezirow, 1991), for example, describes four phases in the transformation resulting from a commitment to religious life: disorientation, search for meaning and peace, self-acceptance, and integration. Similarly, J. Taylor (1989, cited in Mezirow, 1991) describes six steps: encountering trigger events, confronting reality, reaching the transition point, making a shift or leap of transcendence, making a personal commitment, and grounding and development.

This pattern was also confirmed by M. Taylor (1987), who was not deliberately studying transformative learning or using transformative learning theory as a basis for her work. Taylor investigated the stages in becoming self-directed in a graduate level adult education course, a process that involves critical reflection on one's assumptions about oneself as a learner.

Taylor describes four phases and four transition points in the process. *Disconfirmation,* the first phase, is when the learner sees a discrepancy between expectations and experience. This realization is followed by disorientation, discomfort, and confusion accompanied by a crisis of confidence and a withdrawal from people associated with the source of the confusion. A transition phase, identification of the problem, involves naming the problem without assigning blame. This leads to *exploration,* a collaborative, open-ended activity that produces insights and confidence. Reflection is then a transition process in which the learner reviews the process privately. *Reorientation* follows, in which there may be a major insight or a synthesis of the experience. In a transition phase called sharing the discovery, the learner tests the new understanding with others. Finally, there is *equilibrium* — elaboration, refinement, and application of the new perspective and approach.

I have recently proposed a modification of Taylor's model in which learners do not necessarily go through the phases in the same order and in which some phases may be skipped entirely (Cranton, 1992). This model also includes the possibility that learners will reject the process at the beginning or somewhere along the way. The phases I propose include: curiosity, confusion, testing, withdrawal, exploration and reflection, turning to others, renewed interest and excitement, reorientation, equilibrium, and advocacy. Data collected from three groups of adult learners working toward self-directed learning — a total of fifty-one people — provide some evidence in support of the model.

It is probably safe to say, based on the existing models and research results, that the process of working toward transformative learning includes some stimulating event or situation — self-analysis or self-examination, perhaps accompanied by emotional responses such as frustration, anxiety, or excitement; reflection and exploration, including a questioning of assumptions; revision of assumptions (meaning schemes) or meaning perspectives; and a phase of reintegration, reorientation, or equilibrium. Other phases, such as turning to others, may occur for some individuals but not others. I will discuss this possibility in more detail in Chapter Five. It is not safe to say, however, that these stages are in any way sequential or hierarchical or that they are consistent across learners. For example, I suspect that there is a prolonged period of confusion and muddling for some individuals that is followed by a breakthrough or sense of enlightenment. For others, there may be incessant discussion with peers followed by a calm period of integration. As we will see in subsequent sections, the dynamics of transformative learning may influence the length, sequence, and appearance of the stages.

Learner Empowerment

Learner empowerment is both a goal of and a condition for transformative learning. To empower means to give power to, or to make able. An empowered learner is able to fully and freely participate in critical discourse and the resulting action; empowerment requires freedom and equality as well as the ability to assess evidence and to engage in critical reflection. Two scenarios will illustrate this relationship.

As part of a management development program, a senior manager in a government department participates in a performance appraisal. Although she would not have described her relationship with her staff as close, she always thought that her staff respected her; she thought she did a relatively good job as a leader — her unit ran smoothly, the work got done, and she was unaware of any complaints or conflicts. In the appraisal process, she rated her own skills positively on the self-evaluation questionnaire, including her relationship with the staff. When she received her feedback report, however, she was devastated to find that staff ratings of her performance were negative on most items. Staff members indicated that she was an autocrat, that they did not respect her, that there was considerable conflict in their ranks, and that she did nothing about it. Written responses to open-ended questions were vicious. In the series of training workshops that followed the appraisal, this manager felt unable to participate. Although the workshop leader was supportive, encouraging, and apparently knowledgeable, she could not discuss her best and worst experiences as a manager without knowing what kind of manager she really was. She began to consider changing careers, as one person had suggested in the comments on the appraisal form.

A new community college instructor resentfully enrolled in a compulsory summer school program. He had been told by his department head that he would not have a chance to keep his job unless he underwent this training. This new instructor was an experienced carpenter and was enjoying the chance to show his trade to students. He really felt that he could do a good job without having to go to some fancy summer school where he would probably have to read a lot of mumbo-jumbo and maybe even write essays. "I know carpentry," he tried to argue with the department head, "and that's what counts." Actually, he was also worried that his rusty reading and writing skills would be exposed at summer school. Maybe he would lose this job anyway; maybe he would fail. During the first days of the course, there was a lot of discussion in class; several other people seemed to have the same worries he did, though no one actually said so. The teacher, who did not even want to be called the teacher, made it clear that the group would decide how to proceed over the summer. She even said that learners would not be required to write essays and that she would not be judging them. Of course, this would remain to be seen. He had never heard of a teacher like that before, but maybe he could survive summer school after all.

In each of these scenarios, a disorienting event has occurred and the learner is experiencing a dilemma or confusion. According to the models discussed earlier, each learner would now engage in self-appraisal, self-examination, or identification of the problem. The learner in the first scenario, however, has received a shattering blow to her self-concept as a manager. She had believed herself to be competent, had seen herself as relating well to her staff, and now has discovered that this is not the perception of others. She has been disempowered. The learner in the second scenario entered into the learning experience with grave doubts as to his ability to cope and is now being assured that he will not be judged or required to perform tasks beyond his capabilities. He is being empowered.

How is learner empowerment intertwined with the processes of critical self-reflection and transformative learning? In order to engage in honest self-examination, the learner must feel confident, secure, free, equal, or possibly supported by others. There must be a sense of learner empowerment before or during the process of self-examination. With the assistance and support of a sensitive facilitator, the manager from the first scenario could enter the appraisal phase. However, it is just as likely that she will continue to brood over her appraisal results in a less than constructive fashion, withdraw from the workshop activities or participate in a dishonest way, and not confront the dilemma that has presented itself.

This possibility raises a curious point regarding the way transformative learning is described in the literature. Often, dramatic events or life crises such as the loss of a spouse and the loss of a job are described as triggers for the process. It seems just as likely that such events would lead a learner to a sense of helplessness and loss of self-esteem thereby preventing the self-appraisal that is the beginning of working toward transformative learning. A few years ago, by tragic coincidence, I was working with two women in a group whose husbands had died unexpectedly within two weeks of each other. One woman withdrew from the program, took a leave from her position as a trainer, and for more than a year reported powerlessness and helplessness as her reaction to the event. The other woman, equally devastated by her husband's death, first used her work in the course as a means of avoiding her emotions; she grew quite dependent on the group and on me but through these interactions began seriously questioning her personal and professional lives. Her reflections led her to further reading and eventually to a research project on transformative learning, a change in career, and a more open and integrated view of her personal life.

These two stories illustrate the paradoxical nature of the relationship between learner empowerment and transformative learning. The educator's role was critical in the case of the second woman; I will discuss this role further in Chapter Six.

The core of transformative learning in Mezirow's (1991) view is the uncovering of distorted assumptions—errors in learning—in each of the three domains of meaning perspectives. Although questioning assumptions in, say, the epistemic domain (assumptions related to knowledge and the use of knowledge) may not seem threatening, there are many situations in which this would indeed be a difficult and painful process for the learner. Mezirow (1991, p. 128) lists one common type of distorted epistemic premise as "assuming that a phenomenon [the Law, the Church, the Bomb, the Government] produced by social interaction is immutable and beyond human control. . . ." A learner who is questioning his or her belief that the law or the church is immutable will certainly feel threatened.

With regard to reflection on psychological premise distortions, the threat to the learner's self could be even greater.

For example, Mezirow (1991, p. 140) writes of this process, "An educator or therapist may help the learner identify the specific problem to be resolved, its symptoms and the pain it evokes. . . . The strong feelings that impede action also must be dealt with before transformation can occur; simply understanding the situation is insufficient to effect transformative learning." Uncovering sociolinguistically distorted premises may be no less painful. In a recent workshop, learners were engaged in an activity designed to help them make their own assumptions about themselves as learners explicit and to encourage reflection on these assumptions. One learner was discussing the priority that she had given to learning and studying over keeping the house clean. Questioning by her group members led her to an unanticipated, emotional, and painful response—this simple priority was related to her subculture's expectations of women as well as to her own expectations. The learner's basic assumptions about the role of women were uncovered, leading her to a painful questioning of several related issues.

The learner who does not feel empowered during the process of critical self-reflection may not be able to continue. Empowerment is not just a product of critical self-reflection but also a prerequisite for beginning the process and an important component of continuing the questioning of basic beliefs and assumptions. In discussing the enhancement of adult learner motivation, Wlodkowski (1990, p. 83) lists five conditions that repel adult interest, four of which are relevant to our discussion here: *pain* (including psychological discomfort), *fear and anxiety* (resulting from anticipation of the unpleasant or dangerous such as threat of failure or punishment, public exposure of ignorance, or unpredictability of potential negative consequences), *frustration* (reacting to the blockage or defeat of purposeful behavior), and *humiliation* (reacting to being shamed, debased, or degraded). Negative conditions such as these can arise in critical self-reflection. Although he is not discussing transformative learning, Wlodkowski (1990, p. 82) comments that, "to some extent new learning goes against the grain of the personal autonomy and security of adults . . . they have usually found a way to successfully cope with life and have formulated a set of strongly held convictions. New learning . . . is somewhat threatening to them, and their attitudes can easily lock in to support their resistance."

The process may not always be a painful one. Trigger events may be positive events, as described by Belenky, Clinchy, Goldberger, and Tarule (1986) in their research on women's ways of knowing, and by Boud, Keogh, and Walker (1985). For the confident, well-adjusted learner, the experience can easily be positive throughout. Learners may describe transformative learning as joyous, enlightening, freeing, or exhilarating. There is some danger in maintaining gloomy and cautious expectations. One graduate student remarked, "I thought it was transformative—my learning this semester. I truly changed my perspective on my practice and I just see myself in a different light, but then I realized it couldn't be since the whole thing felt so good."

Trigger Events

The literature contains some references to the types of activities that educators might design in order to stimulate critical thinking (Brookfield, 1987) or critical self-reflection (Mezirow and Associates, 1990). I will discuss such strategies in detail in Chapter Seven. But not all critical reflection is stimulated deliberately by an educator—it can be stimulated by a book, a discussion with a friend, an unexpected event, a change in work context, or a sudden insight. In formal educational or training settings, an educator can provoke self-reflection quite unknowingly through the presentation of a new perspective or approach; the learner may then take up the process, perhaps with support from peers or friends. On the other hand, every practitioner who has tried to encourage critical self-reflection through critical incidents, role playing, and the like has probably encountered situations where the learners go through the activity mechanically without ever being affected by it. We must understand what trigger events are, from the learner's perspective, and why some events initiate reflection for some individuals in some situations but not for others. There can be no standard recipe—

no way to say, "hand out one critical incident exercise, carefully add small group discussion, and simmer for one hour."

I will discuss possible precipitating events in relation to the taxonomy of working toward transformative learning presented earlier. Although the epistemic, psychological, and sociolinguistic meaning perspectives may overlap in some ways, and critical reflection in one domain may stimulate reflection in another domain, it is likely that the activities vary for each.

At the least complex level of learning (reflection on epistemic meaning schemes in the instrumental domain), stimulating events are likely to involve being confronted with facts, rules, or principles that directly contradict previously accepted knowledge, particularly knowledge that was acquired from an authority figure. When I was a child, I knew, because my father told me so, that cows chewed gum after they finished their evening feed. My father carried the gum in his pocket and assured me that he handed it out to the cows. When I later encountered a textbook description of the digestive system of cattle, I was taken aback and could not for some time accept the fact that my childhood knowledge was not true knowledge after all. All of us have knowledge obtained from various sources: from parents, books, teachers, and the media. When contradictory information is found, it may provoke reflection on the currently held knowledge and may even lead to reflection on epistemic meaning perspectives. When Louis Pasteur presented evidence that disease was carried by something he called "germs," the medical profession had to deal first with the contradictory knowledge (reluctantly and with hostility), then examine related meaning schemes, and finally, examine their perspectives on practice.

A trigger event in this domain may be something other than simple contradictory information. The learner may come to question the source of knowledge, and this may lead to premise reflection. If a person has always believed in a certain source of information — an author or a political figure — and then that source is discredited in some way, that person might then question any other information from the source. Perhaps many people engaged in collective premise reflection when President Richard Nixon and even the office of the president of the United States were discredited as sources of information.

The nature of events that initiate reflection in the communicative domain of learning will be, by definition, much more varied. Communicative learning as previously described includes "understanding, describing, and explaining intentions; values; ideals; moral issues, social, political, philosophical, psychological or educational concepts; feelings and reasons" (Mezirow, 1991, p. 75). Communicative learning is shaped by "cultural and linguistic codes, and social norms and expectations" (p. 75). Communicative learning can be related to each of the epistemic, psychological, and sociolinguistic meaning perspectives.

The most clearly provocative events here are those that cause the questioning of social norms. The adult male who has never used the household washer and dryer or turned on the kitchen stove might be stimulated to question this norm through discussion with male co-workers who do participate in household activities. The senior university professor who has never conducted a class in a format other than lecture may be challenged to reflect on this norm by seeing his enrollments drop and his classes canceled or by hearing the noise and laughter from a class next door. The young woman from the hills of Tennessee whose family and peers scorn education might be provoked to question this norm when she becomes acquainted with an educated family who has moved into the area. The manager who works in an autocratic organization but experiments with a participatory management style may be stimulated by the success of his experiment and thereby question the norm of the organization. The young man from a Christian family and community who registers in a European literature course that turns out to include only existentialist authors may be led to question his family's and community's beliefs. Examples are as varied as the contexts within which human beings live and work.

Mezirow, particularly in his early writings, saw life crises as precipitators for critical self-reflection. The most commonly cited example is that of the woman who never obtained the skills to live independently and whose husband dies or leaves her. A life crisis thus leads her to reflect on psychological and sociolinguistic meaning perspectives. A man who loses his job is another commonly cited example. The crisis forces change, and this leads to critical self-reflection. The crisis might appear as a positive event from the outside—a promotion to an administrative position, retirement, or the completion of a years-long project. Such events can challenge individuals to reconsider their values, expectations, moral positions, or self-concepts. It is not uncommon, for example, for graduate students to delay completion of a thesis in order to avoid what to them would be the crisis of finishing the degree. Again, a crisis may not lead to critical self-reflection if the learner feels disempowered. The process of transformative learning may take place some time after the crisis but only when security and self-confidence are restored.

Events that initiate critical reflection in the communicative domain of learning may also occur as a person progresses through the developmental stages in an adult's life. Much has been made of the transition periods between developmental phases as states of readiness to learn. Although the validity of some models of adult development can be questioned, individuals do go through some fairly predictable changes over a lifetime. The young woman who is looking for her first job will reflect on her career goals, her personal values, and the expectations of her family. The father who is raising a young family and has the accompanying financial constraints may consider his priorities and values. The individual who in midlife simply wants a change will be stimulated to reflect on his own values, the norms of his subculture, and the expectations of his family. The middle-aged woman who is approaching the end of her career and her retirement will be stimulated to question what she has accomplished so far. She may wonder what she missed in the hectic pace she has maintained. These and other natural passages in the life of an individual can set the stage for critical self-reflection.

Larger societal and political changes will provoke critical reflection for some individuals. The fall of communism, the elimination of the Berlin Wall, the feminist movement, an economic recession or boom, the separatist movement in Quebec, the escalation of violence against women—all such upheavals can lead an individual to question his or her values and beliefs. A good example comes from the protests in the 1960s against the Vietnam War. Many people were led to reflect on values and assumptions related to democracy and communism, peace and war, and the role of the United States in world politics. Many young adults questioned their political views and philosophical beliefs seriously, and rejected traditional views. They acted both individually and socially on their revised assumptions. Social changes also can lead individuals to question racist or sexist beliefs. The man with a sexist attitude may initially react with anger to changes in women's roles but may then be led to question his assumptions about women. Of course, social change does not necessarily lead to individual transformation; in fact Mezirow (1991) makes the opposite point — that individual transformation leads to social action and social change. Changes can take place in both directions.

Distorted assumptions are often revealed through language, as I described in Chapter Two. Changes in acceptable language usage can stimulate reflection on the assumptions underlying the use of words. For example, changes in terminology used to describe individuals with handicaps or disabilities have occurred regularly over the last few years; students of education and psychology have most likely been led to examine their perceptions along with the way language reflects those perceptions. Similarly, the recent emphasis on nonsexist language in journalism, academic writing, and the media can challenge individuals to question their assumptions. Again, change is a two-way street — changes in acceptable language use are a product of individual and group social action, and such changes lead others to critical reflection.

Emancipatory learning takes place through critical self-reflection. As such, it can be an "element in the process involved in validating learning about the environment and other people as well as ourselves; that is both instrumental and communicative learning" (Mezirow, 1991, p. 87). Events and situations that lead to such reflection have already been discussed. When reflection leads to transformed meaning schemes or meaning perspectives, it can be called emancipatory learning. Emancipatory learning includes, however, the critical examination "presuppositions that sustain our fears, inhibitions, and patterns of interaction, such as our reaction to rejection, and their consequences in our relationships" (Mezirow, 1991, p. 87). Life crises such as those I mentioned earlier will be common stimulants of critical self-reflection of this nature. Also, less dramatic changes in an individual's personal life can lead to a critical self-examination. These changes, for example, can be the maturing of an intimate relationship, developing a new friendship, adding new responsibilities at work, taking a course and meeting different people, or joining a club or a new social circle. Several of these potentially provocative events center on the influence of discussion with others. For many people, discussion is likely to provoke critical self-reflection.

Readings also provoke self-reflection. One visible example is the proliferation of self-help or popular psychology books. Whether or not these books actually stimulate self-appraisal and lead to transformative learning can be questioned, but they must lead to change in some individuals, and their popularity indicates a widespread interest in self-reflection. Conversely, it can be argued that learners turn to reading after critical reflection has been initiated by another event. Novels, philosophical writings, and academic books may serve the same purpose for some learners.

As I said earlier in relation to learning in the communicative domain, progress through the developmental phases of an adult's life will often lead to critical self-reflection and emancipatory learning. Transition between developmental phases will, of course, overlap with life crises and other changes in lifestyle.

Although both Mezirow and Brookfield argue that critical reflection is almost always stimulated by the environment and discussion with others, it is also possible that internal processes can lead to self-questioning, especially for persons of an introverted nature. I will discuss this further in Chapter Five. Personal insights may be the product of images, fantasies, dreams, or archetypes (Boyd and Myers, 1988). At times, this is an unconscious product of external stimuli, but it may also be the result of stimuli from the inner world that manifest themselves in conscious insights and seem to appear suddenly in awareness.

Several events that may provoke critical reflection and critical self-reflection have been discussed. These are just some examples of the many situations, contexts, and social interactions that may initiate transformative learning. I will discuss other examples related to the role of the educator in Chapter Seven.

Questioning Assumptions

At the heart of transformative learning theory is the three-part process of questioning assumptions. A learner must first become aware of assumptions and make them explicit. Second, Mezirow and his Associates (1990) propose that the learner then examine the sources of the assumptions and the consequences of holding them. Third, the critical question becomes, Is this assumption valid? If the answer is no and the learner chooses to reject or revise the assumption, transformation of a meaning scheme has occurred. Another way of describing this process is through content, process, and premise reflection, as I described these in Chapter Two.

Any educator who has tried to facilitate this process will readily admit that it is not as straightforward as it sounds. All stages of questioning assumptions are difficult for most learners. In this section, the process will be examined briefly from the learner's point of view. I will discuss the role of the educator in Chapter Seven.

Making Assumptions Explicit

Becoming aware of one's underlying assumptions, particularly in the sociolinguistic and psychological meaning perspectives, is not an easy task in itself. When asked directly about assumptions related to values, moral issues, social views, or self-concept, learners will often respond with trite or superficial statements. Here, Mezirow's point about the importance of critical discourse becomes relevant—with sensitive and intelligent questioning, superficial statements can be translated into underlying assumptions. However, from the learner's perspective, such an exercise can be frustrating and anxiety-provoking and can produce a variety of emotional reactions.

How does this process occur without deliberate provocation? That probably depends on the nature of the individual. Making assumptions explicit, questioning them, and possibly revising them may not be distinct processes but rather, simultaneous or interactive events for some individuals. It may be that some people never make assumptions explicit, and yet revision still occurs. Learners may quickly sense that something is wrong or discrepant and modify it without deliberate thought. Learners may respond to the values and feelings of others around them, again without consciously thinking through the process, or learners may detach themselves from the issue and treat it as a problem to be solved in an analytical way.

Questioning the Sources and Consequences of Assumptions

Questioning the sources of assumptions and the consequences of holding assumptions probably does not consciously occur without the intervention of an educator or others (Meyers, 1986; Wlodkowski, 1990). A person may wonder, Where did that idea come from? or If I continue to act in that way, where will it lead me? But this is probably not done in any systematic fashion as Mezirow's model implies. Discussion with friends or colleagues may serve to focus a learner on these questions. Common advice to people who are making an important decision is to list pros and cons; in effect, this is a consideration of the consequences of holding an assumption or revising it. The consequences of holding an assumption may be more easily described than the sources of an assumption, particularly in the psychological and sociolinguistic meaning perspectives. Unless awareness occurs through therapy or other intensive analysis, the sources of a person's basic assumptions may remain obscure. But awareness may not be necessary for critical reflection to occur.

Questioning the Validity of Assumptions

Questioning the validity of assumptions is a precarious endeavor. As is mentioned throughout the literature, adult learners will cling stubbornly to opinions, values, and beliefs. To change is frightening and threatening. For a person to ask whether his or her underlying assumptions are valid implies a willingness to change them if they are not. Most individuals will avoid making such a step unless circumstances or the challenges of others demand that they do so. Here, interaction with and support from others is probably most crucial if critical self-reflection is to continue.

Consider the senior professor who has begun to question his teaching. He views himself as an expert in his discipline, and his writing and research records support this view. However, his classes are often canceled due to low enrollment, few students ask him to be their adviser for their theses, and he becomes aware of possible weaknesses in his approach to teaching. He may well articulate his assumptions about teaching: "I am a professor, therefore I profess; I am an expert, therefore my job is to share my expertise with students." He may also know the origin of his beliefs about his role — he might have modeled himself on his own professors — and know the consequences of maintaining his assumptions — that students will continue to avoid him. But questioning the validity of his assumptions seriously is another matter entirely. If he realizes that change must occur — a possible outcome of this questioning — how will he do so? He thinks of himself as an expert. How can he go to someone for help? If he does not go to someone for help, how will he know how to change? Clearly, the safest alternative is to leave things as they are and to blame the problem on the low quality of students being admitted to the program.

For adult learners to become aware of and question underlying assumptions is not, as it may seem at first, a simple problem-solving exercise; these assumptions underlie their identity. In the final section of this chapter, I will discuss the importance of support from others in the process of critical self-reflection and transformative learning.

Support from Others

As we saw in the discussion of learner empowerment, events that trigger critical reflection and the questioning of assumptions must be accompanied by support from others if transformative learning is to occur. The educator's role in providing support is discussed in Chapter Eight. Brookfield (1987, p. 29) describes the role of helpers in becoming critical thinkers: "they assist us in breaking out of our own frameworks of interpretation. Trying to . . . identify the assumptions undergirding our apparently objective, rational beliefs is like trying to catch our psychological tail. . . . We hold up our behavior for scrutiny by others, and in their interpretation of our actions we are given a reflection, a mirroring of our own actions from an unfamiliar psychological vantage point." From a theoretical point of view, Mezirow (1991), following Habermas (1984), proposes that learning, particularly communicative learning, depends on consensual validation of the meaning of our assertions. Consensual validation occurs through free and full participation in critical discourse with others. Interaction and support may come from co-learners, co-workers, friends and family, or from an educator. But how does the learner see the role of others?

Self-Concept

Brookfield (1987) describes the process of questioning assumptions as "psychologically explosive" (p. 30). One critical role that others play in the process is that of validation of the self. In order to begin critical reflection, the learner must feel empowered and have a sense of security and confidence. One's self-concept as a learner, as a worker, and as a person must be strong if any critical questioning of beliefs and values is to occur. In an educational setting, the educator and co-learners can provide the crucial atmosphere of acceptance and support. For some learners, the role of family and friends is equally important and must exist in addition to support from the educational setting. A nonsupportive spouse, for example, can lead a learner to withdraw psychologically from the process of critical self-reflection. In a workplace setting, whether learning is concerned with training or retraining, professional development, literacy training, safety, or personal welfare, the learner requires the support and trust of co-workers, supervisors, and a trainer or facilitator to engage in critical reflection. This may be even more important in the workplace than in an educational institution. If an individual feels threatened at work by a supervisor, for example, he or she will probably not be willing to take the risks required to become involved in critical reflection. This point was well illustrated in the implementation of a literacy-in-the-workplace program in Canada; many workers did not want their supervisors to know about their participation in the program (Cranton and Castle, 1990).

For adults involved in critical self-reflection outside an organization—through independent learning projects, community groups, or self-help groups—the support and encouragement of family, friends, or co-learners is just as important. The family that complains about a family member going off to all those meetings or spending all that time with his nose in books can hinder a learning process.

Challenge

Others play a role in questioning and challenging a learner. It is difficult for learners caught up in their perspective to even see the questions that should be asked. Sitting at home in an armchair asking challenging questions may be doomed to failure, even with the assistance of provocative readings. In an educational or workplace setting, the educator and co-learners or co-workers will assume that role after an atmosphere of trust and support has been established. Questioning and challenging should become the norm of a learning setting where critical reflection is a goal. I will discuss how the educator can facilitate this in Chapter Seven. Others can help a person engaged in transformative learning to see his or her assumptions through new eyes. Brookfield (1987, p. 29) aptly compares this to "trying to step outside of our physical body so that we can see how a new coat or dress looks from behind."

The learner working outside an organized setting will turn to family, friends, co-workers, or other group members for this stimulation. Often, by simply describing an issue to another person, even one who is not involved in the same issue, will lead to critical and challenging questions. If no one is available to fill that role, many people will stop at that point, regardless of how much general support is available.

Alternative Perspectives

Closely related to the questioning role is that of providing different perspectives and thus enabling the learner to break out of a way of thinking or a framework within which he or she may be trapped. Sometimes, regardless of how many challenging questions a learner may be asked, it is simply not possible to see things from another perspective. Hearing how another person views an issue can provide a different vantage point, a point from which the learner can then ask questions of her or his own underlying assumptions. The autocratic manager, for example, could be challenged by her staff, her peers, the facilitator of a workshop on leadership, and even her own family. But if she cannot envision any other managerial role, she will have great difficulty in questioning her underlying assumptions about the role of a leader. If another manager from within the same organization were to describe his perspective on leadership style, including concrete illustrations of how he worked with his staff, the autocratic manager might see how to question her beliefs. Depending on whether the learner is in an educational setting, a work setting, or engaging in independent learning, the provision of different perspectives could come from co-learners, educators, co-workers, family, or friends.

Imagining alternatives is another component of transformative learning in which others can provide support. As I will discuss in Chapter Five, some individuals imagine alternatives easily and others do not. For those who do not, help from others is essential. However the stages of working toward transformative learning are described, exploration and seeing alternatives are crucial components. It is one thing for a learner to recognize the flaws in his or her assumptions and quite another to see other ways of viewing the issue. In educational and training settings, brainstorming is often used for this purpose — individuals are free to suggest ideas about possibilities without judgment, comment, or criticism. Only after all suggestions are exhausted does the group analyze or assign priorities. However, the equivalent of brainstorming can take place in any discussion with others. Again, depending on the setting, co-learners, educators, co-workers, family, or friends can assist a learner in generating alternatives. For example, a woman who has lived in an abusive marriage for several years may be incapable of generating alternative ways of viewing her situation. She may have support from others; she may have been challenged and questioned by others; she may have heard the perspectives of other women in a situation similar to hers. In a discussion with friends or members of her support group, she could imagine and express options that might lead her to explore alternative ways of thinking and acting.

Feedback

Others can provide feedback throughout the process of working toward transformative learning. Feedback will play a particularly crucial role during the learner's questioning of underlying assumptions and the exploration of alternatives. Getting feedback may be as simple as expressing ideas to someone else and asking for comment or as complex as writing a paper or a journal for an instructor in an educational setting. As I discussed earlier, feedback can also act as a trigger event for the questioning of assumptions. The manager who receives an appraisal report on her performance or the instructor who collects student ratings of his teaching may be stimulated to reflect on her or his practice, especially if there are discrepancies between what others say and a self-evaluation. One of the few undisputed principles of learning is that learning is facilitated by regular, ongoing feedback; this is as true for transformative learning as for the simple acquisition of knowledge and skills. Feedback from the educator is vital in formal learning contexts, and feedback from co-learners should be built into the discussion and activities of the group. Feedback from others outside the educational setting can be valuable as well but may not be so important as general support. This, of course, depends on the nature of the relationship with the individuals. Outside an educational setting, co-workers, group members, friends, or family members can provide feedback to the learner.

Testing New Assumptions

Finally, others can play an important role for the learner who is testing new assumptions. If a learner has revised basic assumptions or beliefs or rejected and replaced underlying assumptions, that person will feel a certain amount of trepidation about others' acceptance of this change. The learner may act on the revised assumption in order to test it in the real world or may test the ideas through discussion with others. A safe atmosphere will be chosen for this and comments from others solicited. The college instructor may test his revised assumptions about teaching through discussion with a trusted colleague before making radical changes in his course outline. A graduate student may discuss her changed beliefs about her career path with fellow students or her adviser. The husband who has changed his view of men's and women's roles may tentatively do the grocery shopping and hope for praise from his spouse. Any individuals who play an important part in the adult learner's life can provide this kind of support in the process of transformative learning.

Although it may well be possible for learners to engage in critical reflection and self-reflection without support from others, the role of helpers, as Brookfield (1987) describes them, will greatly enhance the process for most individuals.

Summary

In order to better understand working toward transformative learning, the process has been examined from the learner's perspective. I have described strategies presented in the literature for the educator's facilitation of critical reflection and transformative learning; theoretical description is available, and some limited research has been done to determine the stages a learner might go through. However, as educators, we also must develop a clear picture of how the process might look and feel for learners.

I proposed several types or levels of critical reflection and self-reflection: content reflection on knowledge is quite different from premise reflection on psychological perspectives. We should not look for a linear or hierarchical sequence of learning, but be aware that transformative learning is not a single process. Similarly, the phases or stages that a learner goes through in engaging in transformative learning will vary from one person to another. Nevertheless, there seems to be a general pattern to the process.

Learner empowerment is clearly a crucial component of transformative learning. Some sense of empowerment is needed before a learner can engage in critical reflection, and a feeling of empowerment sustains an individual throughout the process. Learner empowerment is also the ultimate goal of transformative learning and of adult education.

I discussed three aspects of transformative learning in detail. A wide range of events, situations, dilemmas, or interactions with others can act to stimulate critical reflection. The process of becoming aware of and questioning basic assumptions is a key component of transformative learning and yet is a difficult task for learners. Support from an educator and others will, for most individuals, make this task easier.

I have shown throughout this discussion that individuals will work through transformative learning in different ways. In the next chapter, we will look at individual differences in transformative learning through the characteristic of psychological type.

FIVE

How Transformative
Learning Varies
Among Individuals

An interesting conundrum exists in the adult education literature. The *diversity of learners* is commonly included in lists of principles of adult learning. Practitioners are cautioned that there
is not much they can do about this diversity except to use a variety of methods and materials. For example, we read such statements as, "Adults are a highly diversified group of individuals
with widely differing preferences, needs, backgrounds, and skills"
(James, 1983, p. 132); "Given the tremendous diversity among
people, the problem seems insurmountable . . . it is obviously
impossible to take all learner characteristics into account when
working with a group" (Cranton, 1992, p. 27); and, "Teaching
and learning are such complex processes, and teachers and
learners are such complex beings, that no model of practice or
pedagogical approach will apply in all settings. A lot of fruitless time and energy can be spent trying to find the holy grail
of pedagogy, the one way to instructional enlightenment" (Brookfield, 1990, p. 197).

On the other hand, theorists and researchers dedicate their
energies to delineating stages and cycles of learning, defining
effective strategies for facilitating self-directed learning, and
predicting which educator behaviors foster critical thinking —
to name but a few current themes in the literature.

Is this the contradiction that it seems to be? Candy (1991)

discusses understanding the individual nature of learning as it relates to constructivism. He says the assumptions of constructivist thought include the following: people participate in the construction of reality; this construction occurs within a context that influences it; commonly accepted categories are socially constructed; given forms of understanding depend on social processes; forms of negotiated understanding are connected with other human activities; the subjects of research should be considered as knowing beings; locus of control rests within the subjects themselves; people can attend to complex communications and organize complexity; and human interactions are based on social roles with often implicit rules (Candy, 1989).

Let us accept the idea that individuals do construct their own perceptions of the world — the way they see events, ideas, values, and possibilities — and let us accept the idea that individuals make decisions related to these perceptions in their own way. This is a constructivist view. It can also be argued that these individuals, regardless of their way of being in the world, change, grow, develop, and learn. The way this change and learning takes place will be different from one person to another, but the process exists for all. If this were not true, we would have no way of explaining learning or maturation. Clearly, although we cannot find a single explanation for it, people do learn and grow.

The literature contains many ways of classifying and explaining individual differences. Developmental phase, learning style, cognitive style, past experience, and self-directed learning readiness have been used, along with learner characteristics, to account for learners' behavior and to predict how they will behave in the future. Most of these attempts to classify learners lead to dichotomies or mutually exclusive categories. People are described as visual learners or auditory learners; they are in the leaving-home phase or the moving-into-the-adult-world phase. There is value in this, of course, as we search for common patterns and trends in human behavior. However, in doing so, we could overlook the diversity and complexity of human learning.

Psychological type theory (Jung, 1971) is one important

way of understanding individual differences in human behavior with less oversimplification. Psychological type can, in fact, be used to explain other individual characteristics such as preferred teaching style, learning style, and leader behavior (Keirsey and Bates, 1984; Kolb, 1984). Research has indicated that psychological type is related to such diverse variables and conditions as cognitive style (Ferguson and Fletcher, 1987), foreign language learning (Moody, 1988), communication patterns (Thorne, 1987), and happiness (Deiner, Sandvik, Pavot, and Fujita, 1992). Although it has not often been incorporated into the adult education literature, psychological type provides a more comprehensive description of the nature of individual differences than does, say, learning style. For this reason, I choose psychological type theory as a means of discussing variations in the learning process; however, individuals should not be stereotyped through any such analysis. Although students of Jung (for example, Myers, 1985) have simplified behavior and categorized individuals, the original theory does not do so. In fact, Jung both accepts the fact that individuals construe their own meaning of the world and attempts to classify those differences without losing complexity.

In this chapter, I will view the process of transformative learning through the lens of psychological type theory. How might individuals of different psychological types engage in transformative learning? How can critical thinking be reconciled with Jung's thinking-feeling type continuum? How do people who prefer to perceive the world rather than make decisions about it engage in critical thinking and transformative learning?

I will first describe Jung's theory of psychological type, then examine the process of transformative learning in light of the individual differences described in that theory.

Psychological Type

Early in his discussion of psychological type, Jung (1971) clarifies his position on the objective and subjective nature of understanding individual differences. "The ideal and aim of science do not consist in giving the most exact possible description of the facts . . . but in establishing certain laws, which are merely abbreviated expressions for many diverse processes that are yet conceived to be somehow correlated. This aim goes beyond the purely empirical by means of the *concept*, which, though it may have general and proved validity, will always be a product of the subjective psychological constellation of the investigator . . . This well-known fact must nowhere be taken to heart more seriously than in psychology" (pp. 8–9). Jung mistrusts "the principle of 'pure observation' in so-called objective psychology" (p. 9) and argues that the observer in psychology must see both subjectively and objectively. "The demand that he should see *only* objectively is quite out of the question, for it is impossible" (p. 9).

Given this perspective, it seems incongruous that Jung would then go about describing eight psychological types. In his introduction to his writing, he comments on the difficulty of describing general psychological types and the difficulty of observing type in others as well as in oneself. Because of the subjectivity of observation, the "picture . . . is extremely difficult to interpret, so difficult that one is inclined to deny the existence of types altogether and to believe only in individual differences" (Jung, 1971, p. 3).

I must make one further cautionary note before proceeding. Jung is clear about the fact that psychological type is but one way of discussing human characteristics: "I have long been struck by the fact that besides the many individual differences in human psychology there are also typical differences" (p. 3). Yet he also believes that the psychological functions forming the framework for type theory can be traced to the beginning of the development of individuality as a concept. By examining psychological typologies in classical literature and philosophy, Jung conveys the power of these concepts as a way of understanding humanity.

Introversion and Extraversion

Jung (1971) began the development of psychological type theory by recognizing the introverted and extraverted preferences among his patients. He describes introversion and extraversion as two basic attitudes an individual may have. No one person is entirely introverted or extraverted; the attitudes exist on a continuum. The following descriptions are of the poles of that continuum.

Introversion "means an inward-turning . . . in the sense of a negative relation of subject [self] to object [external world]. . . . Everyone whose attitude is introverted thinks, feels, and acts in a way that clearly demonstrates that the subject is the prime motivating factor and that the object is of secondary importance" (pp. 452–453). In other words, the introverted individual is oriented by personal or inner factors. A person of this type might say: "I know that my teacher wants me to do so and so, but I don't happen to agree," or, "I see that the weather has turned out bad, but in spite of it I shall carry out my plan. . . . " The introverted person views the world subjectively. As a result, he or she "holds aloof from external happenings, does not join in, has a distinct dislike of society . . . in a large gathering . . . feels lonely and lost" (p. 550).

Extraversion, on the other hand, "is an outward-turning . . . Everyone in the extraverted state thinks, feels, and acts in relation to the object, and moreover in a direct and clearly observable fashion, so that no doubt can remain about his positive dependence on the object" (Jung, 1971, p. 427). The extraverted person is oriented by the external world — the objects, people, and events in the world. Jung describes extraversion as being characterized by "a ready acceptance of external happenings, a desire to influence and be influenced by events, a need to join in and get 'with it', the capacity to endure bustle and noise of every kind, and actually find them enjoyable, constant attention to the surrounding world, the cultivation of friends and acquaintances, none too carefully selected, and finally by the great importance attached to the figure one cuts, and hence a strong tendency to make a show of oneself" (p. 549). For the extravert, the inner world takes second place to the outer world.

Jung placed great emphasis on the integration of the introverted and extraverted attitudes. During the time of this writing (the 1920s), he was arguing against the church and modern science, both of which denied the reality of the inner world and valued objective, empirically determined descriptions of objects and events. His mission was to assert the validity of the internal experiences of ideas and fantasy and to actualize the potential of archetypes in order to achieve individuation or self-actualization. In other words, he saw personal development as the result of the interaction of internal subjective forces and external circumstances. That present-day researchers and theorists (for example, Myers, 1985) dichotomize introversion and extraversion and attempt to quantify them as separate factors is not a criticism of Jung's work.

Functions

Following Jung's original description of introversion and extraversion, he found that this grouping was "of such a superficial and general nature" (1971, p. 6) that it did not "account for the tremendous differences between individuals in either class" (1971, p. 535). Another ten years led Jung to the consideration of psychological functions. He first associated functions directly with attitudes, describing only introverted thinking and extraverted feeling types.

Thinking and feeling became, in the final form of the theory, the two rational (judgmental) functions. "Thinking is the psychological function which, following its own laws, brings the contents of ideation into conceptual connection with one another" (Jung, 1971, p. 481). The use of the thinking function involves the use of logic in judgment. The feeling function, on the other hand, "imparts to the content a definite *value* in the sense of acceptance or rejection ('like' or 'dislike')" (p. 434). Feeling is "a kind of *judgment*, differing from intellectual judgment in that its aim is not to establish conceptual relations but to set up a subjective criterion of acceptance or rejection" (p. 434).

Jung also describes two irrational (perceiving) functions, *sensation* and *intuition*. He does not use the word irrational as meaning illogical but rather outside of or beyond logic or values. "Sensation is the psychological function that mediates the perception of a physical stimulus" (p. 461). "Sensation is *sense perception* . . . it conveys to the mind the perceptual image of the external object . . . " (p. 462). Intuition, on the other hand, "mediates perceptions in an *unconscious* way. Everything, whether outer or inner objects or their relationships, can be the focus of this perception. . . . In intuition a content presents itself whole and complete, without our being able to explain or discover how this content came into existence" (p. 453). The sensing type places an emphasis on sense perception, on facts, details, and concrete events. The intuitive type prefers an emphasis on possibilities, imagination, meaning, and seeing things as a whole.

Psychological Types

Most people have a preferred attitude (introversion or extraversion), a dominant function (judging or perceiving), an auxiliary function (from the opposite domain of the preferred function), and an inferior function. These combinations produce psychological types. For example, if a person's dominant attitude and function is introverted thinking, that person's auxiliary function will be either sensing or intuiting. Everyone both judges and perceives. A person's inferior (or least used) function will be the opposite of the dominant function — in this example, extraverted feeling. Since thinking and feeling are different ways of making judgments, they cannot be used at the same time; hence, if a person's preferred way of making judgments is through thinking, that person will use feeling infrequently.

Overall, the individual whose dominant function is either thinking or feeling will demonstrate an emphasis on reaching decisions and resolving issues. The individual whose dominant function is either sensing or intuition will prefer to perceive as much as possible, whether information or possibilities, before coming to a decision.

In order to delineate differences among individuals, I will present each psychological type as a category; however, each attitude and function exists along a continuum. Two people with the same dominant function will have different strengths to that preference. Also, individuals of the same type may have different overall psychological profiles.

The *extraverted thinking types* make their "activities dependent on intellectual conclusions, which in the last resort are always oriented by objective data, whether these be external facts or generally accepted ideas" (Jung, 1971, pp. 346–347). Using criteria obtained from the external world, these individuals use logical and analytical processes to solve problems and make judgments. The extraverted thinking types aim to establish order in both their personal and professional lives. They tend to be more interested in facts and ideas than in their effect on others. Consequently, they may be seen as cold, unfriendly, or impersonal. They also expect those around them to adhere to their principles; their moral code forbids tolerance of exceptions. They may assume the role of social or organizational reformer or purifier of conscience. They have a tendency to want to "save" others and are seen as idealists. Others may see them as dogmatic or even as tyrants in their pursuit of ideals. Generally though, their thinking is positive, productive, progressive, and creative. They are sure of themselves and their ideals and principles and will pursue these ideals in the face of any opposition.

Extraverted feeling types are "likewise oriented by objective data, the object being the indispensable determinant of the quality of feeling" (Jung, 1971, p. 354). Feeling is also a rational or judgmental function; however rather than using objective criteria, the feeling types use external (traditional or generally accepted) values to make judgments. Jung writes, "I may feel moved, for instance to say that something is 'beautiful' or 'good,' not because I find it 'beautiful' or 'good' from my own subjective feeling about it, but because it is fitting and politic to call it so, since a contrary judgment would upset the general feeling situation" (p. 355). This reliance on generally accepted values leads the extraverted feeling types to a desire for harmony in their surroundings—conflicts in values would upset their process of using these values to determine their own behavior. As a result, they easily adapt their own stance to match that expressed by another. They smooth over differences. This, of course, leads the extraverted feeling type to make friends easily, to work well with others in groups, and to have a harmonious social life.

The lives of *extraverted sensing types* are "an accumulation of actual experiences of concrete objects, and the more pronounced

[the] type, the less use [is] made of the experience" (Jung, 1971, p. 363). They are interested in tangible reality, "with little inclination for reflection and no desire to dominate" (p. 364). Rather than focusing on judgments (either through logic or values), extraverted sensing types perceive the world as it is, "unperturbed by the most glaring violations of logic" (p. 364) and with no desire to understand the relationships among the perceived events and objects. They enjoy things 'of the senses'— good meals and wine, beautiful possessions, and attractive people. For them, the concrete facts and experiences they can perceive with their five senses provide the basis for what comes next. They have little patience for the abstract; rather, they are masters of objective reality. In both their personal and their professional lives, others see them as good company—persons with a lively capacity for enjoyment. Their presence is valued at social gatherings and in their working environment.

For *extraverted intuitive types,* the preferred function is an "unconscious perception . . . wholly directed to external objects. . . . The intuitive function is represented in consciousness by an attitude of expectancy, by vision and penetration" (Jung, 1971, p. 366). The intuitive function transmits images that are not likely to be accessible through the other functions. Individuals who have a preference for this function seek "to discover what possibilities the objective situation holds in store . . . [and to them] every ordinary situation in life seems like a locked room which intuition has to open" (p. 367).

Extraverted intuitive types are intensely interested in new situations, events, and objects; they approach them without judgment. When the novelty wears off, however, these individuals may quickly lose interest. They are likely to be initiators of new enterprises, champions of causes, and visionaries. They are not influenced by thoughts or feelings, either their own or those of others. They are indifferent to everything that is not part of their vision. As a result, others may describe them as lacking in judgment or even as callous and exploitative. They may begin things and never finish them and consequently be seen as frivolous or as frittering away their lives. However, these same characteristics make them particularly suitable for occupations and professions where the ability to see, to perceive, and to visualize possibilities is essential.

The extraverted types are oriented to and connected with the external world, whether that connection is through logical criteria, values, concrete objects and experiences, or images of what could be. The introverted types, on the other hand, are oriented to their inner world. Criteria and values come from within, objects and experiences are filtered through subjective perceptions of them, and images arise from the inner world. This makes the extraverted thinking type as different from the introverted thinking type as from the extraverted feeling type.

Introverted thinking types are "strongly influenced by ideas though [their] ideas have their origin not in objective data but in . . . subjective foundation" (Jung, 1971, p. 383). They use logical and analytical processes to make judgments, but the criteria for those judgments come from within rather than from the external world. Introverted thinking types are uninfluenced by the thoughts and perceptions of others and only become annoyed when others do not understand their thinking. Rather, their thoughts are concerned with developing and presenting new ideas. They enjoy working with theories and models and are less interested in the practical application of these theories. They like to formulate questions, gain new insights, open new prospects, and create new theories, often just for the sake of creating theories. They only collect facts as evidence for their views, not for the value of the facts. Often they tend to force facts into the shape of their ideas. If these facts do not fit, this type may ignore reality altogether and only work with the ideas. Their strength is not in originality or persuasion but in the clarity, organization, and precision of their ideas. Although they may be polite, amiable, and kind to others, they are actually out to disarm them. To do this, they will often say, "I need time to think about this." They have trouble expressing feelings, and often they will not even know how they feel. I think I am angry or I think I like that are typical statements for them.

Colleagues or casual acquaintances tend to describe people of this type as arrogant, inconsiderate, or cold. They are not likely to go out of their way to win others' appreciation; instead, they may discard others' opinions, judge people harshly, and dismiss them as stupid when they do not embrace their ideas. Introverted thinking types have strong inner principles by which they live. They believe that there are absolute truths, some of which they have not yet discovered or fully understood.

In *introverted feeling types,* the valuing or feeling process is "determined principally by the subjective factor. . . . Since it is conditioned subjectively and is only secondarily concerned with the object, it seldom appears on the surface and is generally misunderstood" (Jung, 1971, p. 387). Jung finds this function extremely difficult to describe. Like the introverted thinking process, it is inner; however, it is more difficult to articulate or observe than is the thinking process. Introverted feeling types are described as being "mostly silent, inaccessible, hard to understand" (p. 389). They tend not to reveal themselves, and although their outward demeanor is harmonious, they may be inclined to melancholy. These individuals prefer to live in a quiet inner world of their own values, visions, and feelings. They have an inner intensity that others do not see; it seldom appears on the surface, and they are frequently misunderstood as a result. Their world is not much influenced by what they experience, by the actions of others, or by traditional values. The outside world acts only as stimulation for them. The phrase "still waters run deep" describes this type well. Although unable to express themselves to others, they possess a depth of feeling that no one can perceive or grasp. They enjoy solitude and do not like to be with others for long periods of time. But they have a strong sense of self-containment and at times even feel superior to those who enjoy large gatherings or loud entertainment.

Introverted sensing types are "oriented . . . not by rational judgment but simply by what happens. Whereas the extraverted sensing type is guided by the intensity of objective influences, the introverted type is guided by the intensity of the subjective sensation excited by the objective stimulus" (Jung, 1971, p. 395). In other words, the introverted sensing type is quite different from the extraverted person who has the same preferred function. Extraverted individuals are as intensely interested in objects, events, and situations as they are in reality. The introverted individual sees these same objects but sees them in a subjective way. He or she might, for example, collect paintings but may be primarily interested in how those paintings reflect various facets of himself or herself. If asked to do so, these types would not produce a realistic description of a person or object but rather a representation of their impression of that person or object. In other words, they modify reality by adding their subjective interpretation to what they perceive. Their world is therefore like a psychic mirror; they are more in tune with their own reflections or perceptions of reality than with those of others. In their work and personal lives, they prefer quiet arrangements and routines. They enjoy taking care of the details of life, and feel a sense of accomplishment when all the little chores have been taken care of for the day. Their greatest strength is their sensitivity to people and objects. However, others may see them as unpredictable and arbitrary or inaccessible and difficult to understand. They live in their own perception of the here and now.

Introverted intuitive types "may be stimulated by external objects, [they do not concern themselves] with external possibilities but with what the external object has released . . . " (Jung, 1971, p. 399). They are oriented by inner images that Jung describes as being the contents of the unconscious. "Just as the extraverted intuitive is continually scenting out new possibilities . . . so the introverted intuitive moves from image to image . . . without establishing any connection between them and himself" (p. 400). Reality serves only as a stimulus for releasing images. This type may move from image to image, chase every opportunity, and look for potential, but these images may be fruitless fantasies and have no immediate utility. For that reason, introverted intuitive types may be described by others as day dreamers. In their personal and professional lives, they are the ones who come up with ideas about how things could be; they point out possible views of the world and give life to new ways of being in the world. But they often cannot connect these ideas to reality. In relationships with others they may be frequently misunderstood. They do not reveal themselves to others and may lack good judgment about both themselves and others. Their aloofness to tangible reality is seen by others as either indifference or untruthfulness. Their memory of an event may not coincide with objective reality. People might say they are muddling through life, a statement with which they will agree. Others may misunderstand them or find them to be mysterious.

Auxiliary Functions

Few individuals display all of the characteristics given for any one of these types. First, people are differentiated (to be discussed under the next heading) to varying degrees; second, as I mentioned previously, people have an auxiliary or secondary function as well as a dominant or preferred function. Everyone makes judgments using one of the rational functions and everyone perceives the world using one of the perceptive functions. Jung notes that "investigation shows with great regularity that, besides the most differentiated function, another, less differentiated function of secondary importance is invariably present in consciousness and exerts a co-determining influence" (Jung, 1971, p. 405).

If, for example, a woman has a dominant thinking function, whether it is extraverted or introverted, she still must use one of the perceptive functions to perceive objects, events, and situations. She could then have either sensing or intuition as an auxiliary function. Conversely, the person who has intuition as a dominant function could have either thinking or feeling as an auxiliary function. Jung clearly states, "Naturally only those functions can appear as auxiliary whose nature is not opposed to the dominant function. For instance, feeling can never act as the second function alongside thinking, because it is by its very nature too strongly opposed to thinking. Thinking, if it is to be real thinking and true to its own principle, must rigorously exclude feeling" (pp. 405–406).

An extraverted feeling type who has sensing as an auxiliary function might display quite different characteristics from an extraverted feeling type who has intuition as an auxiliary function. The same is true for each of the types discussed previously. The role of the auxiliary function will be critical in the discussion of the nature of the transformative learning process for different types of individuals.

Differentiation

"Differentiation means the development of differences, the separation of parts from a whole. . . . So long as a function is still so fused with one or more other functions — thinking with feeling, feeling with sensation, etc. — that it is unable to operate on its own, it is an *archaic* condition, i.e. not differentiated . . ." (Jung, 1971, p. 424). The undifferentiated individual does not use the dominant function without having it confused with another function. For example, a person who is undifferentiated on thinking and feeling may continually shift back and forth between logic and value judgments. A person who uses thinking and sensing in an undifferentiated way may not be able to make a logical judgment because of continual interference from sensory stimulation that may contain further information pertaining to the judgment.

Jung writes, "Without differentiation direction is impossible, since the direction of a function towards a goal depends on the elimination of anything irrelevant. Fusion with the irrelevant precludes direction; only a differentiated function is *capable* of being directed" (pp. 424–425). The undifferentiated person, then, will demonstrate ambivalence and perhaps inhibition in the use of the undifferentiated functions.

Individuation

Jung calls the process by which individuals are formed and differentiated individuation. "Individuation . . . is a process of *differentiation* having for its goal the development of the individual personality" (Jung, 1971, p. 448). Some researchers (see Boyd, 1989; 1985; Boyd and Myers, 1988) have focused on this concept specifically in their facilitation of personal transformation. Although their approach does not contradict Mezirow's theory, it is limited in that it involves a concentration on psychological meaning perspectives. Jung is clear that individuation is not the development of a single, separate being, but rather that it leads to more intense and broader collective relationships. Before individuation can be a goal, there must be adaptation to societal norms. Jung (1971, p. 449) also writes, "Under no circumstances can individuation be the sole aim of psychological education." In the following discussion, therefore, I will examine psychological type preferences in relation to the broader perspective of transformative learning theory.

Transformative Learning and Psychological Type

Harry is an extraverted feeling type for whom intuition is a secondary function. He is a senior manager in a department of the federal government. In the yearly performance appraisal, Harry receives very high ratings from his staff on items such as supportiveness of staff, receptiveness to others' ideas, vision, and promoting a good work climate. However, he receives somewhat lower ratings on his organization of work and his decision-making and problem-solving skills. Because his staff members like Harry and do not want to hurt his feelings, they emphasize his strong interpersonal skills and his vision in their comments on his performance as a manager. As a part of a management development program, Harry attends a workshop on leadership. How likely is Harry to be aware of his assumptions and values related to his role? Will he be receptive to questioning what he does, how he performs, and why? How would Harry engage in critical reflection on his leadership style?

Pamela is an introverted thinking type who has sensing as an auxiliary function. She teaches English as a second language in a continuing education program. Pamela enjoys her subject. She particularly likes the structure of language — grammatical structures, the organization of a good composition, and the choice of just the right word to express a thought. Pamela's students have come to expect and appreciate her careful correction of their written English. They like and respect her as a teacher — they especially like her quiet, calm nature — but they would never consider calling her by her first name or discussing any personal concerns with her.

In an adult education course, Pamela experiences journal writing as a learner and decides that this would be a useful activity for her own students to engage in. Her students do as she asks but they do not produce the free-flowing kind of journals that she expects; rather they produce careful, impersonal compositions. They are somewhat disturbed that their teacher does not correct the grammatical mistakes in their journals. In her adult education class, Pamela asks that some time be spent in discussing the most effective way to use journal writing. How likely is Pamela to be aware of her assumptions and values related to her teaching? Will she be receptive to questioning what she does, how she interacts with her students, and why? How would Pamela engage in critical reflection on her teaching style?

Clearly, psychological type influences or perhaps even determines a person's learning preferences. Kolb (1984) reports data from three studies by different investigators of three populations; although the results are not completely consistent across the groups, there is support for the relationship between type and learning style as measured by the Learning Styles Inventory (Kolb, 1984) and the Myers-Briggs Type Indicator (Myers, 1985). Myers (1985) points to some evidence of differences of learning style in children of different psychological types, particularly in relation to test-taking skills. As I mentioned earlier, some investigators have examined the relationship between type preferences and cognitive style and communications patterns. Herbeson (1990) finds that a preference for the intuitive function predicts self-directed learning readiness. Perhaps most relevant to this discussion, Kreber (1993) shows relationships among psychological type preferences and critical thinking factors. Several authors discuss the relationship between learning style and type without basing their predictions on research (see Keirsey and Bates, 1984).

Given the limitations of the research data, the predictions and suggestions made in this chapter should be considered as fully open to questioning and discussion. In Table 5.1, various components of working toward transformative learning are listed on the side of the matrix and the eight psychological types across the top. A prediction is made for each component as to the likeli-

Table 5.1. Individual Differences
in the Transformative Learning Process.

A person of this type is likely to:	ET	EF	ES	EN	IT	IF	IS	IN
Be aware of values and assumptions	Y	Y	N	Y	Y	N	N	N
Be receptive to trigger events	N	Y	Y	Y	N	Y	Y	Y
Question values and assumptions	N	Y	N	Y	Y	Y	N	Y
Engage in content and process reflection	Y	N	Y	Y	Y	N	N	Y
Engage in premise reflection	Y	N	N	R	Y	N	N	R
Engage in rational discourse	Y	N	N	N	Y	N	N	N
Revise values and assumptions	N	Y	N	R	R	Y	N	R
Revise meaning perspectives	N	Y	N	R	R	N	N	R

Note: Y = Yes, likely to; N = No, not likely to; R = Reluctantly

hood that a learner would have a preference for this activity. Auxiliary functions are not considered here but will be included as a part of the subsequent discussion.

This analysis produces some apparent discrepancies with Mezirow's (1991) theory such as indicating that some psychological types are likely to engage in premise reflection but not in revising meaning perspectives and vice versa. This is, in part, because Mezirow does not address individual differences in his theory. I do not suggest that individuals are more or less able to participate in transformative learning, but that transformation may be experienced differently among individuals of different psychological types. I propose that the nature of the process will vary from one person to another. It may be that some people are less likely to be aware of or to question their values and assumptions or to respond to dilemmas with reflection; the process of transformative learning must be different for them.

Awareness of Values and Assumptions

Learners who have a dominant rational function may be more likely to be aware of their assumptions and values and hence more often aware of discrepancies when they occur. Thinking types will tend to gain awareness through their natural interest in logical analyses either through an inner (introverted) or external (extraverted) process. The extraverted feeling type, who is "always in harmony with objective values" (Jung, 1971, p. 354) is by nature aware of his or her own values and how they coincide with generally accepted values. Discrepancies are dealt with by simply adjusting values to restore harmony. To others, especially the opposite thinking type, this awareness may appear to be superficial or even artificial; however, for the extraverted feeling type, the concern for values and feelings is strong and genuine. The introverted feeling types on the other hand are quite different. They demonstrate a strong indifference to the external world and tend to subjectify feelings, images, and values. Self-awareness is probably hampered by the "unconscious effort to realize the underlying images" (Jung, 1971, p. 387).

Among the irrational types, the extraverted intuitives can be expected to display the greatest awareness of values and assumptions. Although they are not interested in values pertaining to the real world, they can be visionaries and can bring these visions to life. This drive to improve the world around them involves making their values and beliefs explicit. If the secondary function is feeling, the improvement drive will center on other people; if it is thinking, it will center on tasks and projects. Either way, values related to the other dimension (people or tasks) may be neglected. Among introverted intuitive types, the passion for images is an internal one that is generated by the unconscious. Without the need to change the world and without an understanding of truth or morality, this type does not have a preference for developing an awareness of values or assumptions. A strong thinking or feeling auxiliary function can modify this profile in some individuals. The same is true of the sensing types, either extraverted or introverted. These types are interested in actual experiences, facts, information, objects, and things of the senses—without a need to look for relationships among them or to form judgments about them.

Receptiveness to Trigger Events

Among the rational types, the feeling types (both extraverted and introverted) are expected to be the most receptive to trigger events (see Chapter Four for a full description of the nature of trigger events). Feeling types, especially extraverted feeling types, are in tune with their environment and the reactions of others. Wanting to maintain that relationship and wanting to please others, they are likely to be sensitive to social norms, the opinions and questions of others, and issues that are raised in the media. The introverted feeling types filter such stimuli, and their perceptions may appear to be distorted to the extraverted type; nevertheless, introverted feeling types are receptive. One would expect thinking types to be equally receptive. However, both extraverted and introverted thinking types possess strong principles and values that are not easily shaken by another's opinion or by an event. The thinking type who by definition does not care about the perception of others is more likely to dismiss a discrepancy in an assumption or value unless he or she is convinced by a good argument. Even in the face of a persuasive argument, the thinking type is more likely to respond with a counterargument than to be stimulated to reflect on his or her own assumptions. Thinking types with a strong intuitive auxiliary function are more receptive.

All of the perceptive types are receptive to trigger events, albeit events of a different nature for the intuitive and the sensing types. Intuitive types, either extraverted or introverted, will respond with enthusiasm to situations that present new possibilities and opportunities for change. Mention to an intuitive type that the department he manages needs restructuring and he will immediately list several ways this can be done. Sensing types, especially the extraverted sensing types, are receptive to events or experiences that are discrepant with past events or experiences. However, this may not lead them to question values and assumptions unless the thinking function is secondary. Introverted sensing types may be less receptive as "an unconscious disposition . . . alters the sense-perception at its source, thus depriving it of the character of a purely objective influence" (Jung, 1971, p. 394). Nevertheless, the introverted sensing type is "guided by the intensity of the subjective sensation excited by the objective stimulus" (p. 395).

Questioning of Values and Assumptions

Among the rational types, both extraverted feeling and intro-verted feeling types seem most likely to engage in questioning their values. As I mentioned earlier, the extraverted feeling types have as a primary interest maintaining harmony with others and with social norms. When their values are in conflict with those of others, they quickly engage in questioning their own values and easily adapt to others. Introverted feeling types have this same tendency, although it would not necessarily be visible to an observer — "their outward demeanour is harmonious, inconspicuous, giving an impression of pleasing repose, or of sympathetic response . . ." (Jung, 1971, p. 389). Extraverted thinking types are less likely to question their assumptions simply because they have developed their own "universal law which must be put into effect everywhere all the time, both individually and collectively" (p. 347). The extraverted thinking type "subordinates himself to his formula, so, for their own good, everybody round him must obey it too . . ." (p. 347).

Intuitive types, both extraverted and introverted, are more likely to question values and assumptions. They may not do this in the same way that a thinking type would do it — unless they have thinking as an auxiliary function. However, imagine the intuitive type who is facing a dilemma. She sees the possibilities in a situation, for example, but encounters resistance from others; since her own principles are not strong or grounded in a concept of 'truth,' she readily questions herself and possibly adapts in order to explore the possibilities. Sensing types, without the need to chase after visions, improvements, or images, have no reason to question their values and assumptions. In fact, they are unlikely to be aware of values and assumptions at all. If someone were to declare that an extraverted sensing type is "at the 'mercy' of sensation" [,] he would ridicule this view as quite beside the point, because sensation for him is a concrete expression of life — it is simply real life lived to the full" (Jung, 1971, p. 363). The introverted sensing type, although directed inward, would be equally disinclined to question himself or herself.

Content and Process Reflection

For thinking types, content and process reflection is a natural process — a part of their nature. Extraverted thinking types focus on the external world and perhaps are more likely to interact with others as a part of the process; introverted types engage in an inner reflective process, commenting that they need time to think and only entering into discussion when the thinking is complete. Feeling types, however, do not operate in the same way. Mezirow (1991, p. 107) describes content reflection as "thoughtful action . . . reflection on *what* we perceive, think, feel, or act upon," and process reflection as "an examination of *how* we perform these functions of perceiving, thinking, feeling or acting and an assessment of our efficacy in performing them" (p. 108). On the surface, these definitions sound as if they incorporate all four typology functions. Closer examination of the concept of reflection reveals it as an analytical, problem-solving process. Mezirow (1991) writes, "We may reflect on the *content* or description of a problem (or a problematic meaning scheme), the *process* or method of our problem solving, or the *premise(s)* upon which the problem is predicated" (p. 117). This kind of thinking is simply not the way a feeling type makes judgments or solves problems. Jung (1971, p. 357) writes, "Nothing disturbs feeling so much as thinking. . . . What she cannot feel, she cannot consciously think. 'But I can't think what I don't feel,' such a type said to me once in indignant tones."

As critical reflection is the core of transformative learning, can feeling types not engage in this process? The answer has to be that the process is different for feeling types or at least that this component of transformative learning is different. The feeling type can enter into an assessment of content or process based on value judgments or like-dislike discriminations. Revision of meaning schemes can still occur as a result of such an evaluation or assessment, but the nature of the critical reflection is different. The goal of an extraverted feeling type is to maintain harmony with the external world; for the introverted type, the process would be subjective.

For the perceptive types, content and process reflection

are somewhat different than for the thinking type but come closer to descriptions in the literature. Brookfield (1987), for example, emphasizes imagining alternatives as a component of critical thinking. Daloz (1986) describes how "it is necessary to leap out from our shell of absolute certainty and construct a whole new world based on some other person's ideas of 'reality,' other assumptions of 'truth'" (p. 228). Imagining alternatives and leaping out of shells are surely the forte of the intuitive type. For the intuitive type, content and process reflection may not be as systematic and logical as Mezirow describes, but it nevertheless achieves the same end. If the learner has a strong secondary thinking function, the reflection more closely resembles the theoretical description. Mezirow includes drawing on prior learning and experience as a part of reflection; here the extraverted sensing type is at ease. This individual reviews previous or similar experiences and problems in order to understand the what and how of the performance. Jung (1971, p. 363) makes an interesting observation of the extraverted sensing type. He says, "since one is inclined to regard a highly developed reality-sense as a sign of rationality, such people will be esteemed as very rational." The introverted sensing type, however, is not guided by real events and experience but rather by the "intensity of the subjective sensation" (p. 395). Reflection most likely takes place through an auxiliary thinking function, or in the case of individuals with an auxiliary feeling function, it resembles the process the feeling type engages in.

Premise Reflection

Premise reflection involves asking why; it is an examination of the reasons for and the consequences of behaviors, thoughts, or feelings. As such, it is a natural process for the extraverted or introverted thinking types, as are content and process reflection. Jung (1971, p. 346) writes that "when the life of an individual is mainly governed by reflective thinking so that every important action proceeds, or is intended to proceed, from intellectually considered motives, we may fairly call this a thinking type." The thinking type is almost defined in terms of premise reflection. Feeling types, on the other hand, do not engage in premise reflection as Mezirow defines it. In relation to content and process reflection, feeling types can evaluate premises not through logical analyses but through value judgments based on like/dislike or pleasure/displeasure.

Irrational types are not inclined to ask why. They do not ask, What are the reasons for and the consequences of my perceptions? These types are driven by images or visions. The sensing types, especially those who are responding to objective reality or to subjective reactions to objective stimuli, are not interested in asking why. Premise reflection occurs through a secondary function. An intuitive type, however, who is pursuing a vision can, albeit reluctantly, engage in premise reflection. For example, consider a college administrator, a strongly extraverted intuitive type, who has a vision of how the college can be. The vision requires the cooperation and participation of faculty and staff, but this is not forthcoming — the faculty union interferes; staff members complain that they do not have time for such changes. In order to bring his vision to life, the administrator can engage in premise reflection. Or, think of the introverted intuitive academic who has an image of herself as a writer. She can imagine her books and their possible contents, but she continually revises her manuscripts and never settles on a feasible and practical outline for a book. If the inner image is strong enough, she can be led to question the premises underlying her self-perception, that is, her psychological meaning perspective.

Rational Discourse

Mezirow (1991, p. 198) argues that participation in critical discourse is essential to the process of transformative learning: "we all depend on consensual validation to establish the meaning of our assertions, especially in the communicative domain of learning, and that an ideal set of conditions for participation in critical discourse is implicit in the very nature of human communication." Participants in rational discourse under ideal circumstances have accurate and complete information, are free from coercion and self-deception, have the ability to weigh evidence and evaluate arguments, have the ability to be critically reflective, are open to alternatives, have equality of opportunity to participate, and will accept an informed, objective, and rational consensus as a legitimate test of validity. Although these characteristics of rational discourse are unattainable, they are viewed as a goal of communication.

Among the rational types, both introverted and extraverted thinking types are more likely to engage in rational discourse. They accept freedom from coercion and self-deception as an ideal since their thinking process rests on 'truth,' and they are relatively uninfluenced by others' opinions. They show a preference for weighing evidence, evaluating arguments, and reflecting critically, and they are likely to accept an informed, objective, and rational consensus. Feeling types, however, are less likely to display these characteristics. They do not tend to see *coercion* as coercion but rather as a conflict of values in which they want to adapt to the accepted norm. Their critical reflection process takes a different form. They do show a preference for evaluating arguments. They can accept consensus as validity but not in Mezirow's sense. They would view consensus as an accepted norm that they can happily adopt—but not because it is informed, objective, and rational.

For the perceptive types, critical discourse takes on yet a different flavor. Sensing types are interested in accurate and complete information but will use their auxiliary function to weigh evidence. Extraverted intuitive types prefer persuasive rather than rational discourse; their goal is to convince others, not to debate rationally. Intuitive types, both introverted and extraverted, are open to alternatives, although they may prefer to follow these alternatives rather than come to consensus with others.

Revision of Values and Assumptions

If content or process reflection leads to a revision of an assumption or a value, the learner has transformed a meaning scheme. Consideration of this process in the light of psychological type leads to an interpretation of transformative learning theory in which learners take different paths to the same end. The thinking types, who are likely to engage in critical reflection and critical discourse, are less likely to transform their meaning schemes. Although they enjoy the process of logical analysis involved in reflection and discourse, they see their assumptions as 'truths' or even universal laws and are reluctant to revise them. Even in the face of strong logical counterarguments, the thinking type prefers to refute the logic rather than revise the underlying assumptions. This suggests that transformation of meaning schemes can take place in two ways for thinking types—either through the acquisition of new knowledge that leads the individual to see the old meaning scheme in a different way or through finding flaws in the logic of the underlying assumptions of a meaning scheme. This is more likely to be the style of the introverted than the extraverted thinking type, as he or she tends to be more self-reflective.

Feeling types, as I have already discussed, easily adapt their values to the values of others or to generally accepted social norms. Yet critical reflection and critical discourse do not take place in the way that Mezirow describes. To the thinking type observer, transformation can appear shallow or inauthentic; to the feeling type learner, this is a genuine change and, depending on the nature of the revised value, can be described by the individual as a profound learning experience.

For intuitive types, both extraverted and introverted, this is a different experience. They tend not to place value on values or assumptions but rather on possibilities and images. The extraverted intuitive type who is working to bring a vision to life or the introverted intuitive type who is following an inner image will revise a meaning scheme that interferes with that pursuit. Sensing types are primarily interested in objects, events, and facts without consideration of the assumptions underlying their perceptions. The sensing types are, nevertheless, receptive to trigger events, and it is easy to envision scenarios in which revision of meaning schemes takes place. For example, an extraverted sensing type may have an underlying assumption that all southern Europeans are lazy, and therefore may also have a sociolinguistically distorted set of meaning schemes about this cultural group. The original assumption could have been based on some set of actual experiences with or observations of individuals — perhaps even on media portrayals. But if that person attends a gathering and meets and talks with several people from southern Europe, all of whom display great ambition and productivity, this fresh experience can lead to a change in attitude, even in the absence of critical reflection per se. Jung (1971, p. 362) writes of the extraverted sensing type, "Objects are valued in so far as they excite sensations, and, so far as lies within the power of the sensation, they are fully accepted into consciousness whether they are compatible with rational judgments or not." Introverted sensing types are not as influenced by an actual experience. "What will make an impression and what will not can never be seen in advance, and from outside" (Jung, 1971, p. 395).

Revision of Meaning Perspectives

Just as critical reflection is at the heart of the transformative learning process, revision of a meaning perspective is a key outcome of the process. Mezirow (1991, p. 111) describes this as "a cardinal objective of adult education." We have all encountered learners who have undergone dramatic changes in their perspectives on life. Similarly, we have all encountered learners who easily acquire new knowledge and skills but do not demonstrate any fundamental changes as a result of their learning. This may be a function of the culture, society, family, or workplace in which learners live, but it also may be a function of psychological and learning preferences.

The likelihood that individuals of different psychological types will engage in revisions to a meaning perspective is, of course, an outcome of the components of transformative learning discussed earlier. Extraverted thinking types may prefer not to revise meaning perspectives because they have a deep urge to stand by their principles and 'truths'; introverted thinking types may reluctantly revise perspectives based on new knowledge or an awareness of flaws in logic, but neither type will want to consider others' values or opinions. Extraverted feeling types can readily transform their meaning perspectives not through a process of critical reflection but through value judgments. The value judgments of introverted feeling types are likely to be in relation to their subjective interpretation of the external world or other people; revision of meaning perspectives, when it occurs, is an intense inner process.

Sensing types are unlikely to transform a meaning perspective unless they are immersed in a very different situation, say, one that provides completely fresh sensations such as a change in environment or culture. Intuitive types can reluctantly revise their perspectives if this becomes necessary for the pursuit of a vision. Intuitives are less tied to assumptions or beliefs underlying a perspective than are thinking types. They do not see or look for absolute truth or one standard of morality.

Theoretical Implications

For the past four decades, educational researchers have emphasized the importance of individual differences in understanding learning. Theoretical constructs and variables such as learning style (Kolb, 1984), locus of control (Rotter, 1966), and field dependence and independence (Holtzman, 1982), to name but a few, have been used in attempts to explain how people approach learning in different ways. Mezirow (1991) partially sidesteps this issue by adopting a constructivist approach and describing individuals as construing meaning in a personal way, as does Kelly (1963). Yet transformative learning theory as a whole, perhaps primarily because of the language used to describe it, does not incorporate readily the very different ways in which individuals perceive the world and make decisions about it. If the predictions from Jung's theory are accurate, thinking types eagerly engage in several components of the process but in the end hold on to their principles and assumptions; feeling types readily revise their values but are not given to critical reflection and discourse. For the perceptive types, even the language used to describe transformative learning may be foreign; transformative learning may not be a systematic and rational process but one of sudden insight or personal illumination such as that described by Boyd and Myers (1988).

Very few educators would deny that fostering critical thinking is a crucial component of the teaching and learning process, that learner empowerment is intertwined with critical thinking, or that transformative learning is one goal of critical thinking. Mezirow's (1991) theory brings these concepts and processes together in an invaluable way. The implications of viewing the process of transformative learning through psychological type theory include the ideas that: an awareness of individual differences is important; the choice of language used to describe the process is critical; and the interpretive, constructivist understanding of learning is of value.

Summary

Jung's model of psychological types provides one powerful and comprehensive way of understanding individual differences, and individual differences clearly need to be considered in any perspective on adult learning. Jung describes people as having different attitudes toward the world: one is an extraverted attitude that entails direct interaction with people, events, situations, and information; and the other is an introverted attitude that allows for indirect stimulation from the world but mainly consists of a subjective, inner set of processes. Psychological type theory also incorporates two preferences in making judgments: the use of logic (thinking) and the use of values (feeling). Finally, Jung describes two ways of perceiving: through the reality of the senses and through intuition. Everyone has attitudes and preferences of different strengths as well as dominant and auxiliary functions that work together in various ways.

The process of transformative learning varies among people of different psychological type profiles. The components of transformative learning theory that I examined included: awareness of values and assumptions, receptiveness to trigger events, content and process reflection, premise reflection, critical discourse, revision of values and assumptions, and revision of meaning perspectives. This examination revealed some interesting ways of looking at transformative learning theory. For example, although the language of the theory is suited mostly to the thinking function, thinking types are not necessarily the most likely to revise their meaning schemes or meaning perspectives. Feeling types, for whom critical reflection does not take place as Mezirow describes it, are still likely to make changes in their values and their perspectives through values-based judgments. Some implications for transformative learning theory were discussed in light of the very different ways in which people see meaning in and act in the world.

Part 2

Promoting Transformative Learning

In Part One, I examined the process of transformative learning, first in the broader context of all adult learning. A description of Mezirow's transformative theory followed; then I viewed the process from the learners' perspective. Finally, I examined the influence of individual learner differences — especially psychological types — on the nature of the process. The focus of the book now shifts.

The purpose of Part Two is to describe the educator's role in promoting transformative learning. Parallel to Part One, I will examine the role of the educator first within the framework of adult educator roles in general. Then I will examine three critical aspects of promoting transformative learning: fostering learner empowerment — or setting the stage for the critical self-reflection, stimulating transformative learning — including consciousness-raising and challenging learners, and supporting the process — providing on-going encouragement and assistance as an educator and through the learning group.

The reader may find some of the educator roles and suggested strategies (such as journal writing or introducing critical incidents) to be familiar from the adult education literature. Promoting transformative learning is not separate from facilitating self-directed learning, encouraging critical thinking, or fostering learner autonomy. Transformative theory integrates and extends these concepts. My intent in Part Two is to incorporate strategies from the general literature and show how they can be used and extended to promote transformative learning.

In the final chapter, I will discuss the educator's role as learner. By engaging in critical reflection on his or her practice, the educator becomes a model for learners, and most important, develops an informed theory of practice.

SIX

The Educator's Role

It is not surprising that adult educators doubt, question, and revise the roles they adopt in a seemingly haphazard way. The literature bombards us with all of the things that we as educators are supposed to be: resource people, facilitators, counselors, mentors, models, reformers, and activists. We read that we should love our subject, share the joys of studying, be knowledgeable, be good listeners, instill confidence, establish a supportive learning climate, use humor, spark disagreement to discourage dependency, encourage involvement, provide positive feedback, use learners as resources, and take motivational factors into account (Brookfield, 1986).

Now, with the emphasis in adult education on developing critical thinkers (Brookfield, 1987), facilitating self-directed learning (Candy, 1991), viewing self-directed learning as a political dimension of practice (Brookfield, 1993), and fostering transformative learning (Mezirow, 1991), educator roles grow even more complex. Discussions of effective teaching techniques have become politically incorrect—we must aim to be social change agents with a critical theory of practice. What does all of this mean for practitioners? How can promoting transformative learning be integrated into our practice?

In this chapter, I will examine the roles of adult educators within the three perspectives used in Chapter One to describe adult learning: subject-oriented, consumer-oriented, and emancipatory learning. These perspectives also provide a framework for the discussion of the sources of power inherent in educator roles. The premise of this book is that learner empowerment through the process of transformative learning is one goal of adult education. The second section of this chapter will introduce educator roles and uses of power from that perspective.

Adult Educator Roles: Framework

The roles that adult educators adopt are derived from their perspective on learning, whether or not that perspective is articulated or even conscious. Educators who see learning as primarily the attainment of a body of knowledge or a set of skills tend to see the educative process as subject-oriented and their role as one of disseminating and clarifying knowledge. Educators who see learning as being initiated by the expressed needs of individuals tend to see the process as consumer-oriented and their role as one of responding to and meeting those needs. Educators who see learning as leading to freedom from personal or societal constraints will see the goal of education as emancipatory learning and will describe their role as one of helping learners become aware of, critical of, and free from constraints. My intention to promote transformative learning is in the latter perspective.

Mezirow (1990, p. 18) defines emancipatory education as "an organized effort to help the learner challenge presuppositions, explore alternative perspectives, transform old ways of understanding, and act on new perspectives." In order to acquire a "more inclusive, discriminating, and integrative perspective" (Mezirow, 1991, p. 167) on educator roles appropriate for promoting transformative learning, I will review the roles used within each of the three perspectives.

Note that this classification of educator perspectives and the roles derived from them is but one way of viewing educator practice. Houle (1980), for example, describes a framework that includes instruction (subject-centered), inquiry (collaborative), and performance (skills-oriented) as the perspectives from which educators work.

Subject-Centered Perspective

When education is subject-centered, the primary role expected of the educator is that of *expert*. The educator describes himself or herself as a mathematician, a mechanic, or a doctor, and as an educator, transmits this expertise to learners. The expert selects the content, orders the content into an agenda or outline, selects materials and readings, presents that content in an instructor-centered fashion (usually), and makes the decisions about whether or not learners have mastered the content. The expert is considered effective when the content is presented clearly, when it is well-organized, when the learners understand what is expected of them, and when the evaluation of learning is fair and objective. This model underlies the research on evaluation of instruction in higher education (see Marsh, 1987).

The *authority* role usually accompanies the expert role. Although authority can be derived from expertise, an authority figure is also one who takes command of a situation. The educator who assumes responsibility for making all decisions related to content will tend to act as an authority figure in other aspects of the process as well. For example, the educator might behave as a manager and be diligent about such activities as keeping attendance records and setting deadlines and penalties for missing deadlines. The authority also manages instructional delivery, that is, determines the pace at which the session is conducted and the timing of question periods. The effective authority makes good and fair decisions and conducts a well-run session.

The subject-oriented perspective most often describes the educator also as a *designer* of instruction. In this role, the educator considers the prior learning and experience of the learners, writes objectives for the instruction, arranges the topics in sequence to make learning progress from one level to another, designs strategies that are appropriate for the learning, and constructs tests for the evaluation of student learning. This perspective is reflected in the practical literature on instructional design (see Dick and Carey, 1978). The effective designer is one who, for example, writes clear objectives at a level appropriate for the learners, distinguishes clearly between major and minor topics, uses a variety of methods and materials, and constructs tests that are clearly related to the objectives. These characteristics are often reflected in standard student rating forms (see Abrami and Murphy, 1981).

The subject-oriented perspective also incorporates some forms of individualized learning such as modularized instruction. Here, an expert and a designer often work together to create materials that present the content in an organized fashion. The learner can then work through the content at his or her own pace.

Consumer-Oriented Perspective

In the consumer-oriented perspective, words such as "instructor," "teacher," and "trainer" are frowned upon; they imply that the educator assumes a central role in telling others what to do. Learners are seen to be self-directed, to have specific problems to solve, to want learning relevant to their immediate needs, and to have experience that serves as a learning resource. The primary educator role becomes one of *facilitator* of a learner-directed process. The facilitator responds to the needs of the learners, fosters an effective group process, provides support and encouragement, builds a trusting relationship with learners, is nonjudgmental, and accepts and respects learners as they are. The facilitator is a people person rather than a content person. This role is discussed at length in the books written for practitioners of adult education (see Brookfield, 1990). The effective facilitator is one who creates a warm and relaxed atmosphere, develops an open and trusting relationship with and among learners, and encourages the learners' pursuit of their own goals.

The consumer-oriented perspective also implies that the educator assumes the roles of *resource person* and *manager*. Although the learner is described as having the skill to seek out his or her own resources, the literature also ascribes this responsibility to the educator. Here, some overlap with the expert role in the subject-oriented model is apparent; however, the learner most often chooses the content area, and the facilitator assists by selecting appropriate materials, readings, experiences, or human resources. The manager role does not imply the management of learners but of resources, experiences, and materials that will facilitate learners' pursuit of their own interests. This might include, for example, arranging visits to a field site, organizing special events, or simply keeping track of the records and paperwork required by the institution in which the education is taking place. The educator who is effective in these roles is flexible and adaptive to the needs of individuals, is resourceful and innovative, provides a variety of resources and experiences, and is knowledgeable about the subject.

Finally, the educator may assume the role of *model* or *mentor* either deliberately or unconsciously. This is not to say that the educator in the expert role may not also take on these roles at times, particularly that of model; however, that tends to be much less likely because of the distance between educator and learner. The model role is more common when the educator-learner interaction occurs in the workplace, as in training for the professions or the trades or in other situations in which the learner can identify with attributes of the educator. The mentor role tends to be more likely in longer-term interactions. These roles are fostered by the nature of the educator's relationship with learners in the consumer-oriented perspective—one that encourages trust, openness, personal disclosure, and closeness. The effective model or mentor displays a love for the subject area, expresses contagious enthusiasm, is available for personal interaction with learners, is open and authentic, and develops good rapport with learners.

Reformist Perspective

There is some debate in the literature (see Chapter Two) as to whether the goal of emancipatory adult education should be primarily social change or personal development. Mezirow writes, "[a]dult learning transforms meaning perspectives, not society" (1991, p. 208) and "[w]hat emerges as common ground is that we must begin with individual perspective transformation before social transformations can succeed" (1990, p. 363). This will be my position here. To reform is defined as "to make or become better by removal of imperfections, faults, or errors" (including distortions and constraints). The reformer sees education as the empowerment of individuals and groups; through empowerment comes individual change and, potentially, social action. Unlike the consumerism model, it is not necessarily expected that learners know what they need; hence an educator's primary responsibility is consciousness-raising or increasing learner awareness. Different educator roles reflect slightly different approaches in working toward this goal.

The educator following Freire's writings (1970) would assume the role of *co-learner*. In this role, the educator works with learners and tries to find out about their lives and experiences even as learners may be questioning their values. For example, the educator working to increase literacy does not simply teach reading as he would under the subject-oriented approach, nor does he assume that people will come to him when they are ready to learn to read; rather, he shares the experiences of the learners, learners of their culture and values, and works within that perspective toward his goal. Similarly, the group leader working in a women's shelter learns about the women's experiences as she works with them to question their views of those experiences. The educator who is a co-learner acts as an equal participant in the process of learning, discovering, and changing. The effective co-learner is one who builds an atmosphere of mutual trust and respect, sincerely engages in learning, stimulates enthusiasm and interest in others, and challenges others' values and beliefs.

The reformist also plays the role of a *provocateur,* one who challenges, stimulates, and provokes critical thinking. Mezirow (1991, p. 206) describes the "empathic provocateur and role model, a collaborative learner who is critically self-reflective and encourages others to consider alternative perspectives. . . ." The provocateur helps to ensure that the norms governing rational discourse are maintained as a goal and encourages the group support that is needed when learners experience challenges to their beliefs and values. The provocateur will guide learners into an awareness of distorted assumptions and help them deal with the discrepancies between their expressed values and their actions. The effective provocateur will foster critical thinking, encourage group support, counsel learners who are threatened by the dilemmas they face, support learners in the choices they make, and assist learners in implementing actions based on these choices. Strategies for working within this role will be the topics of Chapters Seven, Eight, and Nine.

Although the subject-oriented, consumer-oriented, and reformist perspectives on the educative process differ along several dimensions, the power attributed to the educator role is a critical point of differentiation.

Adult Educator Roles: Power

A young and novice adult educator prepares for her first session; she is filled with trepidation and certain that the learners who are older and more experienced than she will question her credibility as an educator. She gathers materials, reads extensively, and is prepared to combat the perception of the group. She is amazed and joyful after the first session because her learners do not question her credibility. However, after the second session, she feels uncomfortable about this and believes that she should in fact question her obvious lack of experience. She says, "Whatever I told them to do, they would do it." This illustrates an issue of power.

In the subject-centered perspective, the educator retains most of the power; in the consumer-oriented perspective, the educator gives up considerable power; in the reformist perspective, power is shared by educator and learners. I will first discuss the nature of power and then will examine power in relation to adult educator roles.

Power

Power can be defined as a person's ability to influence another person's behavior and attitudes (see Mintzberg, 1983; Pfeffer; 1981). The educator who sees his or her job as one of influencing learners' behaviors and attitudes obviously has considerable power. Educators operating under each of the three perspectives described above would probably agree that influencing learners is one of their goals, although this may be less true for the consumer-oriented educator.

Types and sources of power have been described in the professional literatures of sociology, social psychology, and organizational behavior. The role of adult education in changing unequal power relations is a current theme in that literature (see Cunningham, 1992; Hart, 1990b), but the power structure of the educator-learner relationship has rarely been analyzed. A system for examining types and sources of power that comes closest to matching the three perspectives on adult education used here comes from Yukl's (1989) review of leadership theory. He describes position power, personal power, and political power.

Position power has as its sources formal authority, control over resources and rewards, control over punishments, control over information, and ecological or environmental control. Position power resides in the perception of the position itself. For the educator, simply being an educator automatically gives the person power in the eyes of learners and others. Tisdell (1993) finds that even when educators make an effort to share power, "[t]he fact that teachers (and not students) decide on the limits of power sharing is implicitly understood by both teachers and students" (p. 212).

Perceptions of power related to formal authority come from the individual's view of the responsibilities associated with the position in the social system. The person in the position of authority is expected to make decisions and requests. Others have a right to ask for information but are expected to obey the authority figure. The educator is expected to have control, make decisions, know the right answers, and tell the learners what to do.

In a similar vein, this individual controls resources and is the one who provides rewards when behavior meets expectations. This control is accepted because of the position the individual holds. The educator has control over resources that learners do not have, usually through the organization with which he or she is associated — access to photocopying, funds to purchase books, materials — while the learner may be expected to buy or find resources. However, the strongest source of power here is in the control over rewards; the educator is nearly always responsible for grades and is always the source of praise and feedback.

At the same time, the authority figure can punish those who do not behave according to expectations or can withhold rewards. The educator provides negative feedback, lower grades (in credit courses), or poor reports to a supervisor for those learners who do not meet expectations or standards. More informally, in discussions or conversations with learners, the educator has the power to punish by making negative remarks, by ignoring learners' remarks, or otherwise demonstrating a devaluation of the learners.

Because of the individual's position, he or she has control over information, including others' access to that information. If the authority figure decides that certain information is not appropriate, others will not receive it. The educator, of course, has control over information primarily through expertise; the educator has information that the learner does not have. This power source is inherent in the educator-learner relationship.

Finally, the authority figure controls the physical environment, including the organization and design of the tasks that learners engage in. In other words, position power allows the individual in power to make all decisions concerning others' activities, and those decisions are accepted because of the position the individual holds in the social structure of the organization. The educator may select the room in which sessions take place, rearrange the furniture, and arrange for coffee. But most important, the educator usually designs learners' activities.

Personal power has as its source expertise, friendship and loyalty, and charisma. It is partly based on the personal characteristics of the individual and partly on the relationship the individual develops with others. Expertise as a source of personal power is the result of an individual's having specialized knowledge or skill that is valued by others who do not possess it. But this is only seen as power if the knowledge or skill is in demand or if others depend on the knowledgeable person for their own expertise. Note that the individual who has expertise may not have it as a source of personal power if the expertise is derived only from the position itself, such as when a person has control over information.

A person who feels loyalty, friendship, and affection for another person wants to please that person; this results in another source of personal power. Yukl (1989) describes this source of power as being developed when a leader acts in a friendly and considerate manner, shows concern for others, demonstrates trust and respect, and treats people fairly; these characteristics are also among those attributed to being an effective educator. When learners view the educator as a model or mentor, they are likely to identify with the educator and express a desire to please that person. In a co-learner relationship, when the educator becomes a real person to the learner, feelings of friendship and loyalty develop and thus increase the educator's personal power.

Charisma is defined as an intense attraction that develops more quickly than friendship or loyalty. It is based on characteristics such as personal magnetism, persuasive manner, and enthusiasm and conviction. In a classic work by the sociologist, Max Weber (1947), charisma was described as a form of influence based on followers' perceptions that the leader is endowed with exceptional qualities. However, some theorists (Conger and Kanugo, 1987) see charisma as vision and still others (House, 1988) as complex interactions between leader characteristics and behaviors, characteristics of followers, and situational factors. The educator for whom charisma is a source of power is most likely to be the dynamic lecturer, the entertainer, the educator we remember being drawn to but not necessarily close to. Although leadership theorists have tried to list specific behaviors associated with charisma, it is implicit in the definition of the concept that this is a personality trait rather than a set of skills.

Political power, according to Yukl (1989), stems from control over decision processes, coalitions, co-optation, and institutionalization. Although in some sense all power can be described as political, there are processes that increase or magnify the initial bases of power (Pfeffer, 1981), and Yukl refers to these as political power.

Obtaining control over important decisions gives an individual political power; this may involve obtaining membership on committees that make such decisions, working in administrative positions, or having influence on those who do. The educator who works within the organization to control decisions about educational policies, procedures, and programs will have this source of power. For example, an educator who believes in learner self-evaluation but is prevented from using this approach by institutional policy may work to change the policy. The adult educator working outside of educational institutions (business, industry, health professions, and so forth) also may often find himself or herself in the position of working to change policies that determine practice. This type of power may or may not influence individual learners directly or affect the relationship of the educator with learners unless learners are aware of such activities and see their educator as an advocate for better education. In this case, the source of power may become more closely related to personal power from expertise.

Coalitions formed among individuals within an organization or with individuals outside the organization can be used to obtain influence over policies, procedures, or programs. Obviously, this source of power becomes important in informal adult education settings such as community action groups in which the goal of the group is to bring about political change. In this case, learners and educator may form a coalition, perhaps including outsiders, to work toward their goal. Extending the meaning of this strategy beyond its original definition, educator and learners may form a coalition within an educational organization and work as co-learners to achieve some change considered mutually desirable.

Co-optation is a source of political power whereby individuals are invited to participate in decision making and thus become committed to the outcome of the decision when otherwise they might not have been committed to it. This strategy applies to the educator who is interested in making policy changes within an organization or to the one who is working toward social change as a goal. This type of power is also used within a group of learners — that is, learners are invited to participate in making decisions about the learning as in the self-directed model and thereby feeling some commitment to the decisions made.

Institutionalization is described as the process whereby a dominant coalition maintains and protects its power within the organization even if coalition members no longer have the expertise needed for making appropriate decisions. Power resides, unchanging, in the same positions. When this occurs, the organization may fail or the dominant coalition may be overthrown abruptly (Yukl, 1989). An understanding of this concept may be relevant for the educator working toward organizational or social change. It is also interesting to think of the educator who maintains position power, possibly supports the status quo with regard to policy, and yet does not maintain personal or expertise power.

Reexamining Educator Roles

Educators working within the subject-oriented, consumer-oriented, and reformist perspectives have different sources of power. The sources and uses of power vary with individuals, and the nature of a leader's power depends on the characteristics of the followers. But simply adopting a particular perspective on education tends to define the power an educator expects to have. Table 6.1 summarizes this relationship.

The subject-centered educator has been described as adopting the roles of expert, authority, designer, and the like. Clearly, this individual has position power: authority, control over resources, rewards, punishments, information, and eco-

Table 6.1. Source of Power and Adult Education Perspectives.

	Source of Power		
Perspective	*Position*	*Personal*	*Political*
Subject-oriented	yes	yes and no	no
Consumer-oriented	no	yes	yes and no
Reformist	no	yes	yes

logical control — at least within the constraints of the organization. The educator makes decisions about content and then about the learning of the content. The educator working under this perspective may or may not have personal power; expertise, of course, is inherent in the perspective, but friendship and loyalty or charisma are not. This educator is unlikely to have political power simply because it is usually of little interest to the person whose primary concern is in transmitting expertise to learners.

The consumer-oriented educator gives up position power by turning decisions about learning over to learners — who do not necessarily embrace this move; this person works toward helping learners work toward their own goals. Even if institutional constraints prevent the full implementation of this model, the educator does not maintain position power; others in the organization do. Personal power, on the other hand, is maintained by the educator and is a crucial component of the facilitator role, particularly when its source is friendship and loyalty. Expertise may be down-played in the facilitator role, but it should be the basis for this approach, thus yielding a balance of authenticity and credibility. Expertise is a key component of the resource-person, mentor, and model roles. Political power may or may not be important to the consumer-oriented educator. This educator might become involved in trying to change institutional constraints that interfere with meeting learners' needs or perhaps use political strategies to work toward self-directed learning within a group. However, this would not be a central concern or orientation of this perspective.

The reformist educator, by definition, would eschew position power and become an equal participant in the learning process. Although learners may bestow position power on the educator at first, the reformist would work to change that by sharing control over decisions and information and by not assuming formal authority. The provocateur, although not an equal in the sense that the co-learner is, would also shun position power; this contradicts the educator's goal of learner empowerment. The educator working with a reformist perspective would maintain personal power. Expertise as a source of power plays a lesser role for the co-learner, but friendship and

loyalty form an important aspect of the approach. Both expertise and friendship or loyalty are critical sources of personal
power for the provocateur — expertise in challenging and provoking critical thinking and friendship in supporting learners as they
question their beliefs and assumptions. Political power is of interest to the reformer in somewhat different ways from those
included in the original leadership model of power sources.
Mezirow (1991) sees individual learners' changes as steps toward
social change. In this way, learners consider coalition with and
co-optation of learners as strategies for social change. Control
over decision-making processes may not appear relevant here,
but the educator could describe that source of power as a goal
for learners. On another level, the reformist educator is also
interested in political power and change within educational institutions.

In summary, the type of power an educator has and uses
is clearly related to that individual's perspective on education.
Different perspectives, or theories of practice, lead the educator to assume varying roles in their work with learners, and in
these roles, the source of the educator's power varies. Social and
cultural factors may influence educators' development of a theory of practice (see Merriam and Caffarella, 1991) and hence
their use of power. And, of course, within the symbiotic relationship between educator and learners, the educator's use of
power is also in reaction to the responses of the learners. Given
this context for understanding educator power, I will now introduce the notion of learner empowerment.

Adult Educator Roles: Learner Empowerment

Learner empowerment has long been a goal of adult education
practice. Although economic trends, a shift to an information-
based society, and rapid technological developments (Merriam
and Caffarella, 1991) have made job training and retraining a
central focus in adult education, these influences do not change
the notion that adult learning is a process of personal growth
and development. It is interesting to note, for example, that
a recent issue of *Adult Learning* in which technology is a theme,

contains an article on the impact of significant life events (Caffa-rella, 1993). A brief look at the history of learner empowerment will serve to reinforce this notion.

In the 1700s, the Corresponding Societies, whose goal it was to increase literacy, thought adult education was "regarded as a movement for freedom and liberation, both personal (in the sense of widening horizons) and social" (Harrison, 1961, p. xiv). In 1831, an article in *Imperial Magazine* stated that "popular education would lead people to rise above their station in life, make them less happy with their lives, and if they could read they would be corrupted . . ." (Inkster, 1985, p. 64). In North America, in 1848, the *Northern Star* described "educationists [as being] still what they were in Cobbett's time — the pretended friends, but the real enemies of the people" (Jones, 1975, p. 41).

In 1926, Lindeman defined adult education as "a cooperative venture in non-authoritarian informal learning . . . " and stated that "rather than studying 'subjects' the learner begins with his or her own immediate problems impeding self-fulfillment." The educator was seen to move "from acting as an authority figure to become . . . the guide, the pointer-out, who also participates in learning . . . " (Mezirow, 1991, p. 196). Lindeman later saw that "every social action group should at the same time be an adult education group" and "all successful adult education groups sooner or later become social action groups" (Lindeman, 1945, p. 2).

Several decades later, Apps (1985, p. 151) stated that "emancipatory learning is that which frees people from personal, institutional, or environmental forces that prevent them from seeing new directions, from gaining control of their lives, their society and their world."

Brookfield (1986), in criticizing the consumer-oriented perspective, writes that it "is possible to exhibit the methodological attributes of self-directed learning . . . but [still] to do so within a framework of narrow and unchallenged assumptions, expectations, and goals" (p. 57). He redefines self-directed learning as "predicated upon adults' awareness of their separateness and their consciousness of their personal power" (p. 58).

Finally, Mezirow (1991), in his formulation of the theory

of transformative learning, describes learner empowerment in this way: "Emancipatory education is about more than becoming aware of one's awareness. Its goal is to help learners move from a simple awareness of their experiencing to an awareness of the *conditions* of their experiencing (*how* they are perceiving, thinking, judging, feeling, acting — a reflection on the process) and beyond this to an awareness of the *reasons why* they experience as they do and to action based on these insights" (p. 197). Mezirow sees the role of adult educators as helping "learners look critically at their beliefs and behaviors, not only as these appear at the moment but in the context of their history (purpose) and consequences in the learners' lives" (p. 197–198).

Thus, woven throughout the history of adult education, learner empowerment appears as a central theme. This is not to deny the value of the learning of technical and practical information for adults. But learner empowerment, and consequently transformative learning, is the component of adult education that separates it from pedagogy. As Mezirow (1991, p. 3) writes, "Rather than merely adapting to changing circumstances by more diligently applying old ways of learning, [adults] discover a need to acquire new perspectives in order to gain a more complete understanding of changing events. . . . The formative learning of childhood becomes transformative learning in adulthood."

Defining Ourselves as Educators

All educators have assumptions, beliefs, and values concerning their practice. Most educators would have difficulty expressing those assumptions, describing the basis for them, and seeing how they are related to form an overall theory of practice or perspective on education. The how-to literature for practitioners would probably yield a list of dozens of characteristics of effective educators. Many conscientious educators will try to absorb and display these characteristics but without a guiding framework, philosophy of education, or goal, this will prove to be a fruitless endeavor.

I mentioned earlier that learner empowerment through the process of transformative learning is a primary goal of adult education. An acceptance of this goal can provide a meaning perspective on education that can then provide the framework for developing an individual theory of practice. But first, what does this statement mean? What does it exclude? We know that adults can and do learn basic facts, practical information, technical skills, and the like without engaging in transformative learning that leads to empowerment. Likewise, adults often have immediate problems to solve or specific goals, and they can and do seek resources that allow them to meet these needs without becoming involved in transformative learning. These are real and important goals of adult education and may be best met through the subject-oriented and the consumer-oriented perspectives described earlier. On the other hand, much of the theoretical writing underlines the importance of individual and societal development as goals of education.

Adult development has been described from a variety of perspectives. Developmental psychologists see adults as advancing through stages from dependency, to individualism and autonomy, to integration—Tennant (1990) provides a review of this literature. Some writers tie each developmental period to a specific age (Levinson, 1986). Gilligan (1982) argues that women's development follows a different path from men's, one leading to an increased capacity for empathy and attachment rather than autonomy or individuation. Moral development is seen as including a set of hierarchical levels starting with a black-and-white/good-and-bad view of the world and ending with a postconventional, autonomous or principled level (Kohlberg and Turiel, 1971). Psychologists and therapists see self-actualization as a life goal (see Rogers, 1969) or individuation (the development of the psychological individual as distinct from the collective psychology) as a life process (Jung, 1971). Social and cultural factors also are seen to influence development (Dannefer, 1984; Dannefer and Perlmutter, 1990). Going beyond individual psychological development, critical theorists in education write of freedom from oppression as the goal of learning (Freire, 1970). And generally, at any level from preschool to graduate studies, the development of the skills of critical thinking is considered to be a goal of education.

At the same time, the literature for the practitioner indicates that these changes are difficult to make. Brookfield (1990) discusses the resistant learner, the sources of resistance (including a fear of change), a fear of deviating from social norms, and a fear of appearing foolish. Clearly, this is different from providing information in a subject-oriented approach or meeting the needs of learners in a consumer-oriented approach.

Fostering learner empowerment has been defined as working with adult learners to raise their awareness of their assumptions and beliefs, reflect on and challenge their assumptions and beliefs, and support them during the process. If assumptions and beliefs are revised and transformative learning takes place, the process then also includes working with learners to plan and implement actions based on these changes. Note that some degree of learner empowerment is necessary before learners can begin a process of critical reflection (see Chapter Seven), critical reflection and transformative learning are also in themselves empowering processes, and the outcome of transformative learning is empowerment. Under this perspective, what are the adult educator's roles?

Initially, the educator may assume a *facilitator* role. I will argue in Chapter Seven that learners must experience comfort, self-confidence, and a freedom to participate and express their views before consciousness-raising activities or other triggers for critical self-reflection are introduced. The educator who begins a session by asking participants to list their assumptions or values about X and Y is not likely to receive authentic responses; learners will be trying to figure out what their teacher wants them to say. Just as working toward self-directed learning requires an atmosphere of trust, mutual respect, and comfort, so does working toward transformative learning. In fact, to some extent, learners need self-directedness to embark on critical reflection, and the process of critical reflection further enhances self-directedness (see Chapter Seven).

The educator also must establish a sense of equality between himself or herself and the learners early and assume the role of *co-learner*. The educator abandons position power but retains personal power. Learners see themselves as having equal access to participation in discourse and as being responsible for decision making about and in the learning experience. Through this process, which is the topic of Chapter Seven, learners are empowered to question their own beliefs and respond to the challenges of others. Critical self-reflection and potentially transformative learning can now be stimulated.

While remaining an equal member of the group with regard to position power, the educator assumes the role of *provocateur*. Other learners may also assume this role in their interactions with their peers. The educator introduces activities (such as critical incidents, journal writing, simulations, and case studies) that stimulate awareness of and questioning of assumptions, values, and beliefs. Educators and learners question and challenge each other to reflect on their own assumptions. Chapter Eight discusses in detail how the processes of critical reflection and transformative learning can be initiated.

The literature on transformative learning repeatedly describes it as a painful process (see Mezirow and Associates, 1990). Even if transformative learning is not the outcome of critical reflection, learners' open examination of their beliefs can lead to discomfort. The educator should assume the roles of *counselor, friend,* or *supporter,* although perhaps not with all learners. At times, group work will provide the support learners need. Brookfield (1987, 1990) also emphasizes the importance of encouraging learner networks for the fostering of critical reflection. However, the educator also has a responsibility to be aware of and work with the emotional responses of learners during the process. I will develop this topic in Chapter Nine.

Mezirow (1991) emphasizes the idea that transformative learning is not complete until the learner acts on the changed assumptions or values. At times, this part of the process may be impractical for the educator to work with; such changes may not take place until well after the learner leaves the educational environment. But in many contexts, such as in professional development, education in the workplace, or literacy training, the educator may play the role of *resource person* or *manager* as learners plan actions based on changed assumptions.

Summary

The practical literature on helping adults learn leaves the educator with the impression that she or he must not only possess a dazzling list of characteristics but also know just when to implement a specific strategy or technique based on learner needs. Without an explicit theory of practice or a well-thought-out perspective on education, the educator will naturally feel at a loss as to how to follow the many guiding principles of adult education, particularly when learners appear to resist these approaches.

Adult education practice can be described under three orientations or perspectives: the subject-oriented perspective, in which the goal is the transmission of content from educator to learner, the consumer-oriented perspective, in which the goal is the meeting of learner-expressed needs, and the reformist perspective, in which the goal is to foster empowerment of individual learners and ultimately cultural change. Under each of these perspectives, there is a different balance of power between educator and learners.

All educators have and use different types of power over and with learners, sometimes without awareness. But an awareness of power and the roles associated with it is necessary for the development of an informed theory of practice. Educators have, to varying degrees, position power (associated with learners' perceptions of the educator's position), personal power (associated with expertise and the relationship between educator and learners), and political power (associated with control over decisions and influence on others).

Throughout history, learner empowerment has been described as a goal of adult education. Learner empowerment is seen as a prerequisite to critical self-reflection and potentially transformative learning; this process also can be described as an empowering one with increased freedom or autonomy as an outcome (see Figure 6.1). In order to avoid the pitfall of providing yet another set of principles, the educator must work with a fully-informed theory of practice. To this end, the next three chapters will be dedicated to an examination of what such a theory of practice would contain.

Figure 6.1. Learner Empowerment Through a
Process of Transformative Learning.

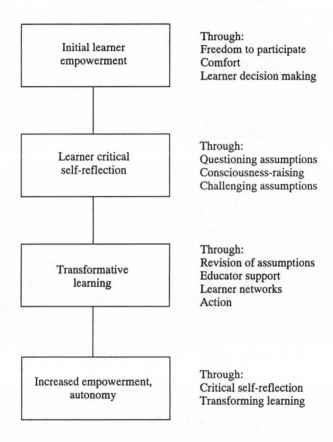

Initial learner empowerment	Through: Freedom to participate Comfort Learner decision making
Learner critical self-reflection	Through: Questioning assumptions Consciousness-raising Challenging assumptions
Transformative learning	Through: Revision of assumptions Educator support Learner networks Action
Increased empowerment, autonomy	Through: Critical self-reflection Transforming learning

SEVEN

Empowering
Adults for
Transformative Learning

"The essence of adult education is to help learners construe experience in a way that allows them to understand more clearly the reasons for their problems and the action options open to them so that they can improve the quality of their decision making" (Mezirow, 1991, p. 203). When such knowledge is gained through critical self-reflection, it is emancipatory knowledge. The learner is freed from the constraints of distorted or inflexible ways of knowing; the learner is empowered or perhaps enfranchised. However, transformative learning clearly cannot take place simply because either the educator or the learner decides that this is a goal of the learning experience. Engaging in the critical self-reflection that may lead to changes in a perspective is, in itself, a process that requires self-awareness, planning, skill, support, and discourse with others. Embedded in that list of requirements is a prerequisite that the learner already be empowered to some extent or at least be working in a context that is empowering and supportive.

As I discussed in Chapter Two, one of the ideal conditions of rational discourse is that the participants be free from coercion; another is that individuals have an equal opportunity to participate. If rational discourse is a key component of working toward transformative learning as Mezirow argues, then it becomes clear that learner empowerment must accompany the entire process rather than be viewed as an outcome of a transformed meaning perspective. Even if rational discourse is not a necessary component of the process, as it may not be for individuals of some psychological types, it seems apparent that the critical questioning of basic assumptions, values, and beliefs cannot take place in an environment in which a learner feels less powerful than others in the group.

An illustration may be useful. Carmen has enrolled in her first course at the local Adult Education Center after several years of being a homemaker. Her assumptions about position power are well developed and are reinforced often. When she was in school, she looked to her teacher for the right answers. As a parent, her children have relied on her for protection, guidance, and authority. In her community, she respects people in positions of authority and is admired for doing so. In her first course in the program, Carmen meets an instructor who provides a detailed and frighteningly difficult looking course outline. He reviews the criteria for evaluation in the course, emphasizing the importance of preparing for the certification examination that everyone must take. He advises the students to obtain a copy of *The Elements of Grammar* immediately so they can refer to it as they write essays. He suggests that anyone who does not have a personal computer should buy one and develop the skills to use it. Carmen thinks momentarily of her restricted budget and the cost of the tuition and textbooks but then quickly returns her attention to the teacher who is now explaining that critical thinking is a key component of modern education since things change so fast in our society. "You are expected not only to read but to be critical of what you read," he remarks. "That is the only way we can deal with all of the information available these days. And you will be expected not only to be critical of others' work, but of your own work and your own thinking." The teacher discusses how they will work together as a group and emphasizes that everyone should feel completely free to interrupt him, ask questions, and express their views. He then proceeds to give his introductory lecture, and, unfortunately, runs out of time to entertain questions. Carmen collects her notes and goes to the bookstore to buy the books, still worrying about the instructor's suggestion that everyone should buy a computer.

This educator, if questioned, would probably say that he encourages learner empowerment. "Of course," he could say, "and I think I make that clear to them from the first class on, especially when I discuss how they need to be critical of what they read."

In this chapter, I will argue that the educator of the reflective learner must give up position power, maintain and use personal power, ensure freedom from coercion and equal opportunity for participation, and support learner-controlled decision making. The first responsibility of the educator in working toward transformative learning is to establish and maintain a working environment in which the learner can become empowered.

I discussed learner empowerment in Chapter Four, describing from the learner's point of view how empowerment leads to and is an outcome of transformative learning. From the educator's perspective (and in the literature on leadership styles and managerial roles, for example, Wellins, Byham, and Wilson, 1993), empowerment unfortunately has become something of a catch word associated with a fashionable trend. Some educators now criticize the use of the term on that basis. However, empowerment simply means to give power or to make able. The argument that the word empowerment should not be used because it inherently implies a power imbalance (in that someone has the power to give to someone else) is deceiving—educators do in fact have more power simply by the virtue of the position they hold. Educators must relinquish that position power in order to ensure learner empowerment and critical self-reflection (see Tisdell, 1993).

Giving Up Educator Position Power

At a recent workshop for university faculty from a broad range of disciplines, Mezirow (1993) asked that some participants identify his underlying assumptions, including those of which he might not be aware. During the workshop, he stated that the participants, as educators, would share the value of equality among all members of a teaching and learning interaction. His point was that no one would tolerate abuse, ridicule, or coercion of learners; however, on another level, he assumed that educators do not want, seek, or use power over their learners. When this was pointed out as an underlying assumption of his own presentation, Mezirow (1993) agreed that it was. Indeed, this assumption is a necessary one for working toward transformative learning. But giving up position power is not automatic, natural, or easy for the educator to do. Educators may often be unaware of the position power they hold. The well-intentioned adult educator in the scenario described earlier probably had not reflected on his power over the new learners. But how does the educator give up position power?

A first step in giving up power is becoming aware of that power. As I described in Chapter Six, position power is based in formal authority and control—control over resources and rewards, over punishments, over information, and over the environment, including what goes on in that environment. The educator could begin the process by listing and analyzing the sources of position power that he or she has.

Let us take the example of Sherry, who works with learners in a job retraining program. Her learners come into the program with a wide variety of backgrounds and goals. Some have undiagnosed learning disabilities; others have dropped out of high school to enter the work force. Some want to improve their literacy skills; others have longer-term occupational goals. At the beginning of the program, learners work with individualized packaged materials, and they move into group work and more traditional classroom experiences as they progress. When Sherry examines the sources of position power she holds, she begins with the following list:

- Learners see her as a teacher in much the same way they viewed their childhood teachers.
- She determines which learning package individuals should use and hands it out at the appropriate time.
- She checks their work, especially their mastery tests, and decides whether learners should proceed to the next package.

- She determines when a group activity would be appropriate.
- She selects additional resources for learners and decides when they should be given to individuals.
- She has designed and decorated the physical environment.

Sherry can make a clear case for her involvement in each of these activities based on the level of her learners and her perceptions of their need for structure and guidance. She cares deeply for her learners; they see this, and over time come to view her as a nurturing person. But Sherry never gives up any of her position power.

If the educator reviews his or her sources of power and carefully considers the context (subject area, characteristics of the learners, institutional constraints), then that educator can decide which sources to relinquish and when and how to do that. Not all of the possibilities can be considered here, but I offer a few suggestions that educators can then adapt to suit their needs.

As for giving up *formal authority,* some fairly simple tactics can have a strong impact: using one's first name, sitting down rather than standing up, sitting close to the learners rather than at the front of the room or at the head of the table, and dressing casually, or appropriately for the group. The educator who does not pretend to have all the right answers will encourage learners to break away from that perception of the teacher—perhaps leading to some initial frustration. Even when working in the instrumental domain of learning where right answers abound, the educator can expect learners to find answers or show that other learners in the group have answers rather than answer all the questions herself. In communicative learning, of course, the perception of formal authority is encouraged even further when the educator's views are presented as the right views.

The educator can avoid making all decisions or controlling what learners do (see Day, 1988). The educator can and should use expertise power sometimes but can resist making *all* decisions. Why, for example, must all learners write an essay on the same topic—or even write an essay at all? Why must all participants engage in a particular group activity or contribute to a discussion? Quite often, upon closer scrutiny, the only reason is that the educator is used to telling learners what to do — in other words, exercising formal authority. Of course, if learning how to work in groups or how to write essays is an agreed-upon goal of the learning experience, this does not constitute a use of educator position power.

Control over resources and rewards can be surrendered in different ways, depending on the context within which the educator works. Brookfield (1993) sees access to resources as one of the two primary political dimensions in emphasizing the individual's standing against repressive interests. Simple strategies include: ensuring that a wide variety of resources are easily accessible in the local library, encouraging learners to share resources with each other rather than providing them oneself, and creating a climate in which learners give feedback to each other as opposed to turning to the educator for feedback on every occasion. In some situations, the educator can work with the institution or organization to ensure financial support for photocopying and for purchasing resources. The educator can work as an advocate for learners when such support is required but is not readily available.

When assigning grades is a requirement of the learning system, this can be the most difficult source of power with which the educator deals. Merriam and Caffarella (1991) describe the evaluation of learning as an ethical dilemma in the teaching and learning process. Decisions about who and what will be judged, which methods will be used, and who has access to results are difficult — especially since position power and expertise power are intertwined. The educator has the expertise to judge the quality of learners' work and is also in a position to control the rewards for quality. To further complicate the issue, grades can be of prime importance to learners. For example, grades serve to meet entrance requirements to further study, or they may bring back old associations with failure. Consequently, grades are often described by educators as motivators of learning.

There are several strategies an educator can use to lessen the disempowering effect of grades on learners. Learning contracts (see Knowles, 1975), either formal or informal, can be used independently by an individual learner or can include some discussion, negotiation, or agreement with the educator. But Mezirow's (1991) clear caution should be noted here. "If a goal of education is to foster transformative learning, dogmatic insistence that learning outcomes be specified in advance of the educational experience in terms of observable changes in behavior . . . result in a reductive distortion . . . " (pp. 219–220). Learning contracts can evolve and need not be formulated at the outset of a learning experience. Some form of learner self-evaluation is the ideal strategy; however most learners should also develop the skills required for self-evaluation. At the very least, it is important that learners participate in the evaluation process by making choices and taking part in on-going discussions.

Control over punishments is not usually a relevant issue for adult educators except perhaps in an evaluation process. The educator who provides poor evaluations either formally or informally to punish a learner who has not lived up to expectations exacerbates the power imbalance inherent in the educator-learner relationship. Educators also can be careful not to use other forms of punishment such as negative or sarcastic remarks, inappropriate humor, or sexist or racist remarks.

Control over information is another problematic aspect of position power since it is also a component of expertise power. In one sense, the educator has control over information based on expertise. Through study and possibly research in the subject and through longer experience, the educator will have a broader, deeper, and better understanding of the content with which the group is working. The educator can make that information as easily accessible as possible to learners. Sharing books, articles, and other resources is a fairly straightforward strategy for giving up control over information. Regularly discussing thoughts, experiences, reactions, and readings also diminishes learners' perceptions of the educator as being in control over information. When this is done in a climate of equality, it will not appear to be a demonstration of superiority or arrogance.

Usually educators have some *control over the environment.* They may be able to select and arrange the room, or, as in Sherry's case discussed earlier, design or decorate the working environment. Whatever aspect of the physical environment the educator has control over can be shared with the learner group. This can be as simple as arranging the tables and chairs and rotating the responsibility for bringing coffee, or it can involve a group working together to create a space for learning.

Control over the environment also includes the design and organization of tasks and activities. To some extent this is linked with expertise power because the educator has more experience in designing tasks. To illustrate the problem, a colleague who wanted to give learners more control in a graduate level class on management asked them to design the remaining tasks for the course about midway through the semester. To his dismay, he saw these learner-designed tasks as superficial and low-level. This need not happen if the educator can involve learners in the design of activities through discussion, collaboration, and choice. Expertise should be used appropriately. Brookfield (1990) comments on the "spuriously democratic teachers [who] will tell students at the outset of a class that the curriculum, methods and evaluation criteria are in students' hands. As matters progress, however, it becomes apparent that the teachers' preferences and judgments are prevailing. This can happen explicitly and overtly, but is more likely to be done insidiously" (p. 168). When sharing control over learning tasks and activities, an educator must remain open and explicit about the process.

Using Educator Personal Power

"Teachers' protestations that they don't really know any more than students do and that they are simply there to help students realize that they already possess the knowledge and skills they need sound supportive and respectful. But such protestations from teachers who are demonstrably more skillful, more intellectually able, and possessed of a much greater range of experience than that of students will be perceived as false" (Brookfield, 1990, pp. 165–166).

As I outlined in Chapter Six, personal power has its sources in expertise, friendship and loyalty, and charisma. The educator who is fostering learner empowerment cannot do so merely by giving up personal power. Brookfield (1990) writes of the importance of maintaining a balance between credibility and authenticity in building trust with learners. The use of *expertise* as a source of power develops one's credibility with learners; however, it is not only in building trust with the learner group that expertise is essential. A consideration of the various components of working toward transformative learning — making values and assumptions explicit, responding to trigger events, questioning assumptions, engaging in reflection, engaging in critical discourse, and possibly revising assumptions and acting on them — makes it clear that the educator needs both content area expertise and a solid understanding of learning and group processes. As Boyd (1989, p. 459) writes, "To facilitate transformations it is necessary to understand what is occurring in a small group." One cannot, for example, facilitate the critical questioning of assumptions without demonstrating expertise, and one cannot engage in critical discourse with learners without using one's knowledge and expertise. The educator is no longer the automaton of the early self-directed learning models but rather is a challenging and reflective practitioner who models these characteristics for learners.

Using *friendship and loyalty* as a source of personal power leads the educator to authenticity. Moustakas (1966) describes the authentic teacher as one whom learners can trust or one who is a real person. The educator who truly cares for his or her learners, believes in their competence, and respects them as individuals is displaying this source of power. Rosenthal and Jacobson's (1968) classic study of the effect of teacher expectations on students' development underlines the importance of this educator attribute. Wang (1983) sees this effect as cyclical. "As the teacher's perception of each student's competence changes, the teacher's behavior toward and expectations of each student are also affected. Positive alterations in the teacher's behavior and expectations, in turn, result in changes in the student's perception of his or her competence and efficacy in acquiring academic and self-management skills" (p. 218). Friendship and loyalty, as described by Yukl (1989), are also attributes the educator needs to provide support for learners as they question their values and assumptions. Mezirow (1991) emphasizes that "educators can provide the emotional support and theoretical insight into transformative learning that is necessary to help learners . . ." (p. 205). Finally, this source of power is critical in acting as a model for learners, and as Brookfield (1990, p. 172) remarks, "More than any other factor, it is a teacher's willingness to display the habits of critical questioning toward his or her own ideas and actions that encourages these same habits in students."

In discussing *charisma* as a source of power, Conger (1989) argues that leaders who have this attribute are most likely to be agents of radical change. He describes four stages of charismatic leadership: detecting opportunities and deficiencies and formulating a vision, communicating the vision and articulating the status quo as unacceptable, building trust, and demonstrating the means to achieve the vision through modeling, empowerment, and unconventional tactics. This model easily applies to the educator working toward transformative learning. If Yukl's (1989) view of charisma as a combination of enthusiasm and conviction is incorporating into these stages, the result may be a description of an educator who displays the ideal characteristics for fostering learner empowerment — assuming, of course, that expertise is also a source of power.

Empowerment Through Equal
Participation in Discourse

Mezirow (1991) sees rational discourse as a means for testing the validity of one's construction of meaning. In the communicative and emancipatory domains of learning in which there is no empirical validity, one turns to consensual validation through discourse. Mezirow (1991, p. 78) writes that "participation in rational discourse under . . . ideal conditions will help adults become critically reflective of the meaning perspectives and arrive at more developmentally advanced meaning perspectives." As such, discourse is a fundamental component of transformative learning.

Participation in rational discourse is also part of the process of learner empowerment. Habermas (1989), in describing the analysis of systematically distorted communication, writes, "Success in the creative use of language is marked by emancipation" (p. 310). Using Habermas's theory of communicative action to examine systematic distortions in classroom communication, Young (1988) sees the teacher's agenda as "hidden throughout the game of 'Guess What Teachers Think' in which at the surface level the speech purports to be a consultation with the students about their opinions, views, etc., but at another, deeper level, the teacher's agenda controls the direction of talk and the inclusion and exclusion of clues along the way to the lesson's (predecided) conclusion" (p. 57). Young notes that the talk in the dominant classroom type is characterized by a low degree of reflexiveness. The scenario of Carmen's first graduate class described at the beginning of this chapter illustrates inequality of participation and describes a disempowering learning situation. But how can an educator foster the equal participation in discourse and freedom from coercion that promotes learner empowerment?

Educators understand the value of learners' involvement in discourse, as demonstrated, for example, by the assignment of a certain portion of the grade in a course for class participation. This strategy, though often well-intentioned, violates another of the ideal conditions of rational discourse, namely, freedom from coercion. Leaners should not be forced into discourse. Rather, the educator can set up a learning environment in which individuals feel supported and feel free to participate. Some possible strategies for ensuring equal participation in discourse follow; their appropriateness will depend on the context of the interaction.

- *Stimulate discussion.* If discussions are slow to start, as they are with some groups, the educator can provide a provocative event for the discussion. This could be a critical incident (to be discussed in Chapter Eight), a controversial statement or reading, or a structured group activity.
- *Develop discourse procedures.* In order to meet its goal of validity testing, rational discourse must stay on the topic. Ideally, the group develops discourse procedures and group mem-

bers check and control the direction of the interaction. This also can be accomplished by agreeing that different learners summarize the discussion periodically.

- *Avoid making dismissive statements.* The educator can avoid using position power during rational discourse by not making either dismissive statements in response to learners' comments or what Brookfield (1990) calls definitive summaries — a distinctly different version of the discussion from what learners said. Young (1988) also remarks on the "implicit regulatory function of the teacher's practice of always being the next speaker and the only commentator on other speakers' speech" (p. 56).
- *Do not let one person dominate.* Individual learners can sabotage the ideal conditions of rational discourse as often as the educator. Learners who dominate the discussion or dismiss others' contributions can destroy equal participation. If the group has established procedures for discourse, other group members may intervene. If not, the educator can suggest this.
- *Allow quiet time.* Silence is important — it provides time for reflection and does not indicate inattention to the discourse. Silence may occur naturally in the group and should be allowed. Cranton and Hillgartner (1981) find that periods of silence predict positive student perceptions of the effectiveness of discussion. Also, some people, introverted learners specifically, often prefer silent reflection.

Encouraging Learner Decision Making

Individuals who do not wish to or who are not permitted to make decisions about their own learning experiences can scarcely be called empowered or be expected to engage in critical self-reflection. Yet this statement masks the complexities inherent in the concepts of learner decision making, learner control, and self-directed learning. In the 1970s, learner decision making was interpreted through an instructional design model that led to the notion that learners should have control over diagnosing needs, setting objectives, sequencing and pacing, choosing methods and materials, and evaluating learners' progress (see Cottingham, 1977; Della-Dora and Blanchard, 1979). This approach is found also in Knowles's (1980) model of andragogy. In the 1960s, researchers used experimental design methodologies in an effort to show that learner control over instruction would lead to increased learning (see McKeachie, 1960; Campbell; 1964). Although the use of these methodologies is now questionable, no significant effects were found; yet the notion of the importance of learner decision making persists.

Since the mid 1980s, writers and researchers have acknowledged that educators cannot simply give control to learners and that self-directedness is neither a personal characteristic nor a method but a multidimensional construct. The educator is still responsible for challenging and questioning learners (Brookfield, 1986; Candy, 1991). As Candy (1991, p. 71) aptly states, "there is nothing inherently undemocratic about [the educator] knowing more than a novice." For practitioners in adult education, however, the pressure to follow the 1970s model has stayed in place, leading to what Candy (1991, p. 237) has called pseudoautonomy, that is, educators espousing a self-directed model and "going through the motions of devolving responsibility onto learners, yet without commitment or conviction."

Now we face a dilemma. Jarvis (1992, pp. 141–142) describes it as "yet another paradox, that while the ideology of society is that people are free and autonomous, a great deal of human learning is other-directed and certainly other-controlled." Decision making cannot be turned over to learners, yet learrners must experience some control over decision making in order to feel empowered. Fostering learner empowerment is necessary if critical reflection and rational discourse are to occur. Aside from theoretical discussions, the adult education literature does not provide practical guidance in resolving this difficulty.

In the management literature, staff participation in decision making has long been an issue of interest. Although Candy (1991) warns us that the notion of equality as it is ordinarily used may become nonsense in the domain of education, perhaps the leader-staff relationship is similar enough to the educator-learner relationship that educators can benefit from applying a participatory leadership model.

Vroom and Jago (1988) describe a model containing five alternative leadership styles (from autocratic to consultative to group decision making) and twelve questions or criteria that can be used to select the appropriate style for a given situation. Some of the questions that may be relevant for the educator include:

- How important is the technical quality of the decision?
- Do learners have sufficient information to make a high-quality decision?
- How important is learner commitment to the decision?
- If the educator were to make the decision, is it reasonably certain that learners would be committed to it?
- Do learners share the organizational [or educator] goals?
- Is the problem well structured?
- How important is it to maximize the opportunities for learner development?

Following the model, it is clear that group (learner) decision making would be most appropriate when: learners have sufficient information, learners would not be committed to an autocratic educator decision, learners already share the educator's goals, learner commitment to the decision is important, and learner development is a priority. These questions, in various combinations, lead to different contexts in which learner decision making could be detrimental. If, for example, the quality of the decision is important, such as in selecting resources, readings, or topics for a learning experience, and if learners do not have sufficient information, learner decision making would not be appropriate. In fact, it would probably lead to learner frustration and poor decisions.

Reviewing the learning situation and considering questions such as those listed may help the educator find a path through the learner-directed versus other-directed dilemma. However, increased learner decision making remains a component of fostering empowerment.

Depending on the learning situation, learner decision making may be encouraged by some of the following strategies described in the adult education literature:

- Providing choices of methods, for example, suggesting that a topic could be dealt with in groups or in a large discussion
- Suggesting that learners select and develop criteria for evaluation activities
- Asking learners for their perceptions of the learning experience and sharing one's own perception
- Encouraging learners to suggest additional or substitute topics for discussion
- Suggesting that learners, working in smaller groups or as a large group, decide on some or all of the topics to be discussed
- Making the decision-making process open and explicit regardless of who is making the decision
- Providing learners with a decision-making model they can use as a guide
- Setting up teams or individuals who are responsible for some part of the decision making such as setting the agenda, forming groups, and coming to closure

When learners make decisions or when some aspect of decision making has been delegated to the learner group, the educator can not overturn the decisions arbitrarily. The educator, however, remains accountable. If a decision is inappropriate, the educator can discuss the problem with learners. The individual or group can then discuss and reconsider the decision in the light of this information. The goal is to foster learner empowerment. At times, the quality of the decision making may not be high, and it may be easy for the educator to think, I should have done this myself. When the quality of the decision is critical (following Vroom and Jago's model), a different leadership style may be more appropriate.

Setting the Stage for Critical Self-Reflection

Critical self-reflection is at the core of transformative learning. Fostering learner empowerment also involves setting the stage for critical self-reflection. If the educator has diminished his or her position power, used personal power appropriately, ensured the opportunity for equal learner participation, and encouraged learner decision making, learners will have a feeling of empowerment. However, critical self-reflection is a difficult and sometimes threatening process. How can we help learners feel prepared for this?

Challenging learners can create a climate conducive to critical reflection if learners are self-confident and knowledgeable when entering the learning environment. Mezirow (1993) describes a doctoral program in which he sets the stage for critical self-analysis. Before attending their first session, learners submit written work to the educator. The educator then provides extensive written critical commentary that the learner also receives before the session. This, Mezirow feels, encourages learners to question their own thinking and models critical thinking—all in preparation for intensive initial studies. However, such a strategy would not be helpful and perhaps even would be destructive with less secure learners.

Challenges can also be provided by setting up less dramatic *discrepancies* between learners' experiences and new or conflicting information. Provocative readings, unusual events, outrageous statements, and unexpected activities can all help create an environment in which differences are not only acceptable but encouraged. This kind of atmosphere leads one to examine long-held assumptions or values.

Brookfield (1987, p. 116) writes, "Asking impertinent *questions* often comes more easily when we are surrounded by others who are doing this." A climate of critical questioning will also be a climate in which learners are encouraged to question their own beliefs. The skill of critical questioning is discussed in Chapter Eight. Making such guidelines available to a learner group so that everyone (not just the educator) can engage in critical questioning will create a climate in which questioning is a norm.

Daloz (1986) describes the delicate balance between supporting and challenging learners. He argues that a high level of challenge combined with a low level of support will lead learners to retreat. If support is given without challenge, learners feel confirmed. Through a combination of a high level of support and a high level of challenge, learner growth can be promoted.

In order to set the stage for critical self-reflection, the learning climate should be one of *openness and supportiveness* as well as one in which challenge is the norm. Educators can model this by being open about their own assumptions as well as some of the dilemmas they encountered in their development as professionals. Early practice with brainstorming techniques in which no judgments are made, even of the most unusual suggestions, fosters such an atmosphere as well. Group-building exercises will encourage supportiveness among individuals in the learning environment. The importance of group processes is stressed throughout the adult education literature. In relation to transformative learning, Boyd (1989) emphasizes the value of support from group members. He describes a group as being composed of three interacting systems: social, personality, and cultural. Each system works on three tasks: establishing identity, developing modes of relating, and furthering reality adaptation. One of the contributions Boyd thinks the group process makes to transformation is "the supportive structure that [the] social system can provide for experimentation, exploration, and disclosure, basic to the realization of personal transformation" (p. 469).

Providing a *model* or models of critical reflection is a powerful climate-setting device because that is a way of fostering continued reflection. The educator need not be the only model. In a recent performance review process in one government department, one group of senior managers participated in collecting feedback, holding staff discussions, and developing action plans for improved management. Later, some lower-level managers emulated this process using their supervisors as models (Knoop and Cranton, 1993). An atmosphere of critical self-reflection had been established in these work units.

Individual Differences

In order to foster learner empowerment, the educator should consider individual differences among learners. Trying to challenge an introverted feeling type into participating in an animated discussion of logical fallacies in a theory may lead only to alienation and withdrawal. Pressing an introverted thinking type to share her innermost emotions with the group in an attempt to encourage openness might well send that learner fleeing from the room. Engaging an extraverted sensing type in a series of analytical questions could produce a confused questioner and an aggravated learner. On the other hand, no educator can function simultaneously in eight different modes in order to match the characteristics of different types of learners.

There are two ways to address this problem. One is to increase learners' awareness of their own learning style, psychological type, values, and preferences. Understanding oneself is a component of critical self-reflection so this serves a dual purpose—fostering learner self-awareness and empowering learners to make decisions as to how they learn best. The other strategy is for educators to develop a strong awareness of how learners vary in the way they think, act, feel, and see possibilities.

Learner self-awareness can be fostered informally or more systematically using various assessment tools. Brookfield (1987, p. 83) suggests that "certain questions can be asked of all learners involved in critical thinking activities. How do they develop and maintain the motivation for various learning activities? To what extent are extrinsic motives (social contact, job advancement) and intrinsic motives (innate fascination with learning, being tantalized by problem solving) interrelated? How do they integrate the new ideas and insights generated by critical thinking into their existing analytical and interpretative framework?" He goes on to suggest other questions the educator could ask of learners; questions can be tailored to the context in which they are used. The educator gains information about the learners; the learners gain insights into their own preferences.

A variety of instruments can be used to measure individual characteristics. Psychological type can be assessed using, for example, the Myers-Briggs Type Indicator (Myers, 1985), the Keirsey-Bates Temperament Indicator (Keirsey and Bates, 1984), and the PET Type Check (Cranton and Knoop, 1992). Learning style can be measured using the Kolb Learning Style Inventory (Kolb, 1984), the Learning Interactions Scale (Fuhrmann and Jacobs, 1980), or the 4-Mat Learning Style Inventory

(McCarthy, 1991). Other useful assessments include those of leadership style (for example, Stogdill, 1963), values preferences (Knoop, 1983), self-directed readiness (see Guglielmino, 1977), and critical thinking skills (see Watson and Glaser, 1980). Of course, formal assessment should be followed by discussion and activities designed to further explore individual differences.

For the educator, it can be difficult to develop a comprehensive understanding of all the ways in which individual learners in a group may vary. As I discussed in Chapter Five, psychological type may be one of the most comprehensive ways to think about individual differences. How would the fostering of learner empowerment vary among the different psychological types? An illustrative case study may be useful. The case is based on actual data from educator journals, observations, psychological type profiles, and learner materials, but the context has been changed to protect the anonymity of the learner.

Roger is an electrician who has worked in his trade for eleven years. He has been teaching a noncredit evening course called "Basic Electricity" at the local college for the past year. When Roger hears from another night school instructor that the college may be looking for full-time teachers and that there is a noncredit Instructor Preparatory Program available for those interested, he decides to enroll. Participants meet daily for two and one-half hours over four weeks in the summer. This is a little inconvenient for Roger, but he is seriously considering a career change so he rearranges his work schedule.

There are seventeen participants in the group, mostly trades people, which Roger finds quite comforting. He writes in his journal that he had been worried about getting in with a bunch of academic types and feeling stupid. The teacher is a woman about his own age who seems calm and knowledgeable. Roger writes on his feedback sheet on the first day that she spends too much time having people get to know each other. He wonders why she does not just get on with the program.

Roger's dominant psychological type preference is for introverted feeling; his secondary function is extraverted sensing. As such, his interactions with others are of a practical nature (his sensing function is extraverted); however, he has a strong inner world in which he subjectifies these experiences and makes decisions based on values while not revealing this side of himself to others. As the educator notes in her journal, "I made a real mistake with Roger—putting him into the feeling type group! He wouldn't even sit down, he stood around the edge of the group. When I asked him what was wrong, he said, 'I don't belong in this group.' Of course! I moved him to the sensing type group where he immediately felt comfortable."

When the educator uses strategies designed to give up position power, Roger indicates in his journal and his feedback sheets that he feels lost. "I need you to tell me what to do," he writes repeatedly for the first two weeks. He finds the learner self-evaluation component of the program particularly troublesome. Even though no grade or credit was given for the program, learners were asked to set their own criteria for learning and to regularly evaluate their progress. Roger refuses to do this for two out of the four weeks. "I can't do this; what do you expect of me?" he says anxiously. The educator spends a good bit of time with Roger, primarily in a supportive role.

It turned out that the use of educator personal power was the major force leading to a successful learning experience for Roger. Initially, he expressed anger that the educator did not behave like an expert. He wrote, "You know all the answers, why won't you just give us a lecture?" and "Aren't you making an easy life for yourself, not teaching us?" When he began to separate position power and personal power about midway through the program, he experienced a short stage of strong dependence on the educator. The educator wrote, "Roger is now following me everywhere," and "Roger was rejected from his group today and came racing to me in what I could only describe as a panic attack. I thought for a moment he would physically hold on to me to keep from passing out." In the third and fourth weeks of the program, Roger took advantage of every scheduled individual consultation time. He set good goals for his learning, although they were not concrete. He read three books and several articles related to his learning goals, each of which he discussed with the educator. He was particularly taken with Brookfield's (1990) concept of the imposter syndrome and identified strongly with this.

Equal participation in discourse was not possible for Roger, at least in this stage of his development. The educator observed that initially Roger would try to participate in group discussions because he thought this was expected of him. These attempts, the educator wrote, "were accompanied by strong emotions and were like strange bursts of inappropriate or irrelevant comments. The group remained silent for a moment, then nervously resumed discussion." Roger's journal contained entries such as, "There's just no way I can make myself talk in front of this group. I feel like I will panic and make a fool of myself." After the first week, Roger no longer participated in large group discussions. He sometimes joined small-group discussions; for the final two weeks, he had many discussions with the educator.

As I mentioned earlier, Roger could not make decisions about his own learning at first. With educator support, he did become able to do this; however, he wrote on his final evaluation sheet, "I probably would have learned more if you had told me what to do from the beginning" and "I wasted a lot of time not knowing what to study."

The key factor in establishing a climate for critical self-reflection appears to have been supportiveness. This relates to his introverted feeling function but not to his sensing preference. In fact, the educator noted that "it is rather odd that Roger focuses his learning goals on abstract concepts when he has a well-developed sensing function."

In spite of the difficulties he encountered, learner empowerment was fostered to some extent in Roger's case. He commented, "I did learn that I can do things" and "I amazed myself for reading those books; I didn't expect that, it's good that you pushed at me to make up my own mind." The educator wrote, "I just hope that Roger doesn't get an instructor-centered approach when he takes another program; he's been left at a critical point."

Summary

This chapter has stressed the importance of fostering learner empowerment. Although learner empowerment is often described as an outcome of an educational experience, I have argued here that powerless individuals cannot engage in critical self-reflection. Further, learner empowerment is a product of transformative learning; however, it is also critical to beginning and maintaining the process. The individual who is insecure, lacking in confidence, anxious, or unsupported, and is then plunged into activities designed to stimulate critical self-reflection may not be able to overcome the emotional barriers to learning and development.

In order to foster learner empowerment, the educator gives up position power but maintains and uses personal power. Possessing formal authority, that is, having control over resources and rewards, punishments, information, and the environment all serve to disempower the learners with whom an educator is working. At the same time, the educator undergoes the complex disentanglement of position power and personal power, leaving the latter intact. This may well be a transformative learning experience for the educator.

Equal participation in discourse and learner decision making were described as important ingredients of learner empowerment. Individuals who are actively involved in the educational environment through discourse and participation in decision making will see themselves as having power over their own learning. Strategies for fostering discourse and decision making will necessarily vary with the learner group, its context, and the characteristics of individual learners.

Feeling ready and able to engage in critical self-reflection is yet another aspect of learner empowerment. The educator can deliberately set the stage for this process by challenging learners, creating discrepancies, asking critical questions, combining support with challenge, and modeling critical reflection.

Individual differences among learners cannot be overlooked or neglected. Critical self-reflection is particularly suited to some individuals; it is not a process that all learners negotiate with equal ease. The educator who is aware of different learner preferences and styles can work toward the empowerment of all individuals.

EIGHT

Stimulating Critical Self-Reflection

The educator who has created an environment conducive to learner empowerment has set the stage for working toward transformative learning, but this does not ensure that learners will engage in critical self-reflection or revise invalid meaning perspectives. Essentially, an educator can do nothing to ensure transformative learning. Learners must decide to undergo the process; otherwise educators indoctrinate and coerce rather than educate. Daloz (1988) describes, for example, his student Gladys who could not imagine, despite his efforts, alternative ways of approaching her job responsibilities. On the other hand, when educators leave learners' critical reflection to chance, they deny some of their responsibilities as educators. How can the educator stimulate or initiate the transformative learning process while not imposing his or her own values, beliefs, and assumptions on learners? Two scenarios may help answer that question.

Tammy, who grew up in a remote rural area of Tennessee, was the first of her family to complete high school. She had wanted to attend college, perhaps to study for a career as a nursing assistant, but the nearest college was a long drive for her, and she decided to begin work in the local furniture factory to earn enough money to buy a car. As time went by, Tammy continued to stay home to care for her parents; she was laid off from her job, and the car and college became more distant dreams. When her parents moved to town to be closer to medical services, Tammy nervously decided to go to college at last. As a mature student, she was assigned to an adviser who encouraged her to take courses called "College Orientation" and "Life Skills" as a part of her regular program. Tammy almost decided to look for a job instead. She could see that college was no place for her. Everyone was younger; the women all dressed differently; she actually could hear her own hillbilly accent. However, Tammy went to her first classes. She was amazed that the teacher called herself by her first name, that they all sat in a circle, and that everyone was friendly and supportive. By following workbook exercises, participating in group activities, and holding discussions with the teacher and the adviser, students were led to determine their own learning needs. The teacher then helped people turn these learning needs into course objectives. Everyone was encouraged to make their own decisions; the teacher would say, "You know best what you need to do." Tammy chose to get rid of her accent to improve her social skills, and to work on her study routines, including managing her time better. She became comfortable with her classmates, her regular courses were not too difficult, and her parents had settled quite happily into town life.

Martin grew up near a small town in southern Ontario's fruit-growing area. His father had immigrated from Yugoslavia when Martin was a baby and had struggled over the years to establish a grape farm. His father had never learned to read or write but did not consider literacy to be especially important for a farmer. Martin knew from an early age that his father would give him the farm, so he always thought it was more important to learn how to care for the grapes than to do well in school. He quit high school as soon as he could do so legally and worked full-time with his father. Martin married a neighborhood girl, and they built their own house next to a stream at the back of the grape field. When the price of grapes fell to one-third of their value and Martin lost most of his crop to mildew, he began to think that he should get some training in a trade to supplement his income. His wife worked on the farm with him, but they also had two small children to support.

Martin enrolled in the local college's academic upgrading program as a prerequisite to taking a program leading to a welding certificate. Martin was dismayed to hear that "Life Skills" was a required course—he figured he had plenty of life skills already and, even if he did not, he could not see what that had to do with learning welding. To make matters worse, the Life Skills teacher was a woman who was much younger than he and who made the students sit in a circle, call her by her first name, and answer fairly personal questions. Everyone had to write a life story and discuss it with someone else; the teacher then asked very impertinent questions about each student's story. Martin could see that he was not the only one who felt uncomfortable. He was interested to find out, though, that some of the fellows had quite similar backgrounds to his. One rather rude question the teacher asked led him to wonder why he had never really considered finishing high school. He mentioned that to his wife over supper the next night.

Although these two scenarios are similar on the surface, it is more likely that the process of transformative learning has been initiated for Martin than it is for Tammy. Martin's educator appears to have challenged him to look beyond his perceived needs. Tammy's educator has, for the time being anyway, simply made her comfortable. Challenging learners can be done in a variety of ways; although it should not be abrasive or destructive, it can be difficult and anxiety-provoking—and exciting and rewarding for both educator and learner.

In this chapter, I will present some strategies for stimulating transformative learning: using questions effectively, constructing consciousness-raising experiences, writing in journals, learning experientially, and introducing critical incidents. For the reader familiar with the adult education literature, some of these suggestions may be familiar. Mezirow (1991) lists twelve goals of andragogy, then comments, "These practice injunctions clearly bear a close relationship to transformation theory. Helping adults elaborate, create, and transform their meaning schemes . . . is what andragogy is about" (p. 201). Transformative learning theory takes us beyond the mere atheoretical application of techniques, however. The goal here is to actively encourage critical reflection through which individuals can investigate the justification for their meaning schemes and perspectives.

Critical Questioning

"Skilled critical questioning is one of the most effective means through which ingrained assumptions can be externalized" (Brookfield, 1987, p. 92). Brookfield goes on to describe *critical questioning* as a specific form of questioning concerned with fostering reflection rather than eliciting information. He emphasizes the sensitivity and skill required in being a critical questioner. As was evident in Martin's case, the questioner may appear to be personal, intimidating, or threatening. The educator should be provocative without intimidating the learner into silence. In a description of *flow experience,* Csikszentmihalyi (1975) suggests that when a challenge far exceeds learner capabilities, learners will experience severe anxiety; when capabilities are greater than the challenge, learners will be bored; however, when capabilities and challenges more or less match, stimulation (flow) is likely to occur. This is similar to Daloz's (1986) description of the interaction of support and challenge.

Brookfield (1987) provides three requirements for effective critical questioning: *be specific* — relate questions to events, situations, people and actions; *work from the particular to the general* — find and express the general themes underlying learners' responses to specific questions; and *be conversational* — avoid the use of academic jargon and describe ideas and experiences in an informal way. Wlodkowski (1990, pp. 164–165) suggests some cautions for educators engaged in questioning: avoid echoing, or repeating portions of learner responses to a question; avoid asking learners to think about an issue, rather, stimulate thinking through the question itself; avoid frequent comments like That's good or Fine answer that suggest that the instructor is the judge of right and wrong answers; and avoid Yes . . . but reactions to learner answers; these are essentially rejections of learners' responses. Wlodkowski also advocates the use of follow-up probes in questioning, particularly when this encourages learners to be clearer or more specific, and he recommends inserting questions into lectures or explanations. These guidelines provide a good framework for communicating with learners through questions, but how does the educator use questions to stimulate transformative learning?

In his description of content, process, and premise reflection (see Chapter Three), Mezirow (1991) provides one way of understanding the role of critical questioning. Content reflection is a consideration of the question, What?, process reflection is an examination of How?, and premise reflection involves asking Why? The What? and How? questions can be asked of psychological, sociolinguistic, or epistemic assumptions or beliefs. Once a learner is asking why, he or she is questioning a meaning perspective. Keeping in mind Brookfield's guidelines and Wlodkowski's cautions, how would this questioning look in practice?

Content Reflection

What? questions serve to raise learner awareness of assumptions or meaning schemes. In the psychological meaning perspective, these questions take the form, What do you know or believe about yourself? The educator might ask, What do you see as your skills in this area? What would you like to improve? What is your perception of yourself as a learner or professional or tradesperson? What aspects of your nature suit themselves to your pursuit of this career? What do you not like about this? What are your beliefs about learning or practicing this profession? or What draws you to this area of study?

In the sociolinguistic meaning perspective, content reflection questions take the generic form, What are the social norms? For example, the educator could ask, What was the perception of this in your home community? What would be the feminist view on this issue? What views do the media present? What are the politicians saying about this? What does the way we use language in this area tell you? What would you say to this if you were the union leader? or What should an educator's response be to this issue?

The most straightforward What? questions exist in the

epistemic domain, taking the form, What do you know? In fact, knowledge questions tend to be overused by instructors (Wlodkowski, 1984). They should be used to stimulate content reflection and not to check or judge the knowledge of learners. The epistemic meaning perspective includes not only knowledge but how knowledge is acquired. The educator might ask, What knowledge have you gained from past experience in this area? What have you read or heard related to this issue? What enabled you to learn this, or what would enable you to learn this? or What is your favorite way of learning?

Process Reflection

Process reflection occurs when learners ask, How did I come to this knowledge, understanding, or value? It is one thing to say, I believe that students should participate in discussions (content reflection), but a deeper level of reflection is achieved when the individual considers how he or she came to have that belief. The educator can stimulate this level of reflection by asking appropriate critical questions. Psychological assumptions can be questioned in the form, How have you come to have this perception of yourself? For example, the educator might ask, How did you come to choose this career? How did you decide that you hated statistics? How did you come to see yourself as a poor writer? How did you become afraid of spiders? or How did you decide that your career goals are more important than your family life?

Sociolinguistic meaning schemes can be questioned using the format, How have social norms been influential? Such questions can be asked in a wide variety of contexts for example, How did the community where you grew up influence that view? How did your high school experiences affect your idea of the role of teacher? How has the women's movement changed your values in this area? How did the media description of this event influence your view? How does advertising affect your choice of products? How do the words you use to describe that event influence the way you see it? or How were you affected by the writings of Mezirow?

To encourage process reflection in the epistemic domain, questions may take the form, How did you obtain this knowledge? As with content reflection on epistemic assumptions, the educator should take care not to trivialize the questioning. Typical questions might include, How did you come to the conclusion that this theory is valid? How did you decide that you need not do further reading in this area? How did you conclude that the experiment failed? How did you come to see yourself as an abstract rather than a concrete thinker? How consistently did you observe this pattern before you came to a conclusion? or How did you develop criteria for making this decision?

Premise Reflection

When engaged in premise reflection, the learner is questioning the question, Why should I care? Why is this relevant? Why is this question worth considering? By its very nature, this type of question no longer focuses on the specific assumption or meaning scheme but has an impact on the learner's broader perspective on the issue. When concerned with psychological perspectives, the educator can ask critical questions such as, Why does it matter that you are afraid of spiders? Why is it relevant that you see your relationship with your mother that way? Why is your self-image as a learner of concern to you? or Why are you questioning your communication skills?

In relation to sociolinguistic meaning perspectives, questioning takes the form, Why are these norms important? For example, the educator could be asking, Why is it relevant what your extended family thinks? Why do you care about the culture of the organization? Why does it matter what others say? Why are you considering the feminist perspective? or Why are you questioning that philosophical stance?

In the epistemic perspectives, the educator encourages learners to consider why they need or do not need knowledge or why they obtain knowledge in a certain way. Relevant questions might include, Why are you focusing on details? Why do you want to read further in that area? Why do you want to learn that? Why do you think that experience will increase your expertise? or Why are you questioning your expertise?

Effective critical questioning challenges learners to consider some aspect of the situation under discussion in a new way. Questioning might set up a sense of uncertainty or unpredictability; Apter (1982) argues that the more unexpected an event, the greater the interest, arousal, and anticipation it generates. Good critical questioning creates a sense of disequilibrium, which Mezirow (1991) would describe as a trigger event for transformative learning and which learning theorists would describe as a prerequisite for learner involvement (see Bigge, 1982). Of course, unpredictability and disequilibrium can become debilitating. Skillful critical questioning requires that an educator know when this might happen and understand how individuals differ in their reactions.

Consciousness-Raising

"Consciousness is a peculiar thing. It is an intermittent phenomenon. One-fifth, or one-third, or perhaps even one-half of human life is spent in an unconscious condition. . . . The conscious mind moreover is characterized by a certain narrowness. It can hold only a few simultaneous contents at a given moment. All the rest is unconscious at the time, and we only get a sort of continuation or a general understanding or awareness of a conscious world through the *succession* of conscious moments. . . . Consciousness is very much the product of perception and orientation in the *external* world" (Jung, 1968, pp. 6–8). From the Jungian perspective, transformation is a change in an individual's consciousness; what was previously unconscious becomes conscious.

Hart (1990b) sees consciousness-raising as understanding the nature of social power structures. "Consciousness raising was not derived from an identifiable, coherent body of theory, but from the experience of oppression" (Hart, 1990b, p. 50). She describes conditions of consciousness-raising as including: acknowledgment of oppression, acceptance of the importance of personal experience, homogeneity of the learning group with respect to social differences, and a structure of equality among all participants of the group, including the teacher or facilitator.

Through the writings of Freire (1970) and others, consciousness-raising has come to be associated with freedom from oppression; the term also is used in this way by feminist theorists. Indeed, individual or personal consciousness-raising as defined by Jung can be seen to form the basis for freedom from oppression as discussed by Hart. The psychological definition of consciousness-raising will be followed here: it is the process of developing self-knowledge and self-awareness (Chaplin, 1985). This definition also parallels the central process of transformative learning—becoming aware of and then questioning one's construction of meaning. What can the educator do to foster consciousness raising?

In some situations, consciousness-raising is provoked by exposure to new information, knowledge, insights, or values, especially if these are discrepant with currently held meaning schemes. More commonly associated with the notion of consciousness-raising is seeing familiar things from a different perspective, thereby increasing one's self-awareness regarding familiar things. I will discuss approaches to encouraging the latter first.

Most learners are firmly entrenched in various roles—as professionals, as persons, and as learners. Experiences that encourage learners to take on the roles and hence the perspectives of others can lead to consciousness-raising. Of these, role playing may be the most commonly used strategy; it is described in most books about working with adult learners (see Brookfield, 1990; Cranton, 1992) and in texts on counseling and group processes (see Johnson and Johnson, 1982; Corey, 1985). The context of the role play is described to learners. The participants (actors) are given a description of the part they are to play—not a script but enough information that a dialogue can be improvised. Ideally, learners and educator together design the scenario for the role play. Some people may be uncomfortable with this; no one should be forced to participate. Those who prefer not to act can be observers with specific reactions or behaviors to look for. Watching for indicators of underlying, unconscious assumptions is a useful exercise. Initially, a role play may seem artificial for both those acting and those observing, but this impression fades. With repetition of the experience, most people become enthusiastic actors.

In order for role playing to lead to consciousness-raising and thereby initiate transformative learning, skillful debriefing is important. Participants should have the opportunity to discuss their experience in the role fully, especially what it was like to view the situation from that perspective. Observers can ask critical questions such as, What were you thinking or feeling? How did you come to that reaction? Why is this important? Observers can describe participants' verbal and nonverbal behavior from their own perspective. Brookfield (1990) recommends that videotaping a role play be used to assist in debriefing. This allows both participants and observers to see discrepancies between their perceptions of the experience and the actual behavior of the actors.

Although role plays can be conducted informally (an impromptu Let's act this out during a discussion), they are usually planned in advance or researched, which leads to a fairly structured experience. Other informal experiences may be useful in some contexts. For example, an educator might suggest that:

• Two people reverse roles and express views they had previously opposed in a discussion
• Two people reverse roles they play in real life (for example, a manager and a staff member, or a union member and a manager)
• A learner or learners participate in a discussion as someone whose work they have read (You take the part of Carl Jung; what would he say?)
• Learners write short autobiographies—of someone else's life, perhaps a theorist, or a colleague, or someone in a different position in the workplace
• Learners write down opinions or views that are antithetical to those they hold and that everyone participate in a discussion maintaining that perspective

As in the more structured role play experiences, consciousness-raising can be initiated when the assumptions, values, and beliefs underlying the roles are made explicit and questioned.

Simulations and games can be used to initiate the viewing of situations or problems from alternative perspectives. Ready-made simulations are available; computer simulations are also available in many disciplines — for example, medicine, dental hygiene, marketing, and quantitative analysis. These may be useful in some situations, but experiences developed by the learners and educator may encourage more involvement and thus match the goals of the learning group more closely.

Useful guidelines have been written for the design of simulations and games (see Greenblatt, 1988; Jones, 1985). Simulations may involve making life and death decisions as in Brookfield's (1987, pp. 107–108) crisis-decision simulations. "Imagine that you are in the aftermath of a nuclear explosion. In the company of eight other people, you are in a radiation-free, protected room that has space and air enough for ten. Three people who are stumbling around in the external environment discover the room, and all ask to be admitted. These are a doctor, a pregnant mother, and a teacher. Which of these three do you choose to admit?" Clearly, such a simulation will provoke learners to make their values explicit and to see their values from others' perspectives. Sensitive and skillful facilitation and debriefing are required here. Less dramatic simulations are equally useful. Some examples from various disciplines are:

- In a gerontology group, suggest that learners simulate loss of hearing, eyesight, and tactile sensation by using earplugs, semitransparent blindfolds, and gloves, and then engage in some routine activity.
- In a management development workshop, suggest that learners simulate a problem such as dealing with a budget cut or a reorganization directive (some participants may act as staff and others as managers)
- In an adult education group, suggest a simulation of an international adult educators' caucus in which each participant acts as a well-known theorist (past or present) and the goal is to agree on how to certify adult education practitioners.

- In a hospitality staff development session, suggest a simulation of a hotel reception area with some participants acting as clients, others as hotel staff, and others as managers.
- In a basic computer workshop, suggest that learners simulate the components of a computer network and pass information from one to the other as the system would do.

Games provide a more abstract representation of reality. By definition, games also have winners and losers, which may not be always appropriate. However, there are situations in which removing experience from reality is useful, for example, when learners are anxious, lacking in confidence, or sensitive to the issues under discussion. With careful design and skillful debriefing, games can serve the same purpose as simulations in consciousness-raising. Games sometimes will demonstrate learner characteristics such as aggressiveness, cooperative preferences, or competitiveness, giving participants opportunity for much insight.

Life histories or biographies are described by Dominicé (1990) as a means of consciousness-raising (although he does not use that term) and fostering transformative learning. Dominicé suggests that individuals first present their life history orally to the learner group. This is followed by questioning and then a discussion of the narrative. Next, the learner prepares a written narrative in no prescribed format; the story determines the style of the life history. In using this strategy in research, Dominicé suggests that content analysis of the narrative be prepared first by a member of the group other than the author; the final interpretation reflects the questions posed by the entire group. In describing the role of the educator, Dominicé (1990, p. 209) writes, "The facilitator helps adults identify the itinerary by which they have become who they are and to reconstruct the process through which they have learned what constitutes their knowledge."

Some form of life histories could be used in a variety of settings as a consciousness-raising experience. Examples include:

- In patient education, to make explicit and critically question lifestyle and health issues
- In adult basic education programs, to foster self-reflection about job choices
- In English as a second language program, to increase self-awareness about perspectives on cultural differences
- In management development, to determine and analyze the assumptions underlying individuals' perceptions of the management role
- In teacher training, to stimulate self-awareness of learners' background and personality as these factors relate to their theory of practice

In such contexts, the educator might want to suggest that the life history be focused on the relevant theme, or this could be the responsibility of the learner group through critical questioning. The educator, of course, must take care not to fall into the role of therapist or to lead learners to believe that past traumas can be dealt with in the learning group. As with other strategies that promote consciousness-raising, the use of life histories can uncover painful incidents in the learner's life.

Exposure to new knowledge also can be a consciousness-raising experience, especially when that knowledge is discrepant with prior knowledge. If an educator has always seen himself as an expert and a transmitter of information and then reads a book or attends a workshop that emphasizes the value of interactive experiences, he may begin to question his approach. If a manager has never considered any leadership style other than assuming responsibility for all decision making, and she meets with a consultant who emphasizes the increase in productivity and staff morale that can result from involving staff in decision making, this could lead to consciousness-raising. If a college instructor has always assumed that she can present topics clearly and explain what students need to know, and then she watches a videotape of her teaching and finds out that students do not follow her, she may reflect on her perception of herself as teacher. New information, knowledge, values, and insights can come from books, art, discussions with others, lectures, or experience.

The educator is an obvious source of new and possibly discrepant knowledge. If he or she provides a variety of resources and readings, presents provocative information, suggests alternative possibilities, and encourages learners to engage in new experiences, consciousness-raising can be fostered.

Journal Writing

Historically, journals and diaries have been used as a means of self-expression, especially for expressing thoughts and feelings for which the writer has no other outlet. Well-known writers, artists, philosophers, scientists, and researchers have used journals to reflect on their life and work (Lowenstein, 1987). Humanistic psychologists and psychoanalysts, including Jung, have also long incorporated journal writing into their work with clients. Progoff (1983), who studied with Jung, has contributed extensively to the literature on using journals. He suggests a variety of formats and journal "sections" that may be used: a life history, a dialogue with a person from the writer's life or with a historical figure, a depth-dimension section containing metaphors, dreams, and images, and a life-study journal written from the perspective of another person.

In order to stimulate transformative learning through journal writing, the educator and learners can select any journal format that seems appropriate for their context. Ideally, individual learners select the format and style that best suits them. However, in order to encourage reflection rather than the production of a log of daily events or a series of descriptions, one or more of the following guidelines could be helpful:

- Suggesting that learners divide each journal page in half vertically and use one side of the page for observations and descriptions and the other side for thoughts, feelings, related experiences, or images provoked by the description
- Stating that journals will not be checked for grammar or writing style or be marked or judged in any way
- Suggesting a theme or a perspective to be explored in the journal such as My thoughts on my career options or My

role as a professional or Past experiences that have influenced me
- Suggesting that learners establish some routine for their journal writing — thus avoiding the situation in which a learner writes a full journal at the end of a learning experience simply to please the educator
- Suggesting that learners experiment with various styles, such as writing to a specific person (perhaps in the format of a letter), writing as someone else, or working with poetry, metaphors, or other creative forms

Two aspects of journal writing can inhibit its potential to stimulate transformative learning; first is the learner's perception of the educator role and any position power imbalance that implies. For her thesis, Gifford (1993) studied dialogue journal writing as a critical reflection process with English as a second language students. In spite of explicit statements to the contrary, her learners viewed the journal as a composition exercise and were resentful when the educator did not correct grammar errors. Only one person in the group showed any indicators of critical reflection. If learner empowerment had been fostered, as discussed in Chapter Seven, this reaction would not have occurred. However, there may be other learner characteristics, such as previous experiences or cultural expectations, that will render the journal ineffective in stimulating transformative learning. Second, the purpose or goal of journal writing should be discussed openly among learners and educators. If this goal is not agreed upon and understood by all participants, critical self-reflection will take place only by chance.

Two critical strategies for encouraging self-reflection and thereby stimulating transformative learning through journal writing are the use of a dialogue journal and the use of self-analysis. In a dialogue journal, another person responds to the journal entries with comments and critical questions. This role may be assumed by the educator, but it could just as well be assumed by another learner in the group. The journal is regularly shared; questions and comments stimulate further reflection. This must be done with care, as journals are ordinarily a private form of self-expression. Responses to the journal should be challenging but not judgmental and provocative but not condescending. Comments should never contradict how the learner sees himself or herself but should question the origin of those perceptions and the consequences of holding them. Questions such as Why do you consider this issue important? What actions would this lead you to? and How did you decide on this view? will tend to provoke further self-reflection. The earlier section on critical questioning contains further examples of appropriate questions.

Learner self-analysis of the journal also will stimulate further self-reflection. Most journals, if kept over a period of weeks, will show a change in thinking and perspective. If the last section of the journal contains an analysis of the journal itself, learners can examine the journal for patterns and themes in content and for changes in opinions, thinking, or feelings.

Experiential Approaches

Experiential learning has long been espoused as an important concept in education; Dewey's (for example, 1933) writings serve as a theoretical foundation for this view. Phrases such as *learning by doing, action learning, action science, reflection in action,* and *praxis* are all used to describe the mixture of doing and reflecting that constitutes experiential learning. Clearly, some areas of learning are best facilitated through doing. Habermas's (1971) technical knowledge, which involves learning to control and manipulate the environment through predictions about observable events based on technical rules, would necessarily involve experience in that environment. Dewey (1933) deals with the notion of reflection as rational problem solving. He defines reflective thought as "active, persistent and careful consideration of any belief or supposed form of knowledge in the light of the grounds that support it and the further conclusion to which it tends" (1933, p. 9). But if one is interested in stimulating critical self-reflection (emancipatory knowledge) rather than, or in addition to, reflection on observable events in the environment (technical knowledge), what is the role of experiential approaches?

Kolb's (1984) model of experiential learning may be useful as a framework. He describes learners as going through a cycle of concrete experience, reflection on that experience, abstract conceptualization, and application of the insights in a new context. Although learners may have preferences for one or more stages of the cycle, a journey through the whole process leads to growth and development. Educators who promote and implement experiential learning often neglect the reflection and abstract conceptualization components of the experience. This neglect places the possibility of stimulating transformative learning in jeopardy. Kolb (1984, p. 31) writes, "Experiential learning is not a molecular education concept but rather is a molar concept describing the central process of human adaptation to the social and physical environment."

The nature of the concrete experience will vary with the learning context. Education for the professions (for example, nursing, teaching, or dentistry) routinely includes a practical component in the program as does trades training. These practica provide concrete experience and can lead to critical reflection. Other examples might include: a visit to or volunteer work in an adult education center by members of an adult education course, attendance at or participation in a play in an English as a second language class, a day spent working at the farm in an agricultural course, participation in a variety of committees in a management development workshop series, or putting on a musical in a continuing education drama course for teachers. Almost every subject area contains some opportunity for concrete learner experience. Experiences can be selected to maximize the potential discrepancy between learners' views or values and the experience. The more learners are involved in a real-life setting and are doing rather than observing, the more likely they are to be influenced by the experience. Schön's (1983) work is interesting in this respect; he describes how individuals engage in reflection as they are involved in action.

To stimulate the transformative learning process, however, the educator must do more than provide concrete experience. According to Kolb's (1984) model, opportunities for reflecting on the experience, for conceptualizing it (fitting it into

currently held views, for developing theories to explain it, gener-
alizing from it), and for applying the insights gained should also
be provided. Kolb (1984, p. 41) says, "The active/reflective di-
alectic . . . is one of *transformation,* representing two opposed ways
of transforming that grasp or 'figurative representation' of experience — either through internal reflection, a process I will call
intention, or active external manipulation of the external world,
here called *extension."* Some strategies that may foster transformation include:

- Setting time aside for critical discourse related to the experience both during and after the experience
- Suggesting that learners write about the experience in journals or other formats
- Encouraging critical questioning, perhaps through having
  learners each develop a series of questions and using them
  with the group
- Emphasizing any discrepancies between the experience and
  the theoretical positions related to the experience
- Suggesting that learners share any related experiences and
  compare them
- Using a brainstorming activity to generate insights, thoughts,
  and feelings derived from the experience
- Encouraging learners to develop hypotheses or plan actions
  based on these insights
- Providing learners with the opportunity to validate their new
  ideas in another concrete experience

Stimulating transformative learning through experiential
learning also can be individualized. Within a group of learners,
one or a few people may benefit from one kind of experience
whereas others have already encountered it. When practical constraints allow it, the educator can encourage different learners
to participate in different experiences. For example, in a farmer's
cooperative learning group, if there is an individual who has
not experienced a marketing board meeting, this could be ar-
ranged as an activity for him or her, either within or outside
of the group; other members of the group who had had that

experience would be encouraged to choose other experiences. Discussions, reflection, and brainstorming to promote critical self-reflection on the political responsibilities of farmers in dealing with marketing boards would take place in the group as a whole.

Critical Incidents

The critical incident was originally developed by Flanagan (1954) as a social science research technique for obtaining qualitative data. Individuals are asked to describe a specific event that is related to a certain topic or theme — one that stands out in their minds as being especially positive or negative. The researcher may ask for both positive and negative events. Usually, a set of questions is provided such as Who was involved in the incident? What were the characteristics of the individuals involved? What made the incident positive or negative? and What insights did you gain as a result of the incident?

Since its development as a research instrument, the critical incident also has become popular as an educational activity. Brookfield (1987, 1990) advocates critical incident exercises in the promotion of critical thinking, pointing out that the primary advantage of the technique is its focus on specific situations, events, and people rather than on abstract concepts. In addition, Brookfield (1987) suggests that a benefit of critical incidents is that they can be used privately; individuals may not wish to discuss their problems in front of colleagues.

The directions for critical incidents usually take the general form, Think back over your last six months (or year) as a . . . learner/teacher/worker/manager. . . . Describe in about one-half page an event that was particularly positive/negative for you. Include when and where the incident occurred, who was involved, what was especially positive — or negative — about the incident, and what insights you gained from it. The degree of structure and the number of questions addressed in the incident will vary with the learner group and the theme being discussed. In some situations, it may be more appropriate to use critical incidents in the third person, for example, Think back over the last six months and describe an event in which a colleague or peer underwent a particularly positive or particularly negative experience.

When used to stimulate transformative learning, the follow-up to the production of the critical incident is perhaps more important than the incident itself. Group discussion or possibly educator and learner discussion of the incident will lead to critical self-reflection. Although learners may privately gain some awareness of their underlying assumptions, this is best facilitated by viewing the incident through others' eyes. Questioning those assumptions is encouraged primarily through interaction with others. Some strategies that can be used by the educator in working with learner critical incidents include:

- Modeling a critical incident either informally or formally and encouraging learners to question that incident
- Suggesting that learners share their critical incidents in pairs with each member of the pair questioning the incident
- Coaching learners to ask indirect questions of each other — not, What are your assumptions underlying . . . ? but rather, Why did you say this? or What led you to describe it this way? or What would your colleague have said at this point?
- Moving critical questioning from the specific to the general and from content reflection (What?) questions through to premise reflection (Why?) questions
- Encouraging learners to share the results of their small-group discussion with the full learner group when an atmosphere of trust exists
- Including some action planning in the discussion by asking, for example, What would you have done differently? or What will you do next time in such a situation? or How will you ensure further similar positive experiences?
- Ensuring that all learner disturbances or residual negative emotions have been fully addressed by each person or by the group (critical incidents can yield a strong affective reaction)

Critical incidents can provide a powerful vehicle for stimulating transformative learning precisely because they are so closely connected to personal experience. Consider the effect of telling an embarrassing story to a friend or relating the details of some negative event to a colleague — the potential power of this as a reflective learning experience becomes obvious. The educator must take care to ensure that all learner concerns are addressed. Recently, at the end of a critical incident exercise with a group of adult education learners, one of the most confident and self-assured members of the group was near tears and called out, "Wait! We didn't finish discussing my incident!" It had not occurred to the group that she needed this discussion, but for her it was traumatic to recall and reveal this event to others.

Individual Differences

By nature, some people are more likely to engage in critical self-reflection and transformative learning than others. And, as I hypothesized in Chapter Five, these processes may vary from person to person. The type of person who continually asks Why? as she surveys her environment or reads a book (thinking type) will more readily respond to questioning as challenging than will the learner who prefers to accept things as they are. The reality-based individual (sensing type) will be more responsive to concrete experiences than the person who dreams of future possibilities but does not know where he left his keys (intuitive type). Kolb (1984) summarizes empirical studies that, at least in part, substantiate these relationships, although the quantification of human complexities is a questionable pursuit. In stimulating transformative learning, the educator must maintain an awareness of individual differences, consider which events will be more likely to stimulate transformative learning in which learners, and expect variation in the processes that individuals go through.

A case study will illustrate the influence of individual differences in reaction to the strategies discussed in this chapter. This case is based on data (psychological type profile, educator journal, and learner and educator materials); however, the context is changed to maintain anonymity. Sally is a senior manager with the federal government. She voluntarily attends a workshop series designed to improve her leadership skills; the workshop promotes teamwork. As a part of the series, several instruments are administered to assess leadership style, psychological type, values preferences, and locus of control. Sally's psychological type profile indicates that her dominant function is extraverted thinking, and her secondary function is intuition. She tends to be a directive leader, highly task-oriented, with a strong internal locus of control.

The workshop experiences include critical questioning, consciousness-raising (though not labeled as such), and experiential assignments that take place outside the workshop but are incorporated into discussions. Journals and critical incidents are not a part of the series for participants.

Sally enjoys the lively discussion that results from critical questioning and comments positively on this in the evaluation of the workshop. However, the educator notes that Sally shies away from any direct questioning of her own behavior with her staff and especially from any critical questioning of her values. Sally responds with statements such as, "One would think that most managers would . . . " Type theory predicts that an extraverted thinking type would not easily express personal feelings or accept criticism. Perhaps related to this, it also appears that others in the group do not feel they really know Sally; there is no evidence that they exchange stories, problems, or confidences with her during breaks.

Sally plunges into a role play with a sense of drama. Without invitation, she helps to organize the role play and sets up furniture and other props. As one of the actors, she appears to assume her role authentically. During debriefing, she has no difficulty describing her reactions while in the role. Sally's intuition preference could contribute to her willingness to imagine herself in a role and hence see things from another perspective. Both her directive leadership style and her preference for thinking (which may be related) would explain Sally's contribution to the organization of the activity. Sally does not comment on this in her evaluation.

The experiential activity involves obtaining staff ratings

on various leadership skills, discussing the results with staff, and reporting back to the workshop participants both on the results and the discussion. Sally's staff gives her low ratings on promoting teamwork, relating well to others, showing flexibility, and some communications skills. They give her high ratings on getting things done, organization of work, and delegation of responsibility and authority. In the debriefing session, Sally defends her results by blaming her staff. When the educator points out that this does not fit with her high internal locus of control, she indicates that some staff members just do not like her, and that is the reason for their low ratings. In a journal, the educator notes that it is impossible to move Sally away from this view. The educator also comments that most others in the group find this activity to be very useful. From Sally's preference for extraverted thinking, her staff's ratings are predictable. Her preference (as an intuitive) is also predictable — she does not prefer practical experiential activities; however Sally's resistance to discussing other possible interpretations within the activity are surprising.

Individuals with different characteristics and preferences do respond in a variety of ways to the strategies used in this workshop. For example, an introverted person probably would not enjoy the role play as Sally did; other participants clearly benefited from the experiential activity while Sally rejected it. Educator understanding of these reactions and their possible basis is critical.

Summary

Critical self-reflection is stimulated by perceived discrepancies between learners' beliefs, values, or assumptions and new knowledge, understanding, information, or insights. Such discrepancies are often encountered in a learning context through reading, talking to other learners, interactions with the educator, or practical experiences. However, the educator who wishes to stimulate critical self-reflection and thus work toward transformative learning can further enhance the process by using strategies designed specifically to reveal and highlight such discrepancies.

Critical questioning can be used to stimulate content,

process, and premise reflection. In fact, these types of questions can lead the learner from making assumptions explicit to questioning meaning perspectives. If the educator initially asks, What do you know or believe? and then proceeds to question the question itself, critical reflection will be encouraged.

Consciousness-raising strategies are used to increase self-awareness and often involve looking at familiar things from a new perspective. Role plays, simulations and games, life histories, and new knowledge can all serve to increase self-awareness. These strategies can take on many configurations in form and content.

The introverted learner will appreciate the opportunity to escape from role plays or simulations and to keep a journal of his or her thoughts, feelings, and insights. A dialogue journal in which the educator or another learner responds with questions and comments adds to its effectiveness as does the incorporation of a learner self-analysis of the journal. The concept of praxis, the combination of doing and reflecting, has long been the basis for educational practice. The provision of concrete experiences for learners, followed by reflection, conceptualization, and application clearly can stimulate critical self-reflection.

Finally, the critical incident provides a unique and effective means of leading learners from the specific to the general in understanding their underlying assumptions and beliefs. As with each of the strategies discussed in this chapter, the subsequent discussion is as important in fostering reflection as the activity itself.

Learners, of course, will not react with equal enthusiasm to each of the efforts to stimulate transformative learning. The individuals who shrink into the background during role plays are probably introverted. Those who write at length and critically about incidents and who fill their reports with facts and details about a recent experience could be sensing types. And the learners who never get around to writing their journals may well be intuitive types. The educator should expect that the process of critical self-reflection will be different for different people and that learners will respond to the various strategies in their own ways.

NINE

Supporting
Transformative Learning

In transformative learning and emancipatory education, learners recognize and work with discrepancies and distortions in the way they see the world. This is a process that the educator cannot take lightly. It can, of course, be a liberating and joyous process, but even the most positive scenario can have a dark side for the person who has changed his or her life by acting on a revised meaning perspective.

Consider Janice who joined a single-parent group when she felt she just could not stand her life anymore. She was juggling part-time studies, part-time work, the raising of three small children, and the care of her home. Janice was continually racing from the day-care center, to class, then home to greet her children when they returned from school, and back to the university for another class, often with a little one in tow. She described her learning in the single-parent group as truly transformative: she changed her career goals, began to feel capable and autonomous, and, to her great joy, was offered a good full-time position. Some weeks later, although she loved her new job, was financially comfortable, and had been able to hire someone to help at home, Janice suddenly felt that she had lost her identity. She found herself unable to concentrate on her work; she complained to her family and slept a great deal. Yet, everything had seemed to work out perfectly.

As Daloz (1986, p. 154) writes, "The struggle to be something more than the person others have made, to construct and then live up to a set of *our own* expectations, is one of the most compelling struggles of our adult lives." He describes the extent to which adult learners are "richly enmeshed in a fabric of relationships which hold them as they are . . ." (1988b, p. 7) and the resulting "gap between old givens and new discoveries (1988a, p. 238). The educator who fosters transformative learning has a responsibility to provide and arrange for support. This does not imply that the educator must act as a counselor to all learners, although I will discuss some ways an educator can help individuals adjust. Nor does it imply that the educator has a lifelong commitment to any learner from a past educational experience who is engaged in action based on a revised meaning perspective. However, the educator must do everything he or she can to ensure that learners have support in negotiating the difficulties they may encounter. Also, learners must gain insight into the process of critical self-reflection so they can see when and where they might encounter problems. As Daloz (1988b) points out, there are strong reasons for adults to refuse to grow. "Sometimes it is just plain simpler to stay right where they are, or at least appear that way" (p. 7).

In Chapter Seven, I presented fostering learner empowerment as a condition of transformative learning; in Chapter Eight, I discussed ways of stimulating transformative learning. I now turn to the critical role the educator plays in supporting the process. Support comes in a variety of forms. If Janice, for example, had been encouraged to maintain a network of women in similar situations, she could have called on those women for support when she felt she had lost her identity. Each educator will have his or her own style of providing or ensuring support, depending on personality characteristics and on the context of the learning experiences. The approaches described in this chapter are general enough to encompass individual differences among educators and a variety of contexts; however, specific strategies are used to illustrate each. If the educator is authentic, fosters healthy group interaction, is skilled at handling conflict, encourages learner networks, gives personal advice when appropriate, and supports learner action, critical self-reflection and transformative learning will be supported (Brookfield, 1987; 1990; Mezirow and Associates, 1990; Mezirow, 1991).

Being Authentic

Learners see educators as authentic when: their words and actions are congruent, they admit to errors and fallibility; they allow learners to see something of them as people outside of the educator role, and they listen to learners' concerns, comments, and suggestions (Brookfield, 1990, p. 164). The educator who is not authentic will have difficulty in conveying true support for the transformative learning process. I mentioned the crucial balance between authenticity and credibility in Chapter Seven, with regard to the educator's use of personal power. But what does it mean to be authentic or to truly believe in learners? Can these characteristics be deliberately developed? If so, is that not already inauthentic? I will discuss educator self-awareness in more detail in Chapter Ten; essentially, self-awareness must precede authenticity. When this is the case, educators cannot play the role of authentic educators, but are simply themselves with learners.

Brookfield (1990, pp. 44–45) writes about the *imposter syndrome*. He describes learners and educators who contrast themselves to others and feel that they really do not belong in the setting, especially as an expert. The educator who simply decides to be authentic may indeed feel like an imposter — perhaps only initially, but perhaps with each learner group. Educators' continual reflection on their own behavior as educators and on the congruency of their basic nature and teaching style may keep the imposter syndrome at bay. Remembering that learners also experience this phenomenon can only enhance educator authenticity; the more the educator identifies with and relates to learners in an honest way, the more supportive the interaction will be.

Continuing with this theme, it can be useful for the educator to think of himself or herself as a learner. If an educator can say truthfully, "I remember how awful and clumsy I felt the first time I turned on a computer and how stupid I was when it came to remembering the simplest commands," this can convey a powerful sense of support to learners through its authenticity. However, an educator may not remember learning subjects or tasks in which he or she is now expert. What seems trivial and mundane to the expert can be traumatic and difficult for the novice. In order to recreate a sense of being a learner, the educator can write a learning history, discuss some of the experiences in the history with a friend or family member who is familiar with them, or simply reflect on past learning experiences.

Most educators are lifelong learners. The educator as learner is discussed more fully in Chapter Ten; however, awareness of this role is vital to supporting transformative learning. Educators may not associate their own learning with that of their students but acknowledging that parallel can foster the authenticity of the educator-learner relationship. This awareness can be enhanced by deliberately engaging in a difficult learning experience. The educator who long has seen himself as lacking in eye-hand coordination could enroll in badminton lessons. The woman who always has thought that philosophy is an intellectual game far beyond her ability could set out to read an introductory philosophy text or take a continuing education course in philosophy. Keeping a journal, discussing the experience with others, or reflecting on being a learner will stimulate further awareness of the experience.

Being authentic also involves acknowledging one's personality and the implications of that characteristic for teaching style. The introverted educator who tries to become a dynamic and inspirational lecturer will not only appear inauthentic to learners but will probably do a poor job of it as well. The analytical scientist who introduces a sharing-of-feelings session into a seminar may come across as artificial and silly rather than supportive of learners' feelings. The authentic educator should perceive a congruence between his or her nature outside the classroom and inside it. If an educator feels exhausted at the end of a session or needs a boost before a session, this congruence probably does not exist. Learners rarely feel supported by an educator who is clearly faking it.

Being oneself with learners requires displaying a congruence between words and actions. The educator who advocates the questioning of assumptions and values should also question his or her own assumptions and values. A common incongruence is the educator who espouses democratic education but then maintains full control over course content, learning activities, and evaluation of learning. Argyris and Schön (see Argyris, 1982; Argyris and Schön, 1974) have examined comprehensively the discrepancies between professionals' espoused theories and their theories-in-use. They suggest that most people are unaware of these discrepancies and even when they are pointed out, practitioners are often unwilling to acknowledge them. The learner, of course, simply sees inauthentic educator behavior. Argyris and Schön (1974) propose that practitioners become aware that they actually are building a theory of practice while they are engaged in the practice and that they reflect on and make explicit this theory-building activity.

Fostering Group Interaction

The educator is not the only one responsible for supporting learners in the process of transformative learning. The importance of the learning group and group discussion is a major theme in adult education (see Bridges, 1989). In a cohesive group, learners will assume much of the responsibility for supporting each other. Boyd (1989), for example, writes that the learner group as a social system "can provide supportive structures that facilitate an individual's work in realizing personal transformation" (p. 467).

Group cohesion is defined as the extent to which the influences on individuals to remain in the group are greater than the influences on individuals to leave the group (Johnson and Johnson, 1982; Keyton and Springston, 1990). Johnson and Johnson (1982, p. 373) elaborate on the characteristics of members in a cohesive group, some of which include: commitment to the group's goals, conformity to and protection of group norms, loyalty to the group, acceptance of responsibility within the group, increased communication among members; willingness to be influenced by group members; acceptance of others' opinions, and willingness to endure frustration on behalf of the group. These group member characteristics would provide extensive support for individual learners. Boyd (1989) reports that small-group participants see the group as an entity on its own and quotes a group member as saying, "I have felt at times that the group was trying to take care of me and it gave me the kind of feeling one gets as a child from one's mother" (p. 463).

Sometimes, simply by virtue of being together over time, having common interests, or having compatible natures, a learning group will become cohesive naturally. However, many forces serve to diminish group cohesiveness as well, for example: disagreement over group activities, unpleasant group experiences, competition, membership in other groups, low group or public image, and disagreeable group demands (Bedeian, 1989, p. 468).

Equal participation in discourse was discussed in Chapter Seven as a means of fostering learner empowerment; to some extent these suggestions are also relevant to encouraging support for transformative learning through group interaction. Empowering learners, stimulating transformative learning, and providing support are not linear in nature but combine to form a holistic process. In addition to the ideas in Chapter Seven, the educator can encourage group cohesiveness and support by:

- Suggesting (if appropriate) that the group act as a unit in some public service context such as writing a letter of protest or applying for increased learning resources
- Suggesting that the group come to consensus on goals, objectives, topics and/or learning activities
- Encouraging the sharing of resources and expertise to establish the interdependence of group members
- Meeting as a group outside the usual learning environment
- Discouraging competition among group members by using individualized evaluation or self-evaluation of learning
- Setting up subgroups based on similarity of psychological type or learning style (long-term use of this technique can create divisiveness in the larger learner group)
- Assuming the roles of observer, adviser, and consultant while the group works together on an activity

Group cohesiveness can be influenced by factors that are beyond the control of the group: group size, interests and backgrounds of individuals, compatibility of individuals in the group, organizational requirements and constraints, administrative structures, and social contexts. Many times, these conditions can be turned into an advantage by working as a group to deal with them. In a large group, teams can be formed and be given different responsibilities; teams may engage in different activities and report to the large group. A diversity of backgrounds and interests can increase learners' use of each other as resources as well as their interest in each other as people if those differences are shared and discussed. Personality differences can be of great interest to learners and can lead not only to increased self-awareness but to the development of new interpersonal skills. Group cohesiveness can be greatly enhanced by using individual differences to the group's advantage rather than treating them as barriers to communication. Organizational or other constraints can be treated as a problem to be solved by the learner group. The educator might say, "This is the constraint we face (for example, no funds for photocopying). What can we do? What are some alternative solutions?" Similarly, administrative structures that interfere with a group's cohesiveness (for example, the requirement that staff feedback on a manager's performance collected in a management development program go into a personnel file) can be presented as a problem to be solved by the group. Research indicates that group cohesiveness increases if the members perceive themselves to be working against an external threat (Stein, 1976). In some social contexts such as in community action groups this is automatic. In other contexts, such as when economic recession leads to job layoffs and retraining programs, this atmosphere can be created within a learner group.

Encouraging Learner Networks

A *learner network* can be defined as any sustained relationship among fellow learners either within a formal setting such as a course or an informal setting such as a self-help group. Learner networks can be fostered deliberately within a learning group through small-group work, project teams, study partners, or peer teaching. Participation in learner networks outside the learning group (professional associations, clubs, self-help groups, and the like) can also be encouraged by the educator. The popular concept of mentoring (Daloz, 1986) also can be seen as a form of learner network. Brookfield (1987, p. 79) emphasizes the importance of learner networks. "When we develop critical thinkers, helping them form resource networks with others who are involved in this activity may make a crucial difference. Because identifying and challenging assumptions, and exploring alternatives, involve elements of threat and risk-taking, the peer support provided by a group of others also trying to do this is a powerful psychological ballast to critical thinking efforts." In support of this view, research indicates that working within a learner network is one characteristic of successful self-directed learning (see Thiel, 1984).

Learner networks may form naturally just as supportiveness within a learner group may occur without deliberate effort. Often, for example, small subgroups that work together in one course will remain in contact throughout a program or even after they have gone on to different learning experiences. This seems to be especially true when the small-group work involves critical self-reflection. Nevertheless, the educator should not leave a process, which has such potential for providing support for transformative learning, to chance alone.

Some strategies that can be used to encourage the development of networks within a learner group are:

- Using small-group activities or discussions during which learners can get to know each other and develop alliances
- Forming project groups or teams in which learners work together over a period of time on a task of common interest
- Encouraging the formation of study partnerships or peer pairs either informally or by systematically matching individuals on some criterion such as common interests, experience, or learning style
- Suggesting peer teaching—when a group member with ex-

pertise shares it with a peer who would like to learn more in that area
- Creating flexibility in meeting times for groups, teams, or pairs by, for example, not convening the regular class or workshop and suggesting that subgroups meet instead where and when it is convenient to them
- Informally fostering liaisons by referring learners to each other when they ask questions of the educator

Some strategies that can be used to facilitate participation in learner networks outside the learner group are:

- Making information available to learners about relevant professional associations, clubs, or existing networks
- Referring learners to support groups (for example, groups for people recently divorced, victims' groups, or unemployment support groups) during particularly difficult personal situations
- Referring learners to special-interest groups such as international students' associations, Christian groups, or feminist groups
- Setting up contacts between learners from different learning groups or between present and previous learners who have common interests
- Suggesting that learners contact other educators or individuals in the community who have relevant interests or expertise
- Encouraging learner participation in computerized networks related to special interests

Usually, helping learners form networks and encouraging them to join existing networks ends the educator's role. Most people enjoy connecting with and maintaining involvement with others who have similar interests. However, in order to further integrate learner networks into the support of transformative learning, the educator can:

- Act as a model by participating in and referring to networks
- Ask learners to share their networking experiences with the group

- Make explicit in group discussions the role of networks in providing support for the learning process
- Build the use of networks into the content of the learning experience

When learners realize how much support is available through networking, they have a lifelong resource. The networks, of course, will change as interests, issues, and developmental phases change, but the option of forming or joining a network will remain open.

Handling Conflicts and Ethical Issues

Conflict immediately undermines a feeling of support from others. If a conflict of values arises between friends or marriage partners, the parties to the conflict cannot turn to each other for support until that conflict is resolved. If a manager is in conflict with a staff member about work priorities, it is difficult to also be supportive. Similarly, if there is conflict within a learner group, a supportive environment will cease to exist. At least three issues are relevant here: conflict among or between learners, conflict between educator and learner, and ethical considerations within the transformative learning process. I discussed the first of these earlier. Managing group conflict also is dealt with comprehensively in the literature; Johnson and Johnson (1982) provide particularly good practical guidelines and suggestions. So this educator-learner conflict will not be addressed further here. I will discuss ethical considerations in transformative learning, however, because conflicts between educator and learners may arise from issues involving ethics.

People usually react initially to the concept of transformative learning with concern over ethics. The process appears to be one in which the educator imposes values or assumptions on learners or tells learners that their assumptions are distorted. Perhaps the use of the term distorted assumptions leads individuals to become immediately defensive and say, "How can anyone call my assumptions distorted?" Clearly, this is not the intention, but such a misunderstanding should be avoided from the beginning of the educator-learner interaction. As Mezirow

(1991, p. 203) writes, "The educator's objective should be only that the learner learns freely and decides, on the basis of the best information available, whether or not to act and, if so, how and when." No educator should try to persuade learners of the superiority of one point of view or value system. In fact, such an approach is in direct conflict with the fundamental tenets of critical reflection, critical questioning, and critical discourse. At the same time, no educational experience is value-free and no educator should pretend that it is or that he or she is value-free. As Mezirow (1991, p. 203) points out, "to avoid the question of values is to opt for perpetuating the unexamined values of the status quo." It is at the heart of transformative learning to make underlying assumptions, values, and beliefs explicit. The educator supports learners in this process, models the process, and is also a learner. Most often, the language of transformative learning theory is not used with learners except in adult education groups; nevertheless, the process itself must be open, explicit, and available for questioning by all participants.

Working openly and explicitly with values and assumptions in a group of individuals who have varied backgrounds and experiences will lead inevitably to some conflicts. Educator and learners are emotionally attached to their value systems. Some people, the introverted thinking types for example, are so committed to their beliefs that they will hold on to them in the face of very convincing evidence for an opposing view. The most democratic group cannot avoid some emotional clashing of views. Among learners, an awareness and acceptance of individual differences and the agreed-upon goal of maintaining ideal conditions for discourse will minimize, but not eliminate, such clashes. However, between educator and learners the problem is different. If the educator maintains an aura of position power, which can happen in spite of intentions to the contrary, this influences the communication and the relationship between educator and learner. Even without the effect of position power, the educator retains personal power and in this sense is never an equal participant in the learner group. What happens, then, when there are value conflicts between educator and learners? This must be examined from two sides, the educator's and the learner's.

As a result of the power differential, the learner may be influenced by the educator's values in ways that he or she would not be influenced by a peer. This is a delicate and difficult point. Usually, this influence is positive; most educators are moral and good people. But what of cultural differences, gender differences, and social norms? Consider the following possible educator-learner combinations: a white Anglo-Saxon protestant female educator working with a group of Asian learners in an English as a second language course, a middle-class white male educator working with a group of unemployed reentry college women, a black self-exiled South African professor working with a group of white Canadians in a politics course, or any other of the possible social, cultural, political, or philosophical mixtures? Each educator may well be a moral and ethical person, a reflective practitioner, and an individual with strong convictions. But, unless the educator takes extreme care while encouraging critical self-reflection, he or she may influence learners in ways that are not at all supportive. Brookfield (1990, p. 153) writes of "committing cultural suicide" as a point of resistance to learning that some learners cannot overcome. Educators, however, should question whether, in fact, this resistance should be overcome. While making their values explicit, educators should always include viable alternatives and should model questioning of their own values. Similarly, educators should respect the values of learners while encouraging the questioning of them. Perhaps most important, educators should reflect continually on their practice, examining the influence they have on learners and questioning the nature of that influence. Anything less fails to provide support and is also unethical.

There may be occasions when, through critical self-reflection, the learner makes choices with which the educator is politically, culturally, or morally in disagreement. Mezirow (1990, p. 204) discusses this possibility. "As long as there is agreement that everyone's interpretation will be open to reflective discourse, there is no reason for an educator to have reservations about working with such learners. However, if the learners decide on a course of action . . . that the educator cannot ethically accept, the educator is quite correct to withdraw from further educational intervention." If the learner's choice were potentially harmful to the learner or others, the educator would also intervene. In some instances, the educator may not wish to, or be able to, completely withdraw from further educational intervention. For example, if a learner is registered in a semester-long course and such a value conflict occurs midway through the course, the educator cannot easily withdraw or ask the learner to withdraw. As difficult as it may be, the educator must be open about his or her position, discontinue support related to that issue, but continue to work with the learner in other areas. Supporting learners who are working toward transformative learning involves handling conflict and dealing with ethical issues in a responsible, professional, and open manner.

Helping Learners Adjust

When can or should an educator help learners with a personal adjustment? Where is the line between helping, counseling, and therapy? There can be no simple answers to such questions; most educators make decisions about when to provide personal help on an individual or situational basis. The decision also depends on the educator's skills and comfort in this domain. Educators regularly counsel learners on job opportunities, courses or programs to take, thesis topics, project activities, readings, and the like. Sometimes this advice can change the course of a learner's life. Yet many educators draw back when a learner's need appears to be personal. This is not to say that educators should engage in counseling if they are uncomfortable with it or that educators should try to treat learners who require psychotherapy. But the nature of transformative learning can be such that educators are responsible for helping learners make personal adjustments.

Mezirow (1991, p. 205) emphasizes that it is "necessary to make a careful distinction between adults who are having commonly encountered difficulties in dealing with familiar life transitions and those who have extreme neurotic, psychotic, or sociopathic disorders and require psychotherapy." If the educator is in doubt at all about making this distinction, the appropriate course of action would be to refer the learner to a professional counselor for an assessment.

On the other hand, providing support through personal advisement has clear benefits. It furthers the relationship of trust between educator and learner. It shows that the educator truly cares about the learner, which encourages further critical self-reflection. It can build self-esteem and allay learner anxiety. It allows the learner to deal with difficult issues in a safe environment. It provides the learner with an opportunity to practice the communication of the assumptions and beliefs being questioned or revised. It increases learners' confidence in their ability to participate in critical discourse. It supports action on revised meaning schemes or perspectives.

Two models presented in Mezirow and Associate's (1990) book of readings on fostering critical reflection may provide a framework for the educator engaged in helping learners adjust. Of course, the nature of each interaction will be unique to that learner. The simplest of these models is Peters' (1990) Action-Reason-Thematic Technique (ARTT). The technique follows an interview-analyze-interview cycle and is essentially a strategy for understanding behavior in problem situations. Five steps are involved:

- Identification of the learner's problem as defined by the learner
- Establishment of the time frame of the problem, the beginning and end of the problem, and its possible solution
- Identification and description of specific actions taken to solve the problem, for example, asking the learner What did you do? or What did you do next?
- Identification and description of reasons for each action taken
- Reduction of actions and reasons to argument themes (or identifying the underlying assumptions that guided behavior)

An interview is followed by an analysis of both the expressed reasons and the hidden premises, making explicit any aspect that has been left unstated. The discussion can then be repeated using the hidden premises as the beginning probes for further discourse.

Peters (1990, pp. 322–323) describes the questioning technique as "the key to an accurate analysis of the interviewee's assumptions." Ten guidelines are provided for asking ARTT questions:

- Ask both What did you do? and Why did you do it? questions
- Ask open-ended questions to allow the learner to describe his or her experiences and reasoning
- Ask probing questions to reveal the learner's reasoning
- Ask only one question at a time and frame questions based on the context of the interview up to that point
- Avoid leading questions
- Mirror learners' answers to enhance understanding and indicate interest
- Postpone judgment of learners' answers
- Use a conversational tone
- Avoid giving opinions or instructions until an analysis of the assumptions is made
- Always focus on the learner and his or her problem

Gould (1990), a psychoanalyst, became interested in the concepts of adult development as a bridge between psychotherapy and learning. He developed the Therapeutic Learning Program, a computer program, as "an organized effort to facilitate transformative learning in educational, work, and treatment contexts" (p. 135). The seven steps of the program may provide a useful framework for the educator engaged in supportive personal advisement:

- Identifying and framing the function to be recovered (identifying the conflict, the problem situation, and the stresses involved)
- Clarifying the action intention, that is, determining action as well as the costs and benefits of the action
- Distinguishing realistic dangers from exaggerated fears (looking at the fear response provoked by the intention to act)
- Isolating and exposing fears as predictions confused with memories (in Mezirow's language, separating the sources

of underlying assumptions from the consequences of acting on them)

- Explaining the origins of catastrophic predictions (understanding the source of old fears)
- Demonstrating and diminishing self-fulfilling prophecies; developing an awareness of the tendency to continue to act in old ways
- Consolidating new views of reality

Gould applies these steps to what he calls units of adult development or units of work—transitions that take place in working through a personal problem. He describes the completion of the process as transformative. "Each time a unit of work has been accomplished, the participants' powers of self-efficacy are enhanced. . . . From the learners' point of view, they have been freed to carry out their most important intentions. They have gained free will as they moved from a divided to a unified self on some very important action issue" (Gould, 1990, p. 145).

Helping learners with personal adjustment often will take the form of more informal discussion or problem-solving sessions. Trust, respect, openness, and genuine caring for the learner are the key ingredients of providing support and assistance. In view of the overall goal of working toward transformative learning, the educator can also work within a framework such as that proposed by Peters or Gould.

Supporting Action

"Action is an integral and indispensable component of transformative learning" (Mezirow, 1991, p. 209). As I discussed in Chapter Three, Mezirow has been criticized for failing to understand the inherent social dimension of critical theory (Collard and Law, 1989; Hart, 1990a; Clark and Wilson, 1991). However, Mezirow (1990, p. 208) describes this as a false dichotomy: "education is the handmaiden of learning, not of politics; but significant learning, involving personal transformations, is a social process with significant implications for social action." Through personal change and development, the individual comes to see flawed, immature, or distorted ways of thinking. As learners revise their perceptions and act on the revisions, these actions may influence interpersonal relationships, organizations, or even societies. The educator has a role in supporting such actions.

One way of viewing this is to see the role of the educator as one of helping learners learn how to develop and implement action plans (see Bedeian, 1989). It is one thing for a learner to say, "I now see the role of women in organizations in a completely new way," and it is something else for that learner to discuss this view with a hostile colleague, to change her behavior at work, to join a fight for pay equity, to establish a committee to investigate women's issues in her own organization, or to take an active role in a national feminist group. But if the learner knows how to plan action based on a new perspective, such steps may not be so formidable.

It may not always be feasible for the educator to support the implementation of an action plan; often learners are with educators for restricted lengths of time, and the action takes place after they have left the educational setting. Also, as Day (1988) says in discussing the consequences of empowerment at the individual level, learning leads to changes that "an educator with the best of intentions has little final control over" (p. 123). Hence, the learner skill of independently planning action is crucial to the success of transformative learning. Although the details will vary from learner to learner, the overall strategy described below should be applicable to most situations.

- *Set a feasible goal or objective that is stated in terms of behaviors or actions.* Actions need not even be observable to others. Some examples include: make a decision to do this, write about this in my journal, discuss this with my wife, write a memo to my boss on this issue, join this group, or argue in this way at the next committee meeting.
- *Distinguish between short-term and long-term goals and include both.* A short-term goal might be to discuss this with a spouse; a long-term goal might be to change careers within the next five years.

- *Set the boundaries for each goal.* These might include the time frame within which the goal will be reached and the people who will be involved or affected by reaching it. Learners are often surprised to realize how many people will be affected by a goal they have set. Other considerations might include: resources required, financial considerations, expertise to be acquired, or practical constraints (for example, the need for day care or transportation).
- *Consider alternatives, options, consequences, and back-up plans.* Could the learner be threatened with the loss of a job, or the break-up of a marriage, or financial complications? If so, what alternative actions would be appropriate?
- *Specify how the plan will be implemented.* This could be as simple as saying, "I'll talk to my wife on Saturday when the kids are at the baseball game," or as complex as in making a long-term plan to gather enough resources to retire in three years.
- *Plan more than one strategy for getting feedback from others.* If, for example, the change involves a revision of a person's role as a manager, plan to collect feedback from both the learner's staff and superior. This could be done informally or systematically. If the change is a personal one, discuss it regularly with family and friends.
- *Be prepared to revise the action plan if or when it does not appear to be working.*

The educator can encourage learners to develop illustrative action plans to practice their planning skills. These can range from making fairly simple and straightforward plans to elaborate long-range planning.

Individual Differences

Supporting adult learners as they work toward transformative learning probably requires a greater understanding of individual differences than does any other of the components of the educator role discussed thus far. To provide support, educators must understand and respect the basic nature of the learner, understand their own nature, and consider how they work with others, especially those who are different from oneself.

Undoubtedly, all educators will have encountered learners with whom good communication is difficult or learners whom they dislike. The standard response is to suppress such reactions and feelings. The espoused theory of practice is usually that all learners should be treated equally, that all are equal members of a group, and that those educators who think otherwise are unprofessional. Likewise, within a group of learners, individuals are expected to be able to communicate easily and to like and respect each other. Given the array of individual differences, however, these are unrealistic expectations indeed.

As in Chapters Seven and Eight, a case study will illustrate the influence of individual differences on the educator's provision of support in the transformative learning process. The case is based on data — a dialogue journal between educator and learner and psychological type profiles of both individuals — but the context is changed to protect the anonymity of the learner.

Chen has been in North America for seven years. He fled from China for political reasons and is here without any contact with his family. In his home country, Chen was in a medical profession; here he hopes to become a teacher of English as a second language. He works mostly at night at a variety of low-wage jobs.

According to his psychological type profile, Chen's dominant function is extraverted sensing. His secondary function appears to be undifferentiated between thinking and feeling, but Chen questions this, pointing out the possible cultural biases in the instrument. He describes his home culture as valuing thinking to the exclusion of feeling and suggests that this has influenced his perspective on many of the test items.

The educator's psychological type includes introverted thinking as a dominant function with intuition as a secondary function. She is Canadian, is about the same age as the learner, and has limited knowledge of Chinese culture. Educator and learner met in a formal credit course. They then continued to work together in an independent study basis; it is from this interaction that the data are available for this case study. Also during this interaction, both educator and learner describe the learning as transformative.

Chen's preference for sensing might explain this strong interest in facts and information. While in the initial stages of the educator-learner meetings, he wanted to accumulate as much information as possible and expressed frustration in his journal when this was not forthcoming. He also questioned the value of keeping a journal, wrote very short entries, and said he did not know what to write about. In relation to authenticity, the educator consistently expressed her belief in the value of journal writing; more important, she included in the journal her belief that learning does not consist in the accumulation of information. Her psychological type profile predicts that she would be more interested in theory than in facts. The journal indicates that the educator communicates authentically; however, this produced frustration on the part of both individuals. There appeared to be no means by which either could make connection with the other. Hostility surfaced in some journal entries. Humor may have been used also to disguise some of the difficulties of the interaction.

Group support was not available, since there is no group of learners meeting at regularly scheduled times. The educator, busily trying to solve the communications problem herself and assuming full responsibility for it, did not suggest to Chen that he turn to other learners for support until midway through their interaction. (This is not to say, of course, that Chen did not do this on his own; in fact he did in discussion with other learners.) Nevertheless, this appears to be a turning point in the journal entries. The educator commented, "I suggest that you discuss this issue with Ric; I know he is interested in that topic and has collected information on it." The next, and subsequent, journal entries are longer. A report on the discussion with the colleague is included. Surprisingly, the emphasis on facts diminished at this time, although information continued to be highly valued. Cultural expectations appeared for the first time as the learner wrote, "In my background, the teacher was always the source of all information." Later in the same entry, he commented, "Ric with whom I discussed this agreed that he, too, expected the teacher to know everything and he has had some trouble with this as well."

Conflict over ethical issues also arose in the latter half of the interaction. Chen wrote, "I see it as immoral that you try to change me to be like you." The educator responded that her only intention was to encourage questioning and that she agreed it would be immoral to change someone in that way. Here, differences in psychological type seem to interfere with the communication. Chen took the educator's comment at face value, remarking, "I'm so glad you agree with me. So, why do you question the information I give you?" This issue was not resolved throughout the interaction.

Chen's psychological type preference predicts that he would emphasize action based on his learning. There was little indication of that during the educator-learner interaction. When the educator commented, "What practical implications do you see here?" or "What will you do as a result of this insight?" subsequent journal entries ignore the questions. In the last portion of the interaction, the educator frequently persisted with such questions and comments. No concrete action plan emerged, but Chen did begin to discuss the application of his learning to his goal of teaching English as a second language.

In this case study, the educator possessed a good understanding of psychological type theory and an awareness of individual differences yet encountered difficulties in providing support for transformative learning. This learner apparently did develop and change over the course of the interaction. His primary support, however, may well have come from sources other than the educator. Evidence for this lies in Chen's having continued in at least one of the relationships he developed with a fellow learner. When an educator works with a learner whom he or she truly cannot understand, one of the most valuable strategies is to turn some of the responsibility for supportiveness over to others.

Summary

The educator's role in fostering critical self-reflection and transformative learning has been described with regard to increasing learner empowerment (Chapter Seven), stimulating questioning of assumptions, beliefs, and values (Chapter Eight), and, in this chapter, supporting learners as they go through these processes. Self-reflection can be rewarding and positive, but it can also be frightening and difficult, even when learners know they are growing from the experience. In a developmental process, the changes can be unnerving. The educator, rather like a parent, has a responsibility to be supportive throughout the change process.

Learners do not experience a sense of support from an educator who they believe is faking it or merely playing a role. Support comes from an authentic person, one whom learners can trust, respect, and talk to freely. The educator who is also a learner and who possesses self-awareness and practices what he or she preaches will be seen as an authentic and supportive individual.

Learners often turn to their peers for support, especially those they identify with and see as going through a similar experience. Effective group interaction leads to group cohesiveness, which in turn increases the likelihood that learners will turn to each other for support. The educator can work deliberately to ensure a good group process.

Support for learners can also come from individuals within or outside the learner group who share an interest in the subject or who have undergone similar experiences. To this end, learner networks can be encouraged. Networks formed within a learner group to work on projects or tasks will sometimes last far beyond the life of the educational experience.

Conflict inevitably arises in a group that works together over time. When critical self-reflection is one goal of the group, such conflict can be even more dramatic than in a task-oriented group. Conflict between educator and learner is especially difficult. In transformative learning, ethical issues can be central to educator-learner conflict. In order to maintain the supportive environment necessary for self-reflection, the educator should deal with conflicts and ethical questions in a sensitive and fair manner.

Helping learners adjust is a part of most educators' practice. When learners are engaged in an examination of their own assumptions and values, educator support can be critical. Of course, educators should determine whether therapy is required — as it may be in rare situations. A problem-solving interview is one model that can be followed in working with individual learners, or Gould's (1990) Therapeutic Learning Program may provide a framework for advisement in some situations.

The heart of learning is action — acting on what is learned. The educator may be able to play a part in supporting learners' actions; however, often learners act on their new insights outside the educational experience. The educator's responsibility becomes one of supporting planning for action. A systematic action plan provides a useful strategy for this endeavor.

Relationships among people is at the core of giving and receiving support. The educator's understanding of his or her own nature and how that influences relationships with others is crucial. Different learners will respond to different styles of support, both from each other and from the educator. There is no point in engaging in an analytical problem-solving session with a feeling type learner just as there will be little response from an intuitive type learner to a discussion of ethical issues. Educator awareness of these individual differences is an essential ingredient of supportiveness.

TEN

Educators as
Transformative Learners

The literature reveals very little about how educators learn to be educators or how they develop and change their practices (see Boice, 1991). In a review of the early literature on the improvement of teaching in higher education, Levinson-Rose and Menges (1981) conclude that most of these experiences are superficial in nature, that is, focused on specific techniques, and are conducted in isolation from any wider context or theory of practice. Only recently has there been some movement away from the discussion of techniques educators use to learn about their practice.

Apps (1985) was an early advocate of improving practice through developing a theory of practice. Brookfield (1990, p. 15) suggests that educators develop a "personal vision of teaching," one that is based on critical thinking about one's teaching. Elrick (1990) describes changing a teaching approach as a very personal process that should be supported by peer interaction. Amundsen, Gryspeerdt, and Moxness (1993) study the effectiveness of faculty discussion groups and collaborative research in encouraging reflection and experimentation among educators. Clark (1992, p. 17) writes, "we must first attend to our own struggles to make meaning of our experience . . . and learn from our learning process. . . . Then having attended to our own meaning making process, we'll be in a position to facilitate that process in others." These are but a few examples of the recent trend toward viewing educators as reflective, possibly transformative, learners.

If we accept the assumption that critical self-reflection is one goal of adult education and that such reflection can lead to development and transformation, and if we accept the assumption that adult educators are also adult learners, we can move easily to the view that educator development includes working toward transformative learning as one goal. The educator, in order to develop the meaning perspective of *being an educator* would: increase self-awareness through consciousness-raising activities, make his or her assumptions and beliefs about practice explicit, engage in critical reflection on those assumptions and beliefs, engage in dialogue with others, and develop an informed theory of practice. The meaning perspective of being an educator would necessarily include psychological, sociolinguistic, and epistemic perspectives. Technical knowledge as defined by Habermas (1971) is not excluded — this is where the techniques training model fits — but its content would be derived from an emerging theory of practice. Technique should not drive an educator's perspective of practice; rather, a perspective of practice should determine what technical knowledge is required.

"It is an experiential sauna bath, a plunge from the reassuring warmth of believing that classrooms are ordered arenas governed by reason into the ice-cold reality of wrestling with the alarming complexities of teaching and learning" (Brookfield, 1990, p. 3). Brookfield is describing vividly the experience of a new educator, but any reflective educator, no matter how seasoned, will find frustration, confusion, bewilderment, and anxiety as common as the joy of working with learners. The educator who is making meaning of the experience, as Clark (1992) puts it, will be going through the same process as the learners with whom he or she is working.

Educator Self-Awareness

Many educators cannot describe what they do in practice let alone say why they do what they do. The most common model for educators to follow is one based on past practice (Amundsen, Gryspeerdt, and Moxness, 1993) or one based on experiences as a learner. The educator who is venturing into critical self-reflection and transformative learning must begin by developing a self-awareness about current practice. Each of the strategies I described in Chapter Eight for stimulating learner reflection are equally appropriate for the educator, whether it is keeping a teaching journal, writing an educator history, writing a critical incident and discussing it with a trusted colleague, or visiting the classrooms of peers. The choice of strategy will depend on the nature and preferences of the educator just as it does with learners.

Each of the three types of meaning perspectives are crucial here. Menges and Mathis (1988, p. 259) write, "The most neglected themes in writing about faculty development concern the personal development of individual faculty members." Likewise, the sociolinguistic context within which educators work is often ignored. Cunningham (1988, p. 143) suggests that professional development for educators include such subjects as peace education and global resource sharing. She also stresses that the training of adult educators should not focus only on technology but the purpose of that technology. Similarly, Apps (1985) suggests that educators examine their assumptions about learners, the purpose of learning in their organization, and the teaching approaches used.

When we go about learning how to be educators, we tend to concentrate only on the epistemic domain — our knowledge and our way of obtaining knowledge. Hence, in this section, educator self-awareness will be discussed in relation to psychological understanding, sociolinguistic understanding, as well as epistemic understanding.

First, through discussion with others, journal writing, or some preferred consciousness-raising activity, the educator can examine psychological perspectives on being an educator. Naturally, this process will vary considerably from one individual to another, but some examples of questions that could be addressed are given below. These questions are mostly at the content reflection level since the initial goal is simply to increase self-awareness not to question assumptions.

- What is my self-concept as an educator?
- How is my self-concept as an educator a part of my self-concept outside my profession?
- To what degree do I feel I have personal control in my work as an educator?
- What do I like and dislike about being an educator?
- When and how did I decide to be an educator?
- What personal needs does being an educator fulfill?
- How does my personality suit or not suit my being an educator?
- What inhibitions or fears do I have related to being an educator?

Second, the educator can develop self-awareness of his or her sociolinguistic perspective on being an educator. Again, questions such as the following can be asked:

- What are the perceptions of an educator in my community?
- How do the media present educators?
- Was my decision to be an educator influenced by my cultural background?
- What social role should an educator take?
- How does society script or determine educator roles?
- What language is used to talk of an educator's work, and what do these terms or phrases imply about others' perceptions?
- Do people treat me differently when they know I am an educator? If so, how?
- What are my learners' expectations of the role of educator?
- What are my organization's or institution's expectations of educators?

Third, an educator can question his or her knowledge of being an educator. Self-awareness in the epistemic domain may be more developed for many educators, especially if they have studied education as a discipline. Some possible questions to consider may be:

- Where and how did I gain my knowledge of being an educator?
- What is my teaching style?
- What is my philosophy of education?
- What is my learning style?
- How much do I know about being an educator? How much more might there be to learn?
- How much do I think about being an educator?
- How do I (would I) evaluate my performance as an educator?
- What do my learners and colleagues say about me as an educator?
- Do I see myself as always being an educator?
- What aspects of being an educator am I most interested in?

By questioning and describing currently held perspectives, an educator can come to a self-understanding that then allows basic assumptions, values, and beliefs to be made explicit. This, of course, is not a clearly delineated step-by-step process; nor is it that way for learners. Consciousness-raising activities naturally yield increased awareness of assumptions and values; however, they do not necessarily lead to being able to explicitly state assumptions and values.

Making Assumptions Explicit

Making our own assumptions explicit is a tricky business. It is far easier to see someone else's assumptions based on what they say and do, especially if the other person's assumptions are different from our own. Our assumptions are the basis for how we see the world; it is extremely difficult to step outside our worldview and explicate the foundation for it. Sometimes it takes a traumatic event such as the loss of a job, death of a mate, or severe illness to pull us out of our comfortable view and face the assumptions upon which we have functioned. On the other hand, some of us continually engage in critical introspection. For most educators, making assumptions about being an educator explicit will require some interaction with a trusted colleague, a friend, or family member. This need not be traumatic. The educator might simply take deliberate steps toward further critical self-reflection.

Any of the techniques I described in Chapter Eight for helping learners make assumptions explicit will be equally useful for the educator if someone else takes on the educator role in these activities. Brookfield (1987) describes two additional strategies that may be particularly suited to educator self-reflection: *criteria analysis* and *crisis-decision simulations.* The characteristics of traumatic events that lead individuals to make their values and assumptions explicit are simulated in both of these activities.

Brookfield (1987, p. 100) describes criteria analysis as "an excellent tool for organizational or group communication and team-building workshops in which the purpose is to make explicit the assumptions underlying people's actions within the group or organization." However, the activity is equally relevant for the educator whose goal is to make explicit the assumptions underlying his or her practice. The strategy consists of three parts: the educator imagines or describes a specific situation in which success or failure in practice has occurred; the standards and judgments (criteria) used to determine the success or failure of the situation are made explicit; and indicators (observable behaviors or actions) of those criteria are identified. Adapting Brookfield's (1987, p. 102) examples, the activity could take one of the following forms:

> Imagine that you are a professional development consultant who has been asked to observe and provide feedback on a colleague's work as an educator. What features would you be looking for as evidence that this educator is effective?
>
> Imagine that one of your colleagues has recently been accused of poor teaching and professional negligence. You have been given the task of serving on a committee to establish a code of conduct for educators. What important indicators would you choose as evidence that someone was behaving in a professional manner?

The critical ingredient in this approach is making the indicators of effective or ineffective practice explicit. Underlying such indicators are assumptions about being an educator. In uncovering these assumptions, discussion with another person can play an important role. Suppose I said, in response to the first scenario:

> I would look for subject-area knowledge and expertise. I would be interested in a dynamic and enthusiastic presentation, one that would stimulate enthusiasm among the learners. But, perhaps most important, I would check for a well-organized lecture in which the expectations of the educator were made clear and learners knew exactly what they had to do.

The indicators are fairly observable, although interpretations of enthusiasm might be somewhat subjective. But what are the assumptions underlying these indicators? If these were my assumptions, I might not be able to explicate them. Critical questioning by a colleague could bring out the following:

- An effective educator is an expert.
- An enthusiastic educator makes enthusiastic learners.
- Organization leads to effectiveness.
- Being an educator is being a lecturer.
- Learners need to be told what to do by the educator.

By describing successes and failures in the educator role, one necessarily uses criteria to make judgments about what is a success and what is a failure. By identifying indicators of those criteria, assumptions are revealed. Through discussion with another person, the assumptions can be made explicit.

Brookfield's (1987) crisis-decision simulation is similar in process, although slightly more dramatic in content. In a crisis-decision simulation, individuals "are asked to imagine themselves in a situation where they are forced to make a decision from among a number of uncomfortable choices" (p. 107). Through a discussion of why those decisions were made, underlying assumptions can be made explicit. For example, the educator might respond to a scenario such as:

> Imagine that you are on a committee required to make a decision about which courses in your program will be cut due to the next year's severe budget restraints. You have to eliminate two of the following courses: a computer literacy course for secretaries who have been required to attend by their managers, an advanced seminar in the use of hypermedia for the computer technicians in your organization, or a computer conference course on action management for the senior managers in your organization. Which courses will you eliminate?

The analysis and discussion of the choices should include speculation about the rationale for making the decision and elaboration on the reasoning used to make it. Making difficult choices often exposes underlying assumptions and values, but again, these may be more apparent to others than they are to the decision maker. Brookfield also suggests that feeling the need for further information in order to make the choice reveals a person's assumptions about what is important. This need could be included in any ensuing discussion.

Critical Reflection on Practice

Once underlying assumptions are made explicit through some combination of activities and discussion of those activities, the educator can question the sources, consequences, and validity of the assumptions. This process can be the same as or similar to that encouraged in learners. However, Schön (1983) emphasizes that for practitioners, critical reflection is more than a cognitive process. His concept of reflective action leading to context-specific theories of practice is one that educators can incorporate into critical reflection on practice. Schön describes reflective action as a mixture of intuitively reacting to events while engaged in practice and reflecting on subsequent events. In other words, the educator can use current and real critical incidents to stimulate reflection, and then use practice to experiment with (or check the validity of) the results of reflection. At the same time, the educator can become aware of how he or she thinks, acts, and makes decisions during practice.

What can the educator do to become critically reflective? On-going introspective questioning, experimentation, or consultation with others can foster and maintain this process.

Asking deliberate questions in the following format will facilitate content, process, and premise reflection on practice:

- What did I do in that course, session, or workshop?
- How did I decide to do that?
- Why should I question what I did?

Asking questions in the format, What is the source of that assumption? and What would be the consequences of continuing to hold that assumption? will lead the educator to question the validity of assumptions and values.

For some educators, experimentation with practice will provide the best vehicle for reflection. This can be as simple as trying a different way of working with a concept—for example, by giving a lecture when normally the educator would use a reading followed by a group activity—and observing and speculating on the result. Or, it can be as complex as participating in collaborative research related to one's teaching with colleagues or instructional development personnel. Zuber-Skerritt (1992, p. 115) outlines a model for action research in higher education in which "the development of critical practice of academics and their critical reflection is one of the salient features." She emphasizes that "observing and reflecting refer not only to the staff [educators] observation of their planned activities and their reflection on the observation results, but also to a critical *self-evaluation* of the whole action research experience in relation to their own limitations and to external constraints. This evaluation and *self-evaluation* may lead to social and personal change and contribute to their *professionalism*" (p. 121).

Interaction and consultation with others fosters critical self-reflection. I will discuss dialogue or discussion with peers next, but the educator can also work with peers through observations of each other's sessions, exchange of course materials, or analyses of videotapes of each other's practice. In a study of mentoring, Sands, Parson, and Duane (1991) find that 72 percent of the educators they surveyed in a university setting saw themselves as engaging in mentoring. The categories that best describe the roles people assumed were: friend, career guide, information source, and intellectual guide. Having an intellectual guide led people to engage in activities that could encourage critical reflection such as providing constructive criticism and feedback. The list of activities was provided by the researchers; more such activities might have been generated if the educators had produced the list themselves.

Consultation with professional development or human resource persons can provide another perspective on one's work as an educator and thus encourage critical self-reflection. Such consultation can take a wide variety of formats (see Zuber-Skerritt, 1992; Menges and Mathis, 1988) including holding on-going discussions about education, conducting observations of sessions, videotaping and analyzing videotapes of sessions, attending workshops, and obtaining readings. Of course, longer-term interactions (as opposed to, say, workshops) are more likely to foster reflection.

Finally, as I have advocated throughout this book, an educator's open discussion with learners about the education process facilitates critical reflection among both learners and educator. Learners can give insightful feedback on their perspective of the educator's work. This can be done systematically through open-ended feedback sheets; comments can be focused on issues the educator is especially interested in. Insight cards—cards on which learners write their insights—can be used regularly at the end of each session. Sometimes such information only serves to confirm the educator's perspective, but when it is discrepant, it can stimulate critical self-reflection.

Dialogue with Others

As rational discourse is an integral component of working toward transformative learning in sessions with learners (Mezirow,

1991), so it is essential for educators. Educators, particularly in more formal settings, tend not to discuss their teaching with their peers. In many cases, adult educators are on their own as a part-time worker, a night school teacher, or as the lone educator in an organization. Apps (1987) notes that educators should not isolate themselves from the rest of the education world. But, some aspects of the educator role seem to be viewed as a solitary activity. Most educators work alone with their learners in isolation from other practitioners. The mere thought of having a colleague observe or participate in a session is intimidating, perhaps because it is associated with evaluation.

In less formal and noncredit contexts such as community action groups or conferences, educators are more likely to engage in dialogue with each other. Panel discussions at conferences, team approaches to workshops, and rotating leadership in action groups all can provide models of the kind of discussion that can take place among educators.

Amundsen, Gryspeerdt, and Moxness (1993) describe educator discussion groups in which the knowledge structure of different subject areas was examined. Wilcox (1993) analyzes the themes that arose in a fifteen-session interdisciplinary educator discussion group and includes *critical reflection on experiences* and *learning to teach by reflecting on unresolved issues* among the themes that emerged. Although the research evidence is still limited, it seems that educators would be stimulated to engage in self-reflection through discussion with colleagues and others.

In order to foster dialogue on their practice, educators could consider:

- Initiating educator discussion groups that meet regularly to discuss participants' practice or specific themes related to their practice
- Participating in adult educator discussion groups via computer networks such as Internet
- Conducting collaborative action research on teaching with colleagues as suggested by Zuber-Skerritt (1992)
- Participating in conferences, such as the Annual Adult Education Research Conference, in which current perspectives on adult education are debated

- Participating in, critically analyzing, and questioning another educator's practice and allowing that person to do the same.

Explicating a Theory of Practice

"But if we view effective practice solely as the improvement of ever more refined practice skills and regard facilitator roles and responsibilities as being primarily those of technicians of design, we denude practice of any philosophical rationale, future orientation, or purposeful mission" (Brookfield, 1986, p. 287). Brookfield goes on to suggest that a philosophy of practice should include at least three elements: a clear definition of the activity concerned, a number of general purposes for the field derived from this definition, and a set of criteria by which the success of the educator's work can be judged. Although Brookfield discusses how a philosophy becomes the rationale for practice, he unfortunately does not address how a philosophy is developed and explicated. Within this general framework, the educator can develop a personal theory of practice in which specific beliefs, assumptions, and values can be grounded. The need for further knowledge of techniques and methods also would be derived from the theory of practice or, in Mezirow's (1991) language, an informed and explicit meaning perspective on being an educator could be developed.

The educator who has engaged in consciousness-raising activities, made assumptions explicit, reflected on those assumptions, and engaged in dialogue with others most likely will have come to a fairly clear theory of practice. What is now important is making that theory explicit.

In writing or in discussion with a colleague, the educator could respond to the following questions that are based on Brookfield's framework:

- What is my definition of an adult educator?
- What are the purposes of adult education in my field?
- How successful am I in working toward these goals?

The theory of practice, for example, could look like the following.

I would define an educator as someone who facilitates individuals' learning and development through sharing expertise, supporting learners, and challenging them to question what they already know and what they are learning.

The purposes of education in my field are: to increase knowledge and expertise; encourage learner self-awareness, promote critical thinking, and support individual and social change and action.

I would judge my success in working toward these purposes through: learners' written work (papers, articles, journals, theses), the quality of interaction among learners and between learners and educator (for example, the degree to which the ideal conditions for critical discourse are met), the quality of group dynamics, and observations of learner behavior, change and action.

This example, of course, could be expanded considerably; however, it illustrates how an educator might respond to these questions.

Using a more detailed set of questions, Kreber (1993) interviewed educators about their theory of practice; an educator could ask these questions of himself or herself or discuss them with a colleague:

- What is my view of my practice as an educator? How would I describe the purpose of education?
- What is my view of the learner?
- How would I describe the role of the educator?
- What methods and strategies do I usually use?
- What is my view of evaluation of learning and how do I evaluate learning?
- Do I experience any constraints or resistances as an educator?

Responding to these questions may lead an educator to a fuller description of his or her theory of practice as it appeared to do in Kreber's (1993) research. The question pertaining to methods and strategies can lead the educator to see discrepancies between espoused theory and action or distortions in the meaning perspectives that guide practice. The question about constraints tends to encourage the incorporation of contextual issues into the theory.

The Role of Professional Development

As I mentioned earlier in this chapter, professional or instructional development has traditionally addressed the development of specific techniques and methods while neglecting the educator's theory of practice (Boice, 1991). However, there is now evidence in the literature that this thinking is changing (Amundsen, Gryspeerdt, and Moxness, 1993). The critically reflective educator should take advantage of any available professional development services and advocate a more philosophically grounded approach when this is appropriate. Professional development need not be only those activities provided by the organization in which an educator works; a wide variety of workshops, seminars, conferences, and courses is available in many areas. Professional development also includes self-directed educator activities such as following the literature related to teaching in one's discipline and subscribing to relevant newsletters and journals.

Some activities that may foster involvement in professional development activities within the organization or institution include:

- Initiate involvement in the activities of a human resource or professional development office (for example, join a committee, offer to work on a special project, suggest a collaborative research project or any activity that will lead to viewing practice from a new perspective)
- Work to turn the organization's view of professional development away from tips and techniques and toward critical self-reflection
- Apply for funding to initiate an innovative educational project — one that will challenge current meaning perspectives on practice

- Apply for funding to conduct an action research project on education, possibly working with a colleague who has a different perspective or set of beliefs about education
- Initiate a newsletter for the exchange of views on education in your institution

Outside the institution or organization, the educator can:

- Join an educators' professional association, such as the American Association for Adult and Continuing Education, the American Educational Research Association, or the Canadian Society for Studies in Education
- Attend, participate in, or present papers at educators' conferences
- Determine what professional development activities and services from nearby institutions might be open to outside educators
- Watch for community events or activities that could be relevant to educational practice (for example, a workshop on psychological type)
- Determine the major publishers of books related to education in the appropriate discipline and ask to be put on their mailing list
- Join special-interest or action groups that are engaged in educational or social change
- Subscribe to relevant journals or magazines (for example, *Adult Learning, Journal of Nursing Education, Journal of Higher Education,* or *Adult Education Quarterly*)
- Volunteer for appropriate positions on boards of directors, advisory committees, lobbyist groups, or political task forces

If professional development becomes more than just attending the occasional workshop or meeting the mandatory requirements for continuing professional education in the discipline, it can provide new insights, stimulate critical reflection, and further the development of an educator's theory of practice. The suggestions given here may be but a small sample of what the creative educator can do to deepen his or her meaning perspective on being an educator.

Summary

Educators must be adult learners continually striving to update, develop, expand, and deepen their professional perspectives both on their subject area and on their goals and roles as educators. The educator who is not a learner becomes an assembly-line worker implementing well-worn habitual tricks and techniques to process learners' acquisition of knowledge and skills. The educator who is not a learner cannot act as a model of learning. The educator who is not a critically self-reflective learner will not be likely to stimulate critical reflection among learners. I described the process of an educator's working toward his or her own transformative learning in this chapter.

Educators' awareness of what they do in practice and how they see themselves as educators is essential for professional and personal growth. Attaining self-awareness can be described in relation to content and process reflection on psychological, sociolinguistic, and epistemic understandings of education. In other words, educators should be considering their self-concept as an educator, their social roles as educators (including the influence of media and language), and their knowledge of education.

Making the assumptions underlying a philosophy of educational practice explicit is a difficult process. Few people would be able to respond directly to the question, What are your underlying assumptions? The learner-educator can use strategies such as writing critical incidents, keeping a journal, completing a repertory grid, writing a life history, conducting a criteria analysis, or engaging in a crisis-decision simulation. For most people, discussion with a colleague or friend will be an essential ingredient of any strategy for explicating assumptions. Even unconscious assumptions can be ferreted out by a keen observer.

Examining the sources and consequences of assumptions (thereby questioning their validity) is the core of working toward transformative learning. The educator who engages in critical self-reflection on practice almost inevitably will revise that practice. An on-going use of the What?, How?, and Why? questions (content, process, and premise reflection) about practice will lead to the habit of being a reflective practitioner. Experimentation with practice, collaborative research on educational practice, discussion with peers, consultation with others, and feedback from learners can all contribute to critical self-reflection.

Of these strategies, dialogue with others is crucial. Educator discussion groups have appeared in the literature as having potential for encouraging critical reflection. Educators can also engage in dialogue about their work in more informal ways.

If educators have made their underlying assumptions about practice explicit, have reflected on them, and discussed them with others, the next logical step is to integrate these assumptions into an informed theory of practice. In Mezirow's language, they would move from questioning meaning schemes toward describing their meaning perspectives on being educators. A theory of practice includes at least three components: a definition, a number of purposes, and criteria for judging success. In addition, the components of implementation or action and contextual issues could be listed.

All of the activities I described in this chapter constitute professional development if that term includes personal growth. Unfortunately, professional development has long been seen as skills training—how to write clearer objectives, how to use audiovisual aids, how to construct multiple-choice tests, and the like. Educators should work to increase their involvement in professional development as well as to change the nature of professional development itself. Activities need not be restricted to institutional offerings but can include a variety of self-directed activities such as initiating discussion groups, joining action groups, subscribing to journals, and participating in conferences.

To be a critically self-reflective educator is to be a lifelong learner. The educator who feels that he or she has found all the answers has stopped questioning, reflecting, and learning. Transformative learning is a continual process of growth and development for the learner and for the educator-learner.

References

Abrami, P., and Murphy, V. *Catalogue of Student Ratings of Instruction.* Montreal: McGill University Centre for Teaching and Learning, 1981.

Amundsen, C., Gryspeerdt, D., and Moxness, K. "Practice-Centred Inquiry: Developing More Effective Teaching." *Review of Higher Education,* 1993, *16,* 329–353.

Apps, J. W. *Improving Practice in Continuing Education: Modern Approaches for Understanding the Field and Determining Priorities.* San Francisco: Jossey-Bass, 1985.

Apps, J. W. "Adult Education and the Learning Society." *Educational Considerations,* 1987, *14*(2, 3), 14–18.

Apter, M. J. *The Experience of Motivation.* New York: Academic Press, 1982.

Argyris, C. *Reasoning, Learning, and Action: Individual and Organizational.* San Francisco: Jossey-Bass, 1982.

Argyris, C., and Schön, D. *Theory in Practice: Increasing Professional Effectiveness.* San Francisco: Jossey-Bass, 1974.

Ash, C. "Applying Principles of Self-Directed Learning in the Health Professions." In S. Brookfield (ed.), *Self-Directed Learning: From Theory to Practice.* New Directions for Continuing Education, no. 25. San Francisco: Jossey-Bass, 1985.

Banta, T. W., and Associates (eds.). *Making a Difference: Out-*

comes of a Decade of Assessment in Higher Education. San Francisco: Jossey-Bass, 1993.

Belenky, M. F., Clinchy, B. M., Goldberger, N. R., and Tarule, J. M. *Women's Ways of Knowing: The Development of Self, Voice, and Mind.* New York: Basic Books, 1986.

Bedeian, A. G. *Management.* (2nd ed.). Chicago: Dryden Press, 1989.

Bigge, M. L. *Learning Theories for Teachers* (4th ed.). New York: HarperCollins, 1982.

Boice, R. "New Faculty as Teachers." *Journal of Higher Education.* 1991, *62,* 150–173.

Boud, D., Keogh, R., and Walker, D. *Reflection: Turning Experience into Learning.* London: Kogan Page, 1985.

Boyd, E., and Fales, A. "Reflective Learning: Key to Learning from Experience." *Journal of Humanistic Psychology,* 1983, *23*(2), 99–117.

Boyd, R. D. "Trust in Groups: The Great Mother and Transformative Education." In L. S. Walker (ed.), *Proceedings of the Annual Midwest Research-to-Practice Conference in Adult and Continuing Education.* Ann Arbor: University of Michigan, 1985. (ED 261 172)

Boyd, R. D. "Facilitating Personal Transformation in Small Groups." *Small Group Behavior,* 1989, *20*(4), 459–474.

Boyd, R. D., and Myers, J. G. "Transformative Education." *International Journal of Lifelong Education,* 1988, *7,* 261–284.

Bridges, D. *Education, Democracy and Discussion.* Lanham, Md.: University Press of America, 1989.

Brockett, R. G., and Hiemstra, R. *Self-Direction in Adult Learning: Perspectives on Theory, Research, and Practice.* New York: Routledge, 1991.

Brookfield, S. *Understanding and Facilitating Adult Learning.* San Francisco: Jossey-Bass, 1986.

Brookfield, S. *Developing Critical Thinkers: Challenging Adults to Explore Alternate Ways of Thinking and Acting.* San Francisco: Jossey-Bass, 1987.

Brookfield, S. *The Skillful Teacher.* San Francisco: Jossey-Bass, 1990.

Brookfield, S. "Self-directed Learning, Political Clarity, and the Critical Practice of Adult Education." *Adult Education Quarterly,* 1993, *43*(4), 227–242.

Brundage, D., and Mackeracher, D. *Adult Learning Principles and*

Their Application to Program Planning. Toronto: Ontario Institute for Studies in Education, 1980.

Bullough, R. V., and Goldstein, S. L. "Technical Curriculum Form and American Elementary School Art Education," *Journal of Curriculum Studies,* 1984, *16,* 143–154.

Caffarella, R. S. "The Continuing Journal of our Professional Lives: The Impact of Significant Life Events." *Adult Learning,* 1993, *4*(3), 27–30.

Campbell, V. N. "Self-Direction and Programmed Instruction for Five Different Types of Learning Objectives." *Psychology in the Schools,* 1964, *1,* 348–359.

Candy, P. C. "Constructivism and the Study of Self-Direction in Adult Learning." *Studies in the Education of Adults,* 1989, *21,* 95–116.

Candy, P. C. *Self-Direction for Lifelong Learning.* San Francisco: Jossey-Bass, 1991.

Chaplin, J. P. *Dictionary of Psychology.* (2nd ed.). New York: Dell Publishing, 1985.

Clark, M. C. "Finding our Way in an Uncertain World." *Adult Learning,* 1992, *4,* 16–17.

Clark, M. C., and Wilson, A. L. "Context and Rationality in Mezirow's Theory of Transformational Learning." *Adult Education Quarterly,* 1991, *41*(2), 75–91.

Collard, S., and Law, M. "The Limits of Perspective Transformative: A Critique of Mezirow's Theory." *Adult Education Quarterly,* 1989, *39,* 99–107.

Collins, M. *Adult Education as Vocation: A Critical Role for the Adult Educator.* New York: Routledge, 1991.

Conger, J. *The Charismatic Leader: Behind the Mystique of Exceptional Leadership.* San Francisco: Jossey-Bass, 1989.

Conger, J., and Kanungo, R. "Toward a Behavioral Theory of Charismatic Leadership in Organizational Settings." *Academy of Management Review,* 1987, *12,* 637–647.

Corey, G. *Theory and Practice of Group Counseling.* (2nd ed.). Pacific Grove, Calif.: Brooks/Cole, 1985.

Cottingham, L. A. "A Classification System for Independent Learning." Unpublished doctoral dissertation, University of New Mexico, 1977.

Cranton, P. *Working with Adult Learners.* Toronto: Wall & Emerson, 1992.

Cranton, P., and Castle, J. "Industrial Tutoring Project." Final Report. Ottawa: Canada Employment and Immigration, 1990.

Cranton, P., and Hillgartner, W. "The Relationships Between Student Ratings and Instructor Behavior: Implications for Improving Teaching." *Canadian Journal of Higher Education,* 1981, *11,* 73–81.

Cranton, P., and Knoop, R. *The PET Type Check.* St. Catharines, Ont.: Professional Effectiveness Technologies, 1992.

Cross, P. *Adults as Learners: Increasing Participation and Facilitating Learning.* San Francisco: Jossey-Bass, 1992.

Csikszentmihalyi, M. *Beyond Boredom and Anxiety: The Experience of Play in Work and Games.* San Francisco: Jossey-Bass, 1975.

Cunningham, P. "The Adult Educator and Social Responsibility." In R. G. Brockett (ed.), *Ethical Issues in Adult Education.* New York: Teachers College Press, 1988.

Cunningham, P. "From Freire to Feminism: The North American Experience with Critical Pedagogy," *Adult Education Quarterly,* 1992, *42,* 180–192.

Curry, L., Wergin, J. F., and Associates. *Educating Professionals: Responding to New Expectations for Competence and Accountability.* San Francisco: Jossey-Bass, 1993.

Daloz, L. *Effective Teaching and Mentoring: Realizing the Transformational Power of Adult Learning Experiences.* San Francisco: Jossey-Bass, 1986.

Daloz, L. "Beyond Tribalism: Renaming the Good, the True, and the Beautiful." *Adult Education Quarterly,* 1988a, *38* (4), 234–241.

Daloz, L. "The Story of Gladys Who Refused to Grow: A Morality Tale for Mentors." *Lifelong Learning,* 1988b, *2,* 4–7.

Dannefer, D. "Adult Development and Social Theory: A Paradigmatic Reappraisal." *American Sociological Review,* 1984, *49,* 100–116.

Dannefer, D., and Perlmutter, M. "Development as a Multidimensional Process: Individual and Social Constituents." *Human Development,* 1990, *33,* 108–137.

Day, M. "Educational Advising and Brokering: The Ethics of Choice." In R. G. Brockett (ed.), *Ethical Issues in Adult Education.* New York: Teachers College Press, 1988.

Deiner, E., Sandvik, E., Pavot, W., and Fujita, F. "Extraversion and Subjective Well-being in a U.S. National Probability Sample." *Journal of Research in Personality, 26,* 205–215, 1992.

Della-Dora, D., and Blanchard, L. J. (eds.). *Moving Toward Self-Directed Learning: Highlights of Relevant Research and of Promising Practices.* Alexandria, Va.: Association for Supervision and Curriculum Development, 1979.

Dewey, J. *Democracy and Education.* New York: Macmillan, 1916.

Dewey, J. *How We Think.* New York: Heath, 1933.

Dick, W., and Carey, L. *Systematic Design of Instruction.* Glenview, Illinois: Scott, Foresman, 1978.

Dominicé, P. F. "Composing Education Biographies: Group Reflection Through Life Histories." In Mezirow, J. and Associates, *Fostering Critical Reflection in Adulthood.* San Francisco: Jossey-Bass, 1990.

Elrick, M. F. "Improving Instruction in Universities: A Case Study of the Ontario Universities Program for Instructional Development." *Canadian Journal of Higher Education,* 1990, *20,* 61–79.

Ewert, G. "Habermas and Education: A Comprehensive Overview of the Influence of Habermas in Educational Literature," *Review of Educational Research,* 1991, *61,* 345–378.

Fenstermacher, G. D., and Soltis, J. S. *Approaches to Teaching* (2nd ed.). New York: Teachers College Press, 1992.

Ferguson, J., and Fletcher, C. "Personality Type and Cognitive Style," *Psychological Reports, 60,* 959–964, 1987.

Ferrier, B., Marrin, M., and Seidman, J. "Student Autonomy in Learning Medicine: Some Participants' Experiences." In D. Boud (ed.), *Developing Student Autonomy in Learning.* London: Kogan Page, 1981.

Flanagan, J. "The Critical Incident Technique." *Psychological Bulletin,* 1954, *51,* 132–136.

Freire, P. *Pedagogy of the Oppressed.* New York: Herder and Herder, 1970.

Fuhrmann, B. S., and Jacobs, R. *The Learning Interactions Inventory.* Richmond: Ronne Jacobs Associates, 1980.

Garrison, D. R. "Critical Thinking and Adult Education: A Conceptual Model for Developing Critical Thinking in Adult Learners." *International Journal of Lifelong Learning,* 1991, *10*(4), 287–303.

Gifford, P. "Dialogue Journal Writing and Critical Reflection."
Unpublished master's thesis. St. Catharines, Ont.: Brock
University, 1993.

Gilligan, C. *In a Different Voice.* Cambridge, Mass.: Harvard
University Press, 1982.

Gould, R. L. "Adulthood." In H. Kaplan and B. Sadock (eds.),
Comprehensive Textbook of Psychiatry (5th ed.). Baltimore: Wil-
liams & Wilkins, 1989.

Gould, R. L. "The Therapeutic Learning Program." In J.
Mezirow and Associates (eds.), *Fostering Critical Reflection in
Adulthood.* San Francisco: Jossey-Bass, 1990.

Greenblatt, C. S. *Designing Games and Simulations.* Newbury Park,
Calif.: Sage, 1988.

Griffin, C. *Adult Education and Social Policy.* London: Croom
Helm, 1987.

Guglielmino, L. M. "Development of the Self-Directed Learning Readiness Scale." Unpublished doctoral dissertation,
University of Georgia, 1977.

Habermas, J. *Knowledge and Human Interests.* Boston: Beacon
Press, 1971.

Habermas, J. *The Theory of Communicative Action.* Boston: Beacon Press, 1984.

Habermas, J. "Hermeneutics and the Social Sciences," In K.
Mueller-Vollmer (ed.), *The Hermeneutics Reader,* 1989.

Hallet, G. *Logic for the Labyrinth: A Guide to Critical Thinking.*
Washington: University Press of America, 1984.

Harrison, J. *Learning and Living 1790–1960.* London: Routledge
and Kegan Paul, 1961.

Hart, M. "Critical Theory and Beyond: Further Perspectives
on Emancipatory Education." *Adult Education Quarterly,* 1990a,
40, 125–138.

Hart, M. "Liberation Through Consciousness-Raising." In
Mezirow, J. and Associates, *Fostering Critical Reflection in Adulthood.* San Francisco: Jossey-Bass, 1990b.

Herbeson, E. *Psychological Type and Self-Directed Learning.* Unpublished master's thesis. St. Catharines, Ont.: Brock University, 1990.

Hoffman, M. "Critical Theory and the Inter-Paradigm Debate,"
Journal of International Studies, 1987, *16,* 231–249.

Holtzman, W. H. "Cross Cultural Comparisons of Personality Development in Mexico and the United States." In D. A. Wagner and H. W. Stevenson (eds.), *Cultural Perspectives on Child Development.* New York: W. H. Freeman, 1982.

Houle, C. O. *Continuing Learning in the Professions.* San Francisco: Jossey-Bass, 1980.

House, R. J. "Power and Personality in Organizations." *Research in Organizational Behavior,* 1988, *10,* 305–357.

Inkster, I. *The Steam Intellect Societies.* Nottingham: University of Nottingham, 1985.

James, W. B. "An Analysis of Perceptions of the Practices of Adult Educators from Five Different Settings." *Proceedings of the Adult Education Research Conference,* no. 24. Montreal: Concordia University/University of Montreal, 1983.

Jarvis, P. *Professional Education.* London: Croom Helm, 1983.

Jarvis, P. *Adult Learning in the Social Context,* London: Croom Helm, 1987.

Jarvis, P. *Paradoxes of Learning: On Becoming an Individual in Society.* San Francisco: Jossey-Bass, 1992.

Johnson, D. W., and Johnson, F. P. *Joining Together: Group Theory and Group Skills* (2nd ed.). Englewood Cliffs, N.J.: Prentice-Hall, 1982.

Jones, D. *Chartism and the Chartists.* London: Allen Lane, 1975.

Jones, K. *Designing Your Own Simulations.* London: Methuen, 1985.

Jung, C. *Analytical Psychology: Its Theory and Practice.* New York: Random House, 1968.

Jung, C. "The Archetypes and the Collective Unconscious." In *Collective Works of C. G. Jung.* Vol. 9, Part I (2nd ed.) Princeton, N.J.: Princeton University Press, 1969a. (Originally published 1934.)

Jung, C. "Forms of Rebirth." In *Collective Works of C. G. Jung.* Vol. 9, Part I (2nd ed.). Princeton, N.J.: Princeton University Press, 1969b. (Originally published 1940.)

Jung, C. *Psychological Types.* Princeton: Princeton University Press, 1971. (Originally published 1921.)

Keane, R. "The Experience of Doubt and Associated Learning in Religious Men." Unpublished doctoral dissertation, University of Toronto, 1985.

Keane, R. "The Doubting Journey: A Learning Process of Self-Transformation." In D. Boud and V. Griffin (eds.), *Appreciating Adults Learning*. London: Kogan Page, 1987.

Keirsey, D., and Bates, M. *Please Understand Me: Character and Temperament Types*. Del Mar, Calif.: Prometheus Nemesis Books, 1984.

Kelly, G. *The Psychology of Personal Constructs*. Vols. 1 and 2, New York: Norton, 1963.

Keyton, J., and Springston, J. "Redefining Cohesiveness in Groups," *Small Group Research*, May, 1990, 234–254.

Kirschenbaum, D., and Perri, M. "Improving Academic Competence in Adults: A Review of Recent Research." *Journal of Counseling Psychology*, 1982, *29*(1), 76–94.

Kitchener, K. "Educational Goals and Reflective Thinking." *The Educational Forum*, Fall, 1983.

Kitchener, K., and King, P. "The Reflective Judgment Model: Transforming Assumptions About Knowing." In J. Mezirow and Associates (eds.), *Fostering Critical Reflection in Adulthood: A Guide to Transformative and Emancipatory Learning*. San Francisco: Jossey-Bass, 1990.

Knoop, R. *Clarifying Values*. St. Catharines, Ont.: Professional Effectiveness Technologies, 1983.

Knoop, R., and Cranton, P. A. *The Self-Staff Review Process: Feedback Report*. Ottawa, Ont.: Department of Indian and Northern Affairs, 1993.

Knowles, M. *Self-Directed Learning: A Guide for Learners and Teachers*. New York: Association Press, 1975.

Knowles, M. *The Modern Practice of Adult Education*. New York: Association Press, 1980.

Knowles, M. *The Adult Learner: A Neglected Species*. Revised. Houston: Gulf, 1984.

Knox, A. *Adult Development and Learning: A Handbook on Individual Growth and Competence in the Adult Years*. San Francisco: Jossey-Bass, 1977.

Knox, A. *Helping Adults Learn*. San Francisco: Jossey-Bass, 1986.

Kohlberg, L., and Turiel, E. "Moral Development and Moral Education." In G. S. Lesser (ed.), *Psychology and Educational Practice*. Glenview, Ill.: Scott Foresman, 1971.

Kolb, D. A. *Experiential Learning.* Englewood Cliffs, N.J.: Prentice-Hall, 1984.

Kreber, C. "The Influence of Faculty's Teaching Philosophy and Behaviour on Students' Critical Thinking and Self-Directedness." Unpublished master's thesis, Brock University, 1993.

Levinson, D. J. "A Conception of Adult Development." *American Psychologist,* 1986, *41*(1), 3–13.

Levinson-Rose, J., and Menges, R. "Improving College Teaching: A Critical Review of Research." *Review of Educational Research,* 1981, *51,* 403–434.

Lindeman, E. C. *The Meaning of Adult Education.* New York: New Republic, 1926.

Lindeman, E. C. "The Sociology of Adult Education." *Journal of Educational Sociology,* 1945, *19*(1), 144–149.

Long, H. *Adult and Continuing Education: Responding to Change.* New York: Teachers College Press, 1983.

Lowenstein, S. "A Brief History of Journal Keeping." In T. Fulwiler (ed.), *The Journal Book.* Portsmouth, N.H.: Boynton/Cook, 1987.

Marsh, H. W. "Students' Evaluation of University Teaching: Research Findings, Methodological Issues, and Directions for Future Research." *International Journal of Educational Research,* 1987, *11,* 253–388.

McCarthy, B. *Learning Styles in Schools: Making it Happen.* Eric Document ED 340 744, 1991.

McKeachie, W. J. "The Improvement of Instruction." *Review of Education Research,* 1960, *30* (4), 351–360.

McLaren, P. "Schooling the Postmodern Body: Critical Pedagogy and the Politics of Enfleshment." In H. Giroux (ed.), *Postmodernism, Feminism, and Cultural Politics.* Albany: State University of New York Press, 1991.

McPeck, J. E. *Critical Thinking and Education.* New York: St. Martin's Press, 1981.

Menges, R., and Mathis, B. C. *Key Resources on Teaching, Learning, Curriculum, and Faculty Development: A Guide to Higher Education Literature.* San Francisco: Jossey-Bass, 1988.

Merriam, S. B. and Caffarella, R. S. *Learning in Adulthood: A Comprehensive Guide.* San Francisco: Jossey-Bass, 1991.

Meyers, C. *Teaching Students to Think Critically: A Guide for Faculty in All Disciplines.* San Francisco: Jossey-Bass, 1986.

Meyers, C., and Jones, T. B. *Promoting Active Learning: Strategies for the College Classroom.* San Francisco: Jossey-Bass, 1993.

Mezirow, J. *Education for Perspective Transformation: Women's Reentry Programs in Community Colleges.* New York: Center for Adult Education, Teachers College, Columbia University, 1975.

Mezirow, J. "Perspective Transformation." *Adult Education,* 1978, *28,* 100–110.

Mezirow, J. "A Critical Theory of Adult Learning and Education," *Adult Education,* 1981, *32,* 3–24.

Mezirow, J. "Concept and Action in Adult Education," *Adult Education Quarterly,* 1985a, *35,* 142–151.

Mezirow, J. "A Critical Theory of Self-Directed Learning." In S. Brookfield (ed.), *Self-Directed Learning: From Theory to Practice.* New Directions for Continuing Education, no. 25, San Francisco: Jossey-Bass, 1985b.

Mezirow, J. "Transformation Theory and Social Action: A Response to Collard and Law," *Adult Education Quarterly,* 1989, *39,* 169–175.

Mezirow, J. *Transformative Dimensions of Adult Learning.* San Francisco: Jossey-Bass, 1991.

Mezirow, J. "Transformative Learning in Higher Education." A workshop given at Brock University, St. Catharines, Ont., 1993.

Mezirow, J., and Associates. *Fostering Critical Reflection in Adulthood.* San Francisco: Jossey-Bass, 1990.

Mintzberg, H. *Structure in Fives: Designing Effective Organizations.* Englewood Cliffs, N.J.: Prentice-Hall, 1983.

Moody, R. "Personality Preferences and Foreign Language Learning," *The Modern Language Journal,* 72, 389–401, 1988.

Moustakas, C. *The Authentic Teacher: Sensitivity and Awareness in the Classroom.* Cambridge, Mass.: Howard A. Doyle, 1966.

Myers, I. B. *Gifts Differing.* (7th ed.). Palo Alto, Calif.: Consulting Psychologists Press, 1985.

Perry, W. G., Jr. *Forms of Intellectual and Ethical Development in the College Years.* Troy, Mo.: Holt, Rinehart & Winston, 1970.

Perry, W. G. "Different Worlds in the Same Classroom." In P. Ramsden (ed.), *Improving Learning: New Perspectives.* New York: Nichols, 1988.

Peters, J. "The Action-Reason-Thematic Technique: Spying on the Self." In J. Mezirow and Associates (ed.), *Fostering Critical Reflection in Adulthood.* San Francisco: Jossey-Bass, 1990.

Pfeffer, J. *Power in Organizations.* Marshfield, Mass.: Pittman, 1981.

Piskurich, G. M. *Self-Directed Learning: A Practical Guide to Design, Development, and Implementation.* San Francisco: Jossey-Bass, 1993.

Progoff, I. *Life-Study: Experiencing Creative Lives by the Intensive Journal Method.* New York: Dialogue House Library, 1983.

Rogers, C. *Freedom to Learn: A View of What Education Might Become.* Columbus, Ohio: Merrill, 1969.

Rosenthal, R., and Jacobson, L. *Pygmalion in the Classroom: Teacher Expectations and Pupils' Intellectual Development.* Troy, Mo.: Holt, Rinehart & Winston, 1968.

Rotter, J. B., *Generalized Expectancies for Internal Versus External Control of Reinforcement.* Psychological Monographs, no. 80, 1966.

Sands, R. G., Parson, L. A., and Duane, J. "Faculty Mentoring Faculty in a Public University," *Journal of Higher Education,* 1991, *62,* 174–193.

Schön, D. A. *The Reflective Practitioner: How Professionals Think in Action.* New York: Basic Books, 1983.

Shaw, M. E. *Group Dynamics: The Psychology of Small Group Behavior.* New York: McGraw-Hill, 1976.

Smith, R. M. *Learning How to Learn: Applied Learning Theory for Adults.* New York: Cambridge Books, 1982.

Stanage, S. M. "Lifelong Learning: A Phenomenology of Meaning and Value Transformation in Postmodern Adult Education," Paper presented at the Annual Meeting of the American Association for Adult and Continuing Education, Atlantic City, N.J., 1989.

Stein, A. "Conflict and Cohesion: A Review of the Literature," *Journal of Conflict Resolution,* March 1976, 143–172.

Stogdill, R. M. *Manual for the Leader Behavior Descriptions Ques-*

tionnaire — Form XII. Columbus, Ohio: Bureau of Business Research, Ohio State University, 1963.

Strike, K. *Liberty and Learning.* Oxford: Martin Robertson, 1982.

Taylor, J. A. "Transformative Learning: Becoming Aware of Possible Worlds." Unpublished master's thesis, University of British Columbia, 1989.

Taylor, M. "Self-directed Learning: More than Meets the Observer's Eye." In D. Boud and V. Griffin (eds.), *Appreciating Adults Learning.* London: Kogan Page, 1987.

Tennant, M. C. "Life-Span Developmental Psychology and Adult Development: Implications for Adult Learning." *International Journal of Lifelong Education,* 1990, *9*(3), 223–235.

Tennant, M. C. "Perspective Transformation and Adult Development." *Adult Education Quarterly,* 1993, *44*(1), 34–42.

Thiel, J. P. "Successful Self-Directed Learners' Learning Styles." *Proceedings of the Adult Education Research Conference,* no. 25. Raleigh: North Carolina State University, 1984.

Thorne, A. "The Press of Personality: A Study of Conversations Between Introverts and Extraverts." *Journal of Personality and Social Psychology,* 1987, *53,* 718–726.

Thorne, E., and Marshall, J. "Managerial Development at General Electric." In M. Knowles (ed.), *Andragogy in Action: Applying Modern Principles of Adult Learning.* San Francisco: Jossey-Bass, 1984.

Tisdell, E. J. "Interlocking Systems of Power, Privilege, and Oppression in Adult Higher Education Classes." *Adult Education Quarterly,* 1993, *43,* 203–226.

Tough, A. *The Adult's Learning Projects: A Fresh Approach to Theory and Practice in Adult Learning.* Toronto: Ontario Institute for Studies in Education, 1979.

Vesey, G., and Foulkes, P. *Dictionary of Philosophy.* London: Collins, 1990.

Vroom, V. H., and Jago, A. G. *The New Leadership: Managing Participation in Organizations.* Englewood Cliffs, N.J.: Prentice-Hall, 1988.

Wang, M. C. "Development and Consequences of Students' Sense of Personal Control." In J. M. Levine and M. C. Wang (eds.), *Teacher and Student Perceptions: Implications for Learning.* Hillsdale, N.J.: Erlbaum, 1983.

Watson, G., and Glaser, E. M. *Critical Thinking Appraisal Manual.* Orlando, Fla.: Harcourt Brace Jovanovich, 1980.

Weber, M. *The Theory of Social and Economic Organizations.* New York: Free Press, 1947.

Wellins, R. S., Byham, W. C., and Wilson, J. M. *Empowered Teams: Creating Self-Directed Work Groups that Improve Quality, Productivity, and Participation.* San Francisco: Jossey-Bass, 1993.

Wilcox, S. *Instructor Support for Self-Directed Learning in Higher Education.* Unpublished master's thesis. St. Catharines, Ont.: Brock University, 1990.

Wilcox, S. "Learning about Teaching." Kingston, Ont.: Queen's University, Unpublished paper, 1993.

Wlodkowski, R. *Motivation and Teaching: A Practical Guide.* Washington, D.C.: National Education Association, 1984.

Wlodkowski, R. *Enhancing Adult Motivation to Learn.* San Francisco: Jossey-Bass, 1990.

Young, R. E. "Critical Teaching and Learning," *Educational Theory,* 1988, *38*(1), 47–59.

Yukl, G. *Leadership in Organizations* (2nd ed.). Englewood Cliffs, N.J.: Prentice-Hall, 1989.

Zuber-Skerritt, O. *Professional Development in Higher Education.* London: Kogan Page, 1992.

Index

245